67 C0:BOD1939

JAPANESE POLICY AND EAST ASIAN SECURITY

WITHDRAWN

JAPANESE POLICY AND EAST ASIAN SECURITY

Taketsugu Tsurutani

PRAEGER SPECIAL STUDIES • PRAEGER SCIENTIFIC

Library of Congress Cataloging in Publication Data

Tsurutani, Taketsugu.
    Japanese policy and east Asian security.

    Bibliography: p.
    Includes index.
    1. Japan—National security.   2. East
Asia—Defenses.   I. Title.
UA845.T85   355'.033052   81-11884
ISBN 0-03-05 9806-0   AACR2

Published in 1981 by Praeger Publishers
CBS Educational and Professional Publishing
A Division of CBS, Inc.
521 Fifth Avenue, New York, New York 10175 U.S.A.

© 1981 by Praeger Publishers

All rights reserved

123456789   145   987654321

Printed in the United States of America

269608

UA
845
.T85
1981

TO CASSEY

Acknowledgments

While researching this book, I incurred large and unrepayable debts to many individuals. I am especially indebted to seven persons not only for their many hours of insightful observations on the subject of the book but also for their generous assistance in enabling me to benefit from other experts in and out of government. They are: Donald Hellmann, Yoichi Itagaki, Takakazu Kuriyama, David Pflug, Noboru Saruwatari, Ichiro Suetsugu, and Shoichi Toda. To those many other individuals, too numerous to mention here, whose candor of observation and natural equanimity to tolerate my naive, often misplaced queries contributed so much to the present volume, I wish to express my particular appreciation.

Research and writing of the book was made possible by a Rockefeller Foundation Fellowship in International Relations, and I am grateful to the foundation for having provided me with an opportunity to acquire an understanding of a field in which I had always been interested but never had time to undertake an inquiry. For crucial additional financial and other support, I owe special thanks to the following offices at Washington State University: the Washington State University Foundation; the Graduate School; the Division of Social Sciences and Humanities, the College of Arts and Sciences; and the Department of Political Science.

The section on the Japan Self-Defense Forces capability in Chapter 5 and parts of the section on Japanese-U.S. force integration and Japan's participation in the maintenance of Western Pacific security in Chapter 7 originally appeared in the author's "Japan's Security, Defense Responsibilities, and Capabilities" published in Orbis 25, no. 1 (Spring 1981). They are presented in this volume by permission of the Foreign Policy Research Institute. Most of the discussion of five specific constraints on Japanese defense policy making in the first few pages of Chapter 5 originally appeared in the author's "The Security Debate" published in Defense Policy Formation: Towards Comparative Analysis, edited by James Roherty, (Durham, N.C.: Carolina Academic Press, 1980). It is included by permission of the University of South Carolina.

Various parts of the first draft of the manuscript were read and criticized by my colleagues H. Paul Castleberry, Maria Hsia Chang, Jack B. Gabbert, William F. Mullen, and Charles H. Sheldon. I am grateful for their friendship and valuable assistance. Numerous errors and other shortcomings that remain are entirely mine in spite of their apposite criticisms and suggestions.

There is one more individual to whom I wish to express my thanks, and that is Joyce Lynd, who typed both the original and final drafts of the manuscript with competence, dispatch, and good cheer.

Contents

List of Tables

Table

1
Introduction

The world in which Japan finds itself in the decade of the 1980s little resembles the one it was accustomed to and took for granted during much of the post-World War II period. Many of the assumptions on the basis of which Japan once conducted its external relations are no longer valid. The pattern of policy that became embedded in its behavior during the previous decades now appears increasingly dangerous. Internal dynamics that shaped Japan's policy predisposition are now seriously challenged by the emerging imperatives of its security requirements and those of the region of East Asia. The dilatory reactionism characteristic of its foreign and security policy can no longer insure national security. Nor do objective circumstances any longer permit Japan to avoid involvement in regional security politics. Its geopolitical location and economic power call on it to play an important, indeed crucial, role in the affairs of the region.

In spite of itself, therefore, Japan now is compelled to reassess its priorities, reexamine its direction, and redefine its role. These are difficult tasks for any nation at any time, for past habits are powerfully inhibitive of action and perilously distortive of perspective. For Japan, these tasks are further compounded by the fact that its new environment, regional as well as global, is characterized by a vastly higher degree of volatility and intractability, and hence unpredictability, than at any other time since 1945. Moreover, as a nation that relied on and took for granted the protection by an unquestionably powerful United States and became habituated to the peace that it once provided, Japan is a novice to the world of realpolitik. Inexperienced and unprepared, it is uncertain of itself, fearful of harm that its unavoidable venture might cause it, and

1

anxious about its own dangerous potentials. To borrow a term that once gained considerable banality as well as currency, Japan is engaged in an agonizing reappraisal.

However uncertain its course ahead may be, there is no turning back, for the world that once was has long ceased to exist. This volume addresses itself to the question of Japan's course in the decade of the 1980s and deals with the issues of its own defense and its role in the promotion and maintenance of East Asian regional security. The book's ultimate purpose is policy recommendation.

There are two fundamental considerations underlying this inquiry. One has to do with the role of the United States not only in the defense of Japan but also in East Asian regional security. By the imperatives and exigencies of international politics since World War II, the United States became inextricably implicated in the security affairs of both Japan and East Asia and acted virtually as the sole guarantor of peace in the Western Pacific. During the last decade its security capability within the region as well as without experienced a significant decline for a range of reasons, causing an increasingly dangerous security gap to develop in East Asia. Given the inability of most of the nations in the region to undertake an effective cooperative enterprise for the maintenance of collective security, however, the United States must continue to play the principal role in insuring peace and stability in the region. The question here is: How can the United States be most effectively assisted in playing its vital and indispensable role? The answer, for a range of critical considerations, is that Japan is the only nation in the region capable of filling the security gap and of assisting the United States. Japan should begin to assume an increasingly explicit role that is supportive of and supplementary to the United States in the maintenance of regional security. Put differently, the existing security arrangements between Japan and the United States should be modified in their internal structure in such a way as to render them more effective for the defense of Japan and for the maintenance of security of East Asia.

The other fundamental consideration underlying this policy suggestion is that the Japanese-U.S. security arrangements that are the basis for regional security require equity and reciprocity, two essential qualities of partnership that have thus far been prominently absent. The bilateral arrangements have been largely one-sided. Strange as it may sound, in the past this one-sidedness was acceptable, in fact preferable, to both Japan and the United States for reasons that were promotive of close relations between them. These same reasons, however, now threaten to disentangle those relations. It is in this light that the above reference to Japan's supportive and supplementary role should at least in part be contemplated. While we do not recommend that Japan become a "major" military power (in fact, as it will become clear, we believe Japan never should), we will suggest that it make proportionately as much sacrifice for the maintenance of regional security as does the United States and that its efforts for its own immediate defense be greater than what the United States expends under the security arrangements. In the end, equity and reciprocity in the arrangements are warranted by Japan's own enlightened self-interest, for they are indispensable to Japanese-U.S. relations if they are to persist and contribute to Japan's defense and the security of East Asia on which its ultimate safety depends.

The decade of the 1980s will prove to be the watershed in the relationship between the two nations, for the future of the relationship will most likely be redefined by the conduct of these nations in the decade. It would not be far-fetched to say that the future security of Japan as well as that of East Asia at large will hinge primarily upon how Japanese-U.S. relations are redefined in the decade.

At this point it may be useful to have a general idea of the literature relevant to Japanese foreign and security policy so that what is to follow in the present volume may be put in some perspective. This is not an exhaustive review of the literature but instead a synoptic and impressionistic view of selective dimensions of the literature that are directly pertinent to the limited discussions in the following chapters, especially to the policy recommendation.

The literature contains three dimensions, among others, that are of interest to this inquiry. The first is characterized by unhappiness about Japan's reluctance or inability to generate active, adaptive, flexible, and long-range policy making. It by and large seeks to explain its failure to measure up to the analysts' expectations and employs, among others, the structure and process of decision making, ideological inhibitions, and the nature of the party and parliamentary system as explanatory devices. Thus the nation's proper external conduct has been inhibited, for example, by intra-bureaucratic operational peculiarities and conflict, vertical and horizontal dispersion of effective policy-making power, and absence of effective mechanisms for policy coordination and central integration. The adaptive capacity of defense policy making in particular has been said to be severely constrained by the character and operative rules of budgetary politics because they were defined and institutionalized around the primacy of domestic economic growth and as a consequence are incompatible with any significant expansion of military expenditure. As for policy leadership, the cabinet is a chance congerie of contending, mutually mistrustful intraparty factions in which the prime minister's tenure depends far more on his skill in avoiding interparty as well as intraparty disputes than on policy commitment or leadership. The Diet, because of its internal structure and process, is incapable of policy initiative or effective policy challenge. Moreover, the pacifism of the postwar Constitution and its corollary, an idealistic liberal view of international relations, both subsequently abetted by the protective U.S. military shield behind which Japan could safely ignore the slings and arrows of international conflict and preoccupy itself in economic pursuits, became virtually internalized in the collective national psyche.

Given these potent inhibitions and stubborn constraints, Japanese external policy making could not but be a dilatory and reactive incrementalism at best. No significant change in defense and security policy should be expected.(1)

The second dimension of the relevant literature is characterized by an uneasiness, if not outright alarm, that Japan has been doing far more than it should be doing or some things it should not do at all. In more senses than one, this contention is rooted in a belief that Japan is vulnerable to internal militarist or reactionary tendencies and, accordingly, it focuses on those sociopolitical and economic phenomena that its authors consider indicative of such tendencies. Japan is viewed as militarily far more prepared and potent than generally thought and its Self-Defense Forces as capable of rapid expansion on short notice. It is the ruling Conservative party's temporary political expediency alone that has thus far caused the nation from nuclearizing its military forces. Some argue that secret military preparations have been going on for some time and that all the three services need is the nuclear explosive. Big business as well as various nationalist and servicemen's organizations and their supporters can be found pushing the government for military expansion and promoting propaganda campaigns for the restoration of prewar moral education at school and traditional discipline in society. There exists, moreover, a subtle but nonetheless potent military-industrial collusion acquiesced in by the conservative political establishment. In many ways this dimension of the literature has mirrored the traditional predilections of the leftist opposition in Japan. While the earlier dimension of the literature reflects the impression that Japan is endangering itself because it is not doing more for defense and security, this one clearly has operated on the notion that the nation is endangering its domestic stability and peace of East Asia because it is doing too much.(2)

A third dimension of the literature imparts great ambivalence with respect to what Japan should do. It consists largely but not exclusively of works by Japanese analysts. Ambivalence emerges in two ways: a conflict between a commitment to the spirit of the postwar Constitution and a nagging fear that the changing international environment may be increasingly incongruent with such a commitment; and a discord between rejection of the idealistic liberal view of international relations on the one hand, and, on the other, an inability or reluctance clearly to ascertain the magnitude and range of danger confronting the nation and thus to specify the level to which the nation's military capability should in fact be raised. The former has characterized proponents of the existing defense policy, and the latter its promilitary-expansion critics. Supporters of the policy have contended that the nation's military capability should be able to cope with indirect and minor aggressions without direct U.S. assistance but sufficiently defensive in character so as not to alarm other states in the region. They have been ambiguous, however, as to exactly what that capability is or should be in concrete terms. Their expansionist critics, in contrast, have argued that the existing level of the nation's military forces is woefully inadequate and dangerously unprepared, but they have been equally vague as to the extent to which they believe it should be raised in both qualitative and quantitative terms.(3)

The literature synoptically reviewed above raises two questions as to what Japan should do, two questions that are largely unanswered in it. One has to do with the specific level to which its security capability should be raised (or, in the case of the antimilitary argument, lowered), and how and why. Second, what is the specific role Japan should or could play in the maintenance of security in the region of East Asia? This volume, therefore, is an attempt to answer these questions.

In the following pages we will attempt to do four things. First, we will provide a context, a backdrop, for Japanese policy and policy making in the new decade through a discussion of selective aspects of the nation's new security predicament. Specifically, we will examine (in Chapter 2) two salient dimensions of the character of international politics in general, dimensions that were neither apparent nor seriously thought of in the heyday of the Cold War during which Japan's postwar posture and orientation were formed. This will be followed by a look (in Chapter 3) at the critical fragility of Japan as a highly industrialized democracy and an island nation and its various aspects that were largely unanticipated but that are inevitable consequences of its very success in achieving democracy and economic superstardom. Chapter 4 will provide a synoptic description and analysis of changes in the security condition of the region of East Asia during the last decade, changes that have come specifically to call for Japan's participation in the task of maintaining regional security.

Second, we will examine (in Chapter 5) the status of Japan's national defense, major features of the security debate in Japan, and those of Japanese-U.S. security arrangements against the context provided in the preceding chapters.

Third, we will inquire into the character, motivation, and dynamics of Japan's unique political psychology as the most crucial source of its external conduct during the past decades (Chapter 6). Rejecting the common argument (variously underlying the existing literature) about the "peace Constitution" as the primary cause for the nation's external conduct during those decades, we will advance a view that the Constitution and its subsequent treatment in the security debate have been symptoms of certain behavioral features of the nation that date back to its "opening" in the midnineteenth century. Japan's vaunted consensual decision making and the leadership style it dictates will be treated more as intervening rather than independent variables in security policy making. They themselves are not inherently incompatible with effective policy making, for they have proven in the past capable of adaptation, innovation, and policy change. Chapter 6 will conclude, therefore, with a discussion of an increasingly ascertainable, albeit still considerably ambivalent, phenomenon in Japan of the kind of political realism regarding its security requirements that was virtually unthinkable several years ago.

Finally, we will make a series of recommendations for Japan (in Chapter 7), some quite specific, others more general but suggestive, on the basis of our findings in the preceding chapters as well as of new expectations that nations in East Asia as well as the United States have come to entertain in recent years. Specific suggestions will be with respect to ways in which Japan could be defended more effectively without massive additional outlays of expenditure and in which Japan would be well advised to play a concrete supplementary and supportive role in the maintenance of regional military security. General suggestions will pertain to Japan's more active and positive participation in international economic development, and in the resolution or management of international crises both within the region of East Asia and beyond by translating its enormous economic power into a means of political and diplomatic suasion.

NOTES

(1) See, for example, Hans Baerwald, "The Diet and Foreign Policy," in The Foreign Policy of Modern Japan, ed. Robert A. Scalapino (Berkeley: University of California Press, 1977); Makoto Momoi, "Basic Trends in Japanese Security Policies," in ibid.; Osamu Kaihara, Nihon Boei Taisei no Uchimaku (Inside Japan's Defense System) (Tokyo: Jiji Tsushinsha, 1977); John Campbell, Contemporary Japanese Budget Politics (Berkeley: University of California Press, 1977); Haruhiro Fukui, "Policy-Making in the Japanese Foreign Ministry," in ibid.; Donald Hellman, "Japanese Security and Postwar Japanese Foreign Policy," in ibid; Taketsugu Tsurutani, "Causes of Paralysis," Foreign Policy 14 (Spring 1974); among many others.

(2) See, for example, Albert Axelbank, Black Star Over Japan (New York: Hill and Wang, 1972); Jon Halliday and Gavan McCormack, Japanese Imperialism Today (New York: Monthly Review Press, 1974): David Hopper, "Defense Policy and the Business Community," in The Modern Japanese Military System, ed. James H. Buck (Beverly Hills, Calif.: Sage Publications, 1975); Ivan Morris, Nationalism and the Right Wing in Japan: A Study of Postwar Trend (London: Oxford University Press, 1960); Hiroshi Osanai, Nihon no Kakubuso (Japan's Nuclear Armament) (Tokyo: Daiamondo, 1975).

(3) See, for example, Kunio Muraoka, Japanese Security and the United States (London: International Institute for Strategic Studies, 1973); Kiichi Saeki, "Japan's Security in a Multipolar World," in United States-Japanese Relations, ed. Priscilla Clapp and Morton Halperin (Cambridge, Mass: Harvard University Press, 1974); Shujiro Kotani, Kokubo no Ronri (Logic of National Defense) (Tokyo: Hara Shobo, 1970); Takuya Kubo, "Kaijo Boei to Kaijo Kotsu no

Kakuho" (Maritime Defense and Security of Maritime Traffic), Kokusai Mondai 217 (April 1978); Kaoru Murakami, Nihon Boei no Koso (A Plan for Japan's Defense) (Tokyo: Simul, 1976); Sankei Shimbun Shuzaihan, Nihon no Anzen (Japan's Security) (Tokyo: Sankei Shimbunsha, 1976), 2 vols.; Tadao Kusumi, "Japan's Defense and Peace in Asia," Pacific Community 4 (April 1973); Hiroomi Kurisu, Watakushi no Boei Ron (A Personal View of National Defense) (Tokyo: Takagi Shobo, 1978). For more detailed discussion of these two patterns of ambivalence, see Taketsugu Tsurutani, "The Security Debate" in Defense Policy Formation: Towards Comparative Analysis, ed. James Roherty (Durham, N.C.: Carolina Academic Press, 1980).

2
An Unstable World Order

The world of the 1980s is confronted with an apparent decline in its ability to manage issues and solve problems among nations and regions. On the one hand, over the last decades its ability has been increasingly encumbered by the steady growth in the number of nations, most of which lack even the most rudimentary tradition of mutual interaction and international cooperation. At the very same time, the world has become burdened with an increasingly wider range of refractory problems – some novel, some old, and still others old but compounded in intractability and magnitude. Many of these problems are pregnant with extremely dangerous potentiality. Deep anxiety pervades the entire world, and international peace and stability have never appeared so threatened since the heyday of the Cold War more than two decades ago. The threat comes only in part from the danger of nuclear confrontation between the two super-powers, though the danger remains the most terrifying of all contingencies. More immediately, it comes from any region of the world in which the declined international ability to manage issues and contain conflicts that would otherwise not lead ultimately to superpower confrontation might tempt spasmodic action and erratic reaction that might sooner than later prompt the ultimate confrontation. Thus, the potential for serious contingencies in the world has vastly increased both in range and likelihood.

Neither the fact of the increase in the number of nations nor that of expansion in the range of international problems can in itself explain the extent of threat to world peace and stability with which the new decade is burdened. Crucial to the understanding of the threat is the manner in which the increase in the number of nations has taken place and the character of the impact it has produced on the expansion in the range of refractory problems. This subject clearly deserves thorough treatment, but we shall leave it to analysts of greater competence. For the purpose of establishing the kind of perspective relevant to the limited inquiry of this volume, therefore, this chapter will confine itself to pointing out some of the salient dimensions of the threat as it pertains to the world in general and the region of East Asia in particular.

THE PASSING OF BIPOLAR STABILITY

That the era of bipolarity – with the world sharply demarcated between a Soviet-dominated camp of nations and a U.S.-led bloc, and international peace maintained by the mutually countervailing balance between the two – has long ended may be a truism. That this bipolarity has since been replaced by the phenomenon of multipolarity is a bit misleading, however, if by the decline of bipolarity is meant that the two power blocs gravitating around two poles were weakened more or less equally. Bipolarization of the world ceased to be a meaningful description of reality because one of these dominant blocs declined in power, influence, and cohesion, while the other has remained basically intact. The weakening has been a phenomenon within the formerly U.S.-led bloc and not within the so-called Soviet bloc.

This did not happen overnight, of course. The decline or weakening of the U.S.-dominant bloc – referred to by its ardent supporters as the "Free World" – began perhaps as early as the 1950s. A bloc may be defined in terms, among others, of internal cohesion and unity (whether enforced or voluntary) of its members, effective superiority and dominance of its leader over its members, and capacity for acting as a collectivity – or for supporting the leader – both to maintain its unity and to meet challenges presented by its adversary or by a nation or nations within its (or its leader's) sphere of influence. In these terms, there has been a clear difference over the last two decades or even longer between the Soviet and U.S. blocs. The difference was initially caused by, among other things, a fundamental variation between the two blocs in sustaining doctrine and ensuing conduct. The Soviet bloc was and is sustained by a totalitarian philosophy that brooks no opposition and is controlled by a leader nation that tolerates no challenge to its preeminent tutelary dominance over its allies. The U.S. or Western bloc, on the other hand, was and is committed to consensual democratic interaction among its members and toleration, if not whole-hearted encouragement, of national autonomy of its former colonies and client states, and this regardless of whatever covert and undemocratic impulses may have constantly lurked beneath. Initial unity of the Western bloc led by the United States, then was largely voluntary, induced by the centripetal force of common fear of the Soviet Union and the exigencies of the task of European reconstruction from the ravages of World War II. The relatively open, egalitarian character of its internal interaction and the ideologically dictated tolerance of autonomy of its former colonies and client states would, however, eventually produce certain consequences for the power, influence, and cohesion of the Western bloc. The first such consequence was the loosening of the bloc's control and influence over its former colonies and semicolonies in what would soon become known as the Third World, giving a progressive rise to the phenomenon of "nonalignment," as well as to certain pro-Soviet tendencies on the part of a number of new nations. A second consequence was an extreme difficulty of containing, let alone suppressing, centrifugal tendencies that are inherent in any large grouping of sovereign states such as nationalistic impulses, changes in individual policy priorities, and differential perceptions and interpretations of both internal and external events among its member nations. These inherent tendencies were, in the case of the Western bloc, further abetted by the widespread and considerably exaggerated credence attached to the "thaw" and then "detente" between the two nuclear superpowers.

The Soviet bloc, in contrast, has remained largely intact as to its basic cohesion − albeit a cohesion enforced by Moscow's military might. While the Soviet Union is not without alliance problems of its own, its resolve to contain and if need be suppress any critical centrifugal or destablizing trend within its own bloc and within what has become its sphere of influence has been repeatedly demonstrated with consistent regularity: in Czechoslovakia in the late 1940s; in East Germany, Poland, and Hungary in the 1950s; in Czechoslovakia in the late 1960s; in Afghanistan toward the end of the 1970s, to cite some of the more dramatic examples. Its attempt to repress Yugoslavia in the late 1940s was not carried through, at least in part, because the Western bloc led by the then indisputably powerful United States was perceived by Moscow as willing and prepared to counter it. In the subsequent Soviet repressions of intrabloc dissent, rebellion, or instability, the West has shown increasing signs of unwillingness as well as unpreparedness to take any effective countermeasure beyond essentially rhetorical and symbolic gestures of disapproval. The fact that its bloc or its sphere of influence is of considerable geographical size and of ethnic, cultural, linguistic, and national diversity compels the Soviet Union to tolerate degrees of internal political, cultural, and economic autonomy of its member states. This is the cost Moscow recognizes as necessary in order to maintain stability of its position of dominance over the entire bloc. Moscow's tolerance, however, has a clear limit, as has been repeatedly demonstrated and, we suspect, will be demonstrated in the future − for example, with respect to Romania, if Nicolae Ceausescu or his successor steps out of bounds, and (at this writing) Poland, if the Warsaw regime fails to resolve its problem with workers and peasants. Soviet methods of insuring its intrabloc cohesion may change, but there is little or no indication that Moscow would ever tolerate the kind of centrifugal tendency that has weakened the cohesion and unity of the Western alliance.

If there is a phenomenon of multipolarity, it is to be found in what once was called the "Free World." (How free most of that world was in fact is beside the point here.) In it, the United States, of course, remains the most formidable single pole, but there are others that challenge it with varying degrees of effectiveness, frequency, and audacity: the European Community, the Arab world, Latin America, Black Africa, or even such individual states as Cuba and Iran, and, with overlapping membership, the so-called non-aligned nations. Differently put, in the world outside of the Soviet bloc, there has been a steady increase in the number of national actors capable of acting independently of the preference of the Western bloc in general, and its leader nation, the United States, in particular. However we might choose to group nations outside the Soviet bloc, we could not escape the fact of diffusion and fragmentation of power in the former Free World. It is this fact that boosts the potency of the Soviet bloc far above the level to which its recent expansion of influence into Africa, the Middle East, Southeast Asia, and Southwest Asia would in itself have raised it. Today, therefore, it might be argued that a unit of Soviet power, political or military, is relatively much greater than it was, say, a decade or two ago. Conversely, a unit of U.S. or Western power, one could say, is much weaker than it ever was. It is precisely this very context of relative potency that encouraged what one U.S. official characterized to the author as "declining restraint of Soviet conduct."

The decline of the stable bipolar system in the world, precipitated by the inevitable unleashing of centrifugal forces and trends under the very democratic character of the internal relations within the Western bloc and its external relations with its former colonies and client states, makes the task of maintaining peace in the world far more difficult than when the world was clearly polarized, and this for at least three reasons. First, the Soviet Union, which could still count on the basic cohesion of its bloc, can and often is tempted to engage in probing actions, by itself or through proxy and with increasing impunity, in many parts of the world over which the West in general and the United States in particular have lost their control and influence. Second, any number of Third World nations (or nonaligned states) would and often do attempt to play one super-power against the other, the Western bloc against the Soviet, or even one Western state against another (including the United States). Third, the Western bloc, of which the United States remains at least militarily the most powerful member, is increasingly unable either to take a resolute joint countermeasure or to permit and support the United States to take a prompt and effective countermeasure in those contingencies, thus encouraging them to proliferate and worsen. Thus, the erosion of cohesion of the Western bloc — combined with the rising autonomy of nations within its former sphere of influence — has come to create a seriously destabilizing condition in much of the world.

The world of the 1980s is more unstable than it has ever been since the early 1950s. Its volatility is of increasingly dangerous proportions. This volatility, however, now contains an additionally disturbing dimension that suggests further weakening and disarray of nations that formerly constituted a cohesive Western bloc capable of countervailing the Soviet bloc. This new dimension is the change in the character of international interdependence.

A NEW CHARACTER OF INTERNATIONAL INTERDEPENDENCE

Interdependence among nations is an old concept as well as phenomenon. In an objective sense, larger and larger numbers of sovereign states have become mutually more dependent since 1945. In this sense, the pattern has been linear. Presumably, this should lead to more intimate relations among nations and encourage cooperation and peace among them. This, however, still remains a mere proposition, however fervently believed in by all people of good will. Beyond this discouraging recognition, there is another important fact to consider, and that is a significant change in the character of international interdependence in recent years that is producing a critical impact upon relations of power in the world, especially outside of the Soviet bloc. We are again referring to the current phenomenon of the growing instability of the world.

Interdependence is a matter both of objective fact and subjective perception of that fact, and the latter is more important in terms of its impact on the behavior of nations concerned and patterns of relations among them. Prior to the last decade, the fact of international interdependence was commonly perceived as favoring advanced industrial states of the West and Japan in their relations with resource-producing nations of the Third World. They not only were affluent, with modern consumer economies and advanced industrial technology, thus viewed with envy and strong desire for emulation by those Third World nations, but they also retained an ascertainable upper hand in their economic, hence political, relations with those underdeveloped or developing nations that had once been their colonies or client states. It was generally those advanced industrial states that called the tune in the world marketplace regarding supply and demand, the marketplace in which those resource-supplying nations did not seem to have an ability to deal with them on an equal footing. Industrial states, with their finances, technology, managerial manpower, and political favors that they could supply or withhold at will, could make or break those underdeveloped nations, and there was little the latter felt able to do to counter the former. The proposition that Western states – the former colonial powers – were now ideologically or rhetorically committed to helping the underdeveloped nations (unless, of course, they were procommunist) in itself did not assuage the fundamental sense of inferiority and vulnerability of those Third World nations vis-à-vis the whim and potential machination on the part of the industrial states. Thus, whatever the public protestations of international cooperation, equality, and interdependence, the relationship between industrial nations and resource-supplying Third World nations, in the perception of both, was unequal, largely one-sided, characterized by enormous freedom of action and policy on the part of industrial states and relative lack thereof on the part of the others. In part, this was a crucial element in the power and influence of the Western alliance and especially of the United States in the world arena, augmented, no doubt, by their relative willingness covertly or otherwise to use their political, economic, and even military capability in case any of the underdeveloped nations had the temerity to challenge or threaten the existing pattern of interdependence as, for example, against Guatemala and Iran in 1953, Egypt in 1956, and Indonesia in 1958. Thus, while the Western industrial world was objectively dependent for its growth and well-being on the resource-supplying Third World nations, the latter were subjectively far more dependent upon it for their survival and viability.

It is well-nigh impossible to establish or ascertain the precise date when the old pattern of interdependence (in which the industrial West enjoyed undisputed superiority) began to change in the direction of potential reversal. The first dramatically incipient stage of the potential reversal arrived in 1973 with the successful attempt by oil-producing Arab states to use their possession of this vital energy source as a political weapon of devastating potency against the industrial West and Japan. This was the Arab oil embargo to protest the West's support for Israel (or nonsupport for the Arabs) in the Middle East conflict. The impact of the embargo upon the economies of industrial states that had taken a constant supply of oil for granted was immediate and widespread, causing a near panic in some precipitating a heretofore unending period of increasingly severe economic dislocations combining inflation, unemployment, and stagnation in virtually all of them. The event was a vivid harbinger of the character of potential future interdependence between the industrial world and the resource-producing Third World and was quickly followed by the firm establishment of OPEC (Organization of Petroleum Exporting Countries) control over oil prices that turned the whole oil matter overnight into a seller's market. Today, the industrialized world outside the Soviet bloc (and, before long, including it) is at the tender mercy of periodic and unfailing raises in oil prices by OPEC nations individually and in collusion. One of the most critical consequences of the rise of petropolitics, then, is the new perception on the part of industrialized nations that the relationship between them and oil-producing nations of the Third World is unequal, largely one-sided, characterized by enormous freedom of action in matters of price and supply on the part of the latter and lack thereof on their part as well as nonoil producers in the Third World. For much the same reason that leaders of those Third World nations used to flock to the capitals of industrial Western states periodically, hat in hands, so to speak, in an effort to seek favors and to remain in their good graces, leaders of these Western states and Japan today find frequent pilgrimages to the capitals of major oil states increasingly essential to their nations' stability, even survival.

This perception of unaccustomed and often frightening vulnerability on the part of industrial nations might soon extend beyond the matter of oil. While oil is the only major commodity over which its Third World producers have managed effectively to establish control in order to reverse the traditional character of interdependence, there are other key industrial raw materials over which their respective producers could sooner or later establish similar control. Table 2.1 indicates production by Third World nations and Soviet bloc states of some of those key materials as a proportion of their total world production in 1972. Industrial nations require most of these raw materials as well as oil produced in the Third World in order to maintain their current levels of economic activity. This, of course, has always been the case, but now the same case has come to be perceived differently by those industrial states, that is, perceived with a growing fear that the supply of not only oil but also other commodities essential for their economies may be disrupted through embargo or excessive price hikes by their producers — contingencies that until a decade ago had been largely unthought of. In long-range political consequences, this change in the character of international interdependence may be the most crucial and historic development in the last third of the twentieth century, equal in magnitude and ramifications to the spread of communism in the first third and the emergence of nuclear technology in the second.

The magnitude of the changed character of international interdependence is compounded further by the fact that the change came about at the very time when industrialized nations had just entered a period of unprecedently intractable internal trials. We are referring to some of the new phenomena of advanced industrial society, sometimes called postindustrial society. These phenomena, a few of which we shall briefly touch on shortly, are consequences of economic growth, prosperity, and rapid expansion of welfare in industrialized states of the West and Japan, all veritable instances of good things producing unintended destabilizing events. One of the conventional liberal convictions was that there was, at least in democratic and industrialized society, a positive correlation between prosperity and welfare, on the one hand, and sociopolitical stability on the other. The vitality of democracy, accordingly, would be strengthened as the distribution of material benefits of an industrial economy became more equitable and the general standard of living higher. Corollary to this conviction was the belief that discontent and subsequent instability in society would decline as more and more groups were permitted to participate in the political process. This was the notion that emancipation would strengthen democracy. Advanced industrial society, indeed, has come to

TABLE 2.1

Third World and Soviet Bloc Production of Key Raw Materials, 1972 (percent)

	Third World	Soviet Bloc
Manganese	67	30
Copper	63	26
Lead	37	14
Nickel	40	20
Bauxite	50	14
Tungsten	38	38
Chrome	80	15

Source: Kokusai Tokei Yoran 1975 (International Statistical Abstract 1975), ed. Sorifu Tokei Kyoku (Tokyo: Okura-sho Insatsu Kyoku, 1975), pp. 75-80.

approximate these propositions insofar as more equitable distribution of economic benefits and wider popular participation in the political process are concerned. The trouble is that only one side of each of these equations has materialized, but not the other. In fact, the other side of each of these equations has suffered regress, not progress. Whence this seeming paradox?

Postwar economic growth in industrialized society led not only to a rising affluence but also to an increasingly wider distribution of that affluence in part because the very dynamic and logic of further economic growth dictated an increasingly more equitable distribution of the benefits of modern industrialism. Increasing welfare, then, was the function of a combination of ideological preference and systemic imperatives in postwar industrial society. This, of course, produced salutary effects on the gradual reduction of serious gaps in material well-being among classes and groups and the increasing mitigation of poverty and other forms of deprivation to which the elderly, the uneducated, the unemployed and unemployable, among others, would otherwise have been consigned. This development, once it gained certain momentum, however, gave rise to some unanticipated tendencies that would soon prove irreversible. Two of the more inclusive tendencies are particularly salient, one on the part of the public at large and the other on the part of government.

As the trend toward the welfare state continued, groups that were its beneficiaries as well as others began to perceive new needs and wants to be satisfied, needs and wants that in earlier times would have entered the minds of few but that were now demanded not only as legitimate but also as a matter of rights. This was what one analyst called the "revolution of rising entitlements," involving minimum household incomes, the floor of a decent standard of living, access to higher education, certain employment practices, elimination of inconveniences for the physically or mentally handicapped, and the like.(1) These demands kept expanding both in level and in range, without any sign of abatement.

The government of an advanced industrial and democratic society, inasmuch as it was the product of electoral competition among parties vying for power, was induced to address these expanding popular demands, that is, meet them, and politicians as well as competing parties were compelled to promise to meet them, even to do more. The convergence of these two trends eventually reached the point where popular expectations increasingly exceeded not only the ability of government prudently to afford to satisfy but also the rate of economic growth itself because, as one British analyst observes, of "the lack of a budget constraint among voters," and he terms this phenomenon an "economic contradiction of democracy."(2) Chronic deficit spending, therefore, has become a new feature of the government of an advanced industrial society, seriously weakening its fiscal integrity, eroding the value of its currency, and repressing the rate of economic growth.

The impact of rapid expansion of welfare in advanced industrial society is not solely economic; it is also sociocultural. Corollary to the expansion of demands to be satisfied by government, an expansion that does not seem to know its limits, is the lowering of ability or reticence to tolerate hardship, inconvenience, and other impediments to a life of abundance and comfort. There has emerged a growing tendency on the part of individuals and groups alike to politicize private disputes that used to be resolved through face-to-face, voluntary, patient, and informal negotiations, and personal inconveniences that they once viewed themselves as having to overcome by their own efforts. Today, they rush to the court, start political agitation, appeal to public authorities for intervention, and otherwise make public issues out of private matters, because they crave a quick-fix, instant gratification. Resilience of individuals and groups alike has apparently declined greatly, and their relations have become increasingly characterized by contentiousness and asperity. This creates enormous strains on the capacity of government. Every problem, when viewed as such by any aggregate of individuals, is a problem. There are, however, different levels of magnitude among various problems and different degrees to which they may or may not deserve authoritative resolution or management. Additionally, it is necessary to consider the basic political capability of government in determining whether and to what extent a given problem or issue really warrants critical exertion by government relative to its existing capability as well as to the magnitude of other problems calling for authoritative management and resolution.

The impact of the expansion of welfare is also political. Government in an advanced industrial society is burdened with the range and kinds of problems that are beyond its ability effectively to manage or resolve. It suffers from the phenomenon called "overload."(3) Inasmuch as the stability of government in democratic society is the function of proper equilibrium between popular expectations and its ability to meet them, governments of advanced industrial societies have become increasingly unstable. Also, advanced industrial democracies during the past decade and a half have been commonly characterized by growing "regime instability,"(4) with expanding political fragmentation of the electorate, tenure insecurity of incumbent governments, intraparty discord, proliferation of single-issue politics, legislative difficulty – all reflecting the impact and ramifications or consequences of the manner in which welfare has in the past been expanded as well as of the cummulative effects of industrial diseconomies such as pollution, inflation, and so on. At the level of the state, advanced industrial society, much like the Western alliance discussed a few pages earlier, has lost much of its internal discipline and political cohesion, for the forces unwittingly unleashed by expanding welfare under a democratic political system were in their fundamental character and inevitable tendency largely centrifugal and destabilizing, reflecting the particularisms of self-interest of various contending groups.

All this has serious implications for each industrial state's external behavior and, collectively, for the behavior of the group of advanced industrial states of the West and Japan in the international political arena. For one thing, internal political instability and economic difficulty would aggravate the magnitude of external vulnerability of industrial states vis-à-vis resource-producing Third World nations inasmuch as the governments of those industrial states are less and less able to make, let alone effectively implement, rational, long-range policies to cope with and reduce the level of their external vulnerability. Oil policies of these nations are currently the prime example of this problem. What is difficult for individual industrial nations to do, then, is clearly far more difficult for them jointly to do as a group faced with a common problem.

Existence of an International Energy Agency to coordinate efforts to manage the problem of oil supply is largely cosmetic, and industrial states are unable to formulate and implement effective joint policy on the matter precisely because of their respective internal political weaknesses. Much as Third World nations were once so divided because of their internal weaknesses that they permitted advanced Western nations to manipulate and in effect rule them, industrial states today may become easily susceptible to efforts of OPEC nations to divide and rule them. While oil-producing Arab states could with relative dispatch impose an oil embargo upon the entire industrial world in effective concert, those industrial states could not even agree on any meaningful economic sanction against a single oil-producing nation. Instead, the industrial states often demonstrate great willingness to compete for favors and good graces of those oil-producing nations by exploiting or taking advantage of one another's predicament, much in the same way that those Third World nations once competed among themselves for favors and good graces of industrial Western states. These industrial states are in danger of intensifying their mutual competition for oil and soon, perhaps, for other raw materials from Third World nations unless they somehow manage to restore a certain necessary degree of domestic political discipline and coherence, and then establish a minimally requisite extent of unity and consensus among themselves regarding individual and collective approaches to their relations with Third World nations. Never before has advanced industrial society been internally so fractious and unstable; and never before has the industrial world of the West and Japan been so divided. Yet, never before has the requirement of unity within each of these states as well as among them been so pressingly imperative.

Internal instability of advanced industrial society aggravates the magnitude of its external vulnerability vis-à-vis resource-producing Third World nations in yet another way, and here we consider relative resilience or imperviousness to material hardship, however caused. In this respect, the industrialized world, with all its sociopolitical and cultural sophistication, technological and organizational superiority, would seem to fare rather badly. The very tradition of poverty and underdevelopment of their masses would confer upon Third World nations, including the nouveaux riches among them, an enormous advantage of time and perseverance over the industrial nations. Even supposing that those advanced industrial states somehow managed to take a common stand in dealing with Third World nations producing key industrial raw materials and energy, and supposing further that negotiations between the two groups reached an unbreakable impasse, with the result of mutual trade embargo, such an event, which may not be quite as unlikely as we would wish to think, could affect both parties concerned immediately for obvious reasons. However, the degree to which each would be adversely affected would be quite different, and the principal reason for this is that one would be able to withstand the resultant hardship and dislocation much better and longer than the other. Masses in Third World nations by and large contine to be poor, thanks in part to persistent and widespread corruption and greed of their tiny elites. They are, moreover, still predominantly rural and retain a potent tradition of mutual help and community within the extended family, clan, village, tribe, or region, a tradition that was long ago lost in industrial nations by virtue of that very industrialism involving as it did urbanization, depersonalization of interpersonal and social relations, nuclearization of the family, and increasing reliance on government for services, even for basic sustenance. These factors – poverty and community – commonly viewed by Westerners as elements of underdevelopment, would help assuage whatever adverse effects such a mutual trade embargo might produce on the masses in Third World nations. In contrast, masses in advanced industrial states are not only affluent and increasingly soft, but have become addicted to affluence and a soft life, including most of those groups that still claim to suffer from inequity and inequality. Any significant reduction in their standards of living would wreak havoc in their midst, compounded by the loss of community and mutual help, and, worse yet, this would immediately translate itself into a diversity of disruptive, destabilizing, even violent political conduct, both individual and organized, thus further reducing the ability of government to cope with the initial impact of the embargo. To what sort of ultimate consequence these developments would lead could not be readily contemplated. In any game of patience and perseverance, industrial nations would most likely be the sure losers, for their internal life-support systems, physical and organizational, are so complex, variegated, and sophisticated, full of delicate joints and sensitive connecting links, that even a slight environmental fluctuation could cause a chain reaction of damage and malfunction that might render them inoperable. The effects of such dislocation would be pervasive, touching every part of the population and society. Third World nations, on the other hand, would be far more impervious to such events, for their most direct effects would be restricted to those few elites who monopolize the benefits of external trade with advanced industrial state. Geographically, too, effects would largely be concentrated in urban centers. Rural masses would be relatively untouched by such events as they are by the benefits of trade in the commodities involved. Governments, dynasties, and individual political leaders might fall, but that, too, would affect the masses little or not at all. Internal life-support systems for the masses of these nations are relatively simple, hence more adaptable, flexible, and versatile, for they are maintained largely by individual efforts and communal innovativeness. Any decline in material well-being caused for the masses in the event, while inevitably considerable, would be viewed as no more severe than one caused by intermittent natural misfortunes to which they have long been accustomed.

The current instability of the world is thus the function primarily of two phenomena in the position of the Western industrial world: its politicomilitary decline relative to the Soviet bloc and its politicoeconomic decline in its relationship with the Third World. These phenomena, in turn have become aggravated and compounded by certain debilitating and seemingly intractable internal socio-political trends that are increasingly common among advanced industrial societies of the West and Japan. The relationship among the Soviet bloc, the Western industrial world, and the Third World (especially its resource-producing members) is fundamentally con-flictual, if not irrevocably incompatible, for reasons of differential development, outlook, and interest. It has always been so, but today it is rendered more explicit by the very decline of the Western industrial world and the concomitant rise of Soviet boldness and Third World vigor. Transformation of this conflictual relationship into a harmonious one is the most important task that the world must undertake, for, otherwise, the present status of world order already dangerously unstable would deteriorate progressively. Three things, among others, would be essential to this end: stabilization of Soviet conduct, orderly economic modernization and political development of the Third World, and recultivation of resilience and cohesion of the Western industrial states. The subject, of course, is outside the purview of the present volume, for our concern is East Asia and Japanese policy in that particular region of the world, but the basic principles required would seem the same whether we are discussing the world at large or East Asia. Of the three principles, the third – the recultivation of resilience and cohesion of industrial states – would seem crucial in both immediacy and potential impact. This, we hope, will soon become clear within the context of East Asia in the following chapters.

NOTES

(1) Daniel Bell, "The Public Household – On 'Fiscal Sociology' and the Liberal Society," Public Interest 37 (Fall 1974): 39.

(2) Samuel Brittan, "The Economic Contradictions of Democracy," British Journal of Political Science 5 (April 1975): 139 and passim.

(3) Compare, for example, Anthony King, "Overload: Problems of Governing in the 1970s," Political Studies 23 (June-September 1975), and Leopold Bellak, Overload: The New Human Condition (New York: Human Sciences Press, 1975).

(4) Morris Janowitz, Social Control of the Welfare State (New York: Elsevier, 1976).

3

Japan: The Fragile Superpower

Political implications of a nation's economic and physical conditions are crucial ingredients of its external policy and domestic politics. Japan's policy regarding East Asian security cannot, therefore, be sufficiently discussed without taking into account its economic and physical conditions, which have undergone vast transformations during the past three decades. These conditions, the current predicament of which could not have been fully anticipated three decades ago, cannot but critically influence the nation's perception of its external environment, its range of policy options, and, therefore, its international conduct.

AN ECONOMIC GIANT WITH AN ACHILLES' HEEL

Japan is not only a highly advanced industrial state but also an economic giant — and a very unique one at that inasmuch as it is Asian, while all other advanced industrial nations are Western. Japan's economic presence in the world is well-nigh ubiquitous, with its industrial products ranging from digital wrist watches to cameras and automobiles, from stereo sets to mammoth oil tankers, from cosmetics to high-grade steel, flooding markets from one end of the globe to the other. It has become so ubiquitous, indeed, that customers of these Japanese goods in some countries are often unaware that such brand names as Panasonic, Olympus, and TDK are Japanese. Japan not only saturates other nations with its manu-

---

The chapter title was borrowed from Frank Gibney, Japan: The Fragile Superpower (New York: Norton, 1975).

factured goods but also invests heavily in many of these nations both to acquire sources of raw materials it requires for its advanced industrial economy and to produce goods locally with greater economy. The rise of Japan as an economic giant from the ashes of the devastating defeat in World War II has been so spectacular and the inventiveness and vitality of its economy seemingly so boundless that more than one foreign observer in the last decade was moved to predict the coming of an economic Pax Japonica as the future world order.(1)

Simple statistics confirm Japan as an economic giant. By 1980 its per capita GNP was nearly equal to that of the United States. In 1978 Japan surpassed the Soviet Union in GNP and now clearly ranks as the second largest economic power after the United States, whose population is twice as great. In 1960 Japan's gross fixed capital formation was less than one-sixth that of the United States ($13 billion versus $89 billion), but by 1976 it had grown to 63 percent ($206 billion versus $327 billion),(2) markedly surpassing the United States in per-capita figures. This was precisely what was behind one analyst's finding several years ago that, as of 1972, 65 percent of the plant and equipment in Japan's manufacturing sector was less than five years old, while the same percent of those in the United States was more than ten years old.(3) The modernity of the Japanese plant and equipment in large measure accounts for a consistently high annual increase in labor productivity, which in recent years averaged approximately 10 percent.(4)

Investment in plant and equipment alone, however, would not generate economic growth. A nation needs trained and disciplined manpower, sophisticated technical knowledge, and efficient managerial expertise in order to turn investment into growth and create and expand a variety of support logistics such as effective and extensive communications and transportation networks, systems of efficient allocation of resources, and administrative mechanisms to insure their proper functioning, adjustment, and improvement. It is for this reason that such suddenly rich nations as the Persian Gulf states, whose per capita income either equal or exceed Japan's and whose ability to generate investment capital is therefore considerable, cannot become powerful industrial states overnight, for they lack these crucial human, technological, and social resources. The Japanese are not only literate (100 percent literacy) but also highly educated, producing increasingly larger numbers of trained personnel to manage and operate an expanding range of productive and support activities funded by a rising level of investment, as reflected, albeit indirectly, in Table 3.1 on changes in university enrollment. It is no coincidence that the extent of increase in university enrollment closely paralleled not only that of capital formation but also that in real economic output. Nor is it an acident that 135 of Fortune's 500 largest corporations in 1979 were Japanese.

It should be noted at this point that Japan's world stature as an economic giant has not been achieved and maintained at the expense of social progress at home. Japan was a highly stratified society before the war, stratified both in sociopolitical status and in level of income among its population. Postwar political reforms, carried out directly by or at the insistence of the U.S. occupation administra-

TABLE 3.1

University Enrollment, 1950, 1965, and 1977
(excluding junior colleges)

	Faculty	Students
1950	19,332	224,923
1965	83,204	937,556
1977	158,904	1,839,363

Source: Japan Statistical Yearbook 1979 (Tokyo: Statistics Bureau, Prime Minister's Office, 1979), p. 583.

tion, eliminated all forms of formal sociopolitical status differentiation and turned the nation into a democratic state that has since been fervently supported by an overwhelming majority of its people. Political democratization, however, was one thing; pursuit of economic equality is quite another and vastly more difficult matter. In this pursuit, too, Japan has been largely successful. True, poverty still does exist and there also are enormously wealthy individuals. What is significant, however, is the extent of the economic leveling effect that has been brought about during the postwar period, thanks largely to the combination of a rapid growth in the national economy and the systemic imperatives of advanced industrialism discussed briefly in Chapter 2. Most of the poor as well as most of the rich have been effectively eliminated through the years and traditional income differentials between the blue-collar and the white-collar workers (or, to use a very simplistic contrast favored by Marxists, between the proletarian and the bourgeoisie) have steadily declined.(5) This leveling effect has been reflected in Japanese self-perceptions. In 1962, for example, well into the era of rapid growth and rising prosperity, three out of every four Japanese viewed themselves as middle-class; by 1969 nine out of every ten came to identify themselves as such.(6) Another concrete indication of the economic leveling effect is the change in the size of welfare clientele. There were approximately 2 million welfare recipients in 1955, but, two decades later, despite the facts that the government had expanded the eligibility for an increasingly wider range of welfare benefits (the national government's welfare expenditure rose by an average annual rate of 24 percent between 1965 and 1978), the population has consistently increased, and traditional popular inhibitions against receiving welfare benefits had declined in the meantime, there were only slightly more than 1.25 million individuals receiving direct benefits from the state.(7)

To return to the matter of Japan's economic stature, one of the crucial factors promoting the nation's rapid recovery and subsequent growth has been the role the government plays in the national economy. Modern Japan has never had what is called "free enterprise" or laissez-faire capitalism, due primarily to a coincidence of an authoritarian tradition and exigencies of the times.

During the Meiji period when Japan was seeking to transform its feudal society into a modern state, rapid economic development and modernization were the principal tasks requiring concerted national efforts so as to minimize waste and error and maximize progress. This necessarily placed the government in the position of direct and extensive leadership. In the preceding Tokugawa period, economic activities, from which the samurai class had been explicitly excluded, had been under close governmental direction, supervision, and control. This tradition now was conjoined with the requirements of rapid modernization. The government bureaucracy presided over by the modernizing elite therefore planned, formulated, financed, and implemented an increasingly wider range of economic projects and enterprises, operated and managed them, especially since there was no private sector or class with sufficient capital and technical competence to undertake them. Japan's modern economy thus started as a planned economy. It did not lead to socialism or state capitalism, however, because the government, in its unusual wisdom, would, as soon as those new economic enterprises became viable and self-sustaining, turn them over to the private sector (selling them at cost), thus fostering the growth of a capitalist modern national economy. At the same time, the government retained its powerful role in the growth of this modern private economic sector by institutionalizing the practice of guiding its expansion, directing its conduct, providing subsidies and technical assistance in various forms, and issuing general policy directives. It was in this fashion that a tradition was established regarding the character of relationship between government and economy, and it was this tradition that came powerfully to define the postwar policy of rapid economic recovery and growth. The enormous, seemingly insurmountable task of economic recovery from the ashes of defeat and subsequent growth and prosperity dictated careful allocations of scarce resources to, judicious coordination of, and authoritative setting of priorities and targets for various sectors of the national economy from the center, that is, the government. The government thus undertook the responsibility of restructuring the nation's economic system, planning its activities, regulating its conduct, and guiding its growth. The role of government throughout the postwar period became as crucial and potent in the nation's economic affairs, therefore, as it had been during the Meiji period of economic modernization. With respect to its economy, then, Japan's decision making is neither socialist nor laissez-faire, but a "carefully guided democracy."(8) It has clearly provided a high degree of coherence and rationality to the national efforts and helped obviate numerous bottlenecks and other obstacles and pitfalls that would otherwise have been unavoidable.

Another important factor to be noted in passing regarding Japan's spectacular postwar economic performance is labor-management relations. We should not exaggerate the putative efficacy of Japanese labor-management relations,(9) but it is necessary to take into proper account their impact on the pace and extent of Japan's economic change in the postwar period. One outstanding feature of relations between labor and management or between employee and employer in Japan's private sector is a strong sense of community, a feeling that "we are all in this together." A company or firm is a virtual family in which all members, workers and managers, employees and employers alike, are bound not by a legal contract but by this sense, this feeling. The worker does not "sell" his labor to the employer during whatever number of hours, days, and years he works at the company. He is part of the company, his ties to it extending far beyond the working hours. "Employers do not employ only a man's labor itself," writes an eminent Japanese sociologist, "but really employ the total man, as shown in the expression marugakae (completely enveloped)."(10) The company "provides the whole social existence of a person" and there is "an exceedingly high degree of . . . emotional involvement" between the company and the workers, for the company is a "household" and is viewed by the worker "as more important than all other human relationships."(11) However, it is not only the worker who becomes the member of the "household" but also his family. The company pays special allowances for his dependents over and above his wages and sometimes even housing allowances; it organizes and subsidizes a range of recreational, cultural, and social activities for him and his family, takes individualized interest in the health, education, and careers of his children, and comes to his or his family's aid in case of serious illness or other kinds of family misfortune. To the extent at all possible, the company also insures life-time employment to him, regardless of fluctuations in its business fortune. Personal loyalty is reciprocal. The company goes to any length to insure harmony and an almost organic unity among its employees. Thus, while there are occasional labor strikes, they tend to be more ritualistic. Labor unions are influential, but inasmuch as they are mostly enterprise unions, their relationship with management is entirely accomodative of economic imperatives of sound and viable operation of those enterprises. Labor demands for wage increases, for example, are tempered by the knowledge of the workers of the financial conditions of their employers and are consequently adjusted closely to the rise in productivity and revenue, which the employers find generally acceptable.(12)   More important insofar as Japan's postwar economic performance is concerned is the fact that the sense of community that characterizes typical Japanese labor-management relations induces an astonishingly high degree of diligence and devotion in the employee's work.   For example, one Japanese economist reported to the author after a series of visits to corporate offices in Japan that supervisory and administrative personnel in Japanese firms put in an average monthly overtime of 60 hours without overtime pay. (Employees below a certain rank or level must by law be paid overtime.)   As "family" members, employees of a company do not compete among themselves; they compete, as a family, with other families (companies) in productivity, sales, and revenue. Even among Japanese, a common phrase referring to workers is hatarakibachi (working bees), and managerial employees are called moretsu shain (workhorse employees.) Foreigners have been constantly amazed at the obvious "workoholism" of the Japanese, but to the Japanese it is just a matter of course. There is nothing artificial or contrived about it at all.

Statistics pertaining to Japan's economic power are impressive, to put it rather mildly. The nation's economy appears formidable, massively capitalized, undergirded by intricate and sophisticated educational, technological communications, and transportation infrastructures, manned by competent managers, diligent and skilled workers, and assisted by a benevolent and helpful government. This awesome economic giant, however, has a mortal Achilles' heel. This fact is nothing new; Japan's attack on Pearl Harbor was at least in part precipitated by the nation's fear of this fatal weakness. In the postwar period, awareness of this weakness existed but the magnitude of the danger was first driven home only early in the 1970s.

No major nation in the world is as constrained by fear of economic pressure as is Japan today. The United States, despite its obvious economic trials and tribulations, is fundamentally strong and resilient in its economic capability. In case of another OPEC oil embargo, it could weather resulting shortage of oil by tightening its belt by a small notch or two, for, after all, it still is fabulously endowed with natural resources, including oil, and the degree of its external dependence for oil is such that, with proper government policy, it would experience little more than inconvenience.   The European Community, too, is fundamentally autonomous in terms of most of its economic requirements and, with close mutual cooperation among its members, it, too, possesses a high degree of resilience.   The same would be generally true of such other industrial states as Canada, Australia, and New Zealand. Disruption, for example, of oil supply to Japan, whether it be brought about gradually, barrel by barrel, or suddenly as would be the case with a total moratoriuim by major OPEC nations, or by physical harassment of its long but narrow sealanes, would wreak havoc in its economy if it lasted longer than a few months.

TABLE 3.2

Indexes of External Dependence for Selected Commodities, 1977

Commodity	Percent	Commodity	Percent
Sulphur ore	100.0	Tin	97.8
Bauxite	100.0	Copper	97.2
Cotton	100.0	Soy beans	97.0
Wool	100.0	Wheat	96.0
Natural rubber	100.0	Barley	91.2
Nickel	100.0	Manganese	91.2
Crude oil	99.8	Salt	85.9
Iron ore	99.6	Coal	76.9

Source: Asahi Nenkan 1979 Bekkan (1979 Asahi Yearbook Supplement), p. 338, and Gaimusho, ed., Waga Gaiko no Kinkyo (Recent State of Our Diplomacy) (Tokyo: Okurasho Insatsu Kyoku, 1979), p. 499.

Japan is virtually without industrial raw materials of its own and with few sources of energy — it is one of the poorest nations on earth in this regard. Consider Table 3.2 indicating Japan's degree of poverty in some of the most basic raw materials. Even in grain, the most important dietary item in any society, Japan was able to meet only 43 percent of its domestic requirements in 1975, for example, which was by far the lowest among advanced industrial states. (Figures for other industrial states in the same year were: 64 percent for Great Britain, 74 percent for Italy, 80 percent for West

Germany, 152 percent for France, and 174 percent for the United States.) The figure delined to 39 percent two years later.(13) Japan's annual fishing catch, an important traditional source of protein, is approximately 10 million tons, but nearly half of that is caught within 200 miles of other nations.(14) Insofar as its energy needs are concerned (petroleum, coal, electricity, atomic energy), 87 percent must be purchased abroad, again by far the highest figure among the industrial nations.(15) This extremely high degree of external dependence for basic materials in order to keep its gigantic industrial economy running and people alive renders Japan danger- ously vulnerable to circumstances over which it has little or no control. In other words, Japan is hostage to events in and among nations that supply it with those key commodities without which it would readily collapse.

The extent to which Japan may be vulnerable to events abroad is influenced not only by the degree of its external dependence for a given key commodity but also by the pattern of distribution of sources of that commodity as well as by the relative importance of that commodity in its domestic economic activity. In this sense, Japan is definitely most vulnerable with respect to oil. Japan's sources of oil supply are highly concentrated geopolitically in one of the most unstable areas of the world, an area that is pregnant with imminent likelihood of paralyzing upheaval and instability: the Persian Gulf region. From this area, Japan imports 83 percent of its oil (combined with imports from Indonesia, another potentially unstable nation, the figure goes up to nearly 98 percent). This smacks of putting all your eggs in one questionable basket, but, of course, Japan has no choice in the matter. In fact, none of the major and medium oil exporters to Japan is really stable; virtually every one of them is in imminent danger of internal chaos. It is this internal instability, actual or potential, and consequent long-range unpredictability of external behavior of these oil-producing states and the volatility of their region at large that vastly raise the level of saliency of Japan's vulnerability. To compound this danger, Japan relies on oil as an energy source more heavily than all other major advanced industrial states except for Italy. (See Table 3.3). Indeed, the growth in the extent of Japan's dependence on imported oil has been virtually exponential: between 1955 and 1977, the volume of import had grown 33 times, with the value of imports rising 119 times.(16) As of 1977, three-fourths of Japan's energy requirements were met by imported oil, in contrast to three-fifths ten years earlier. (An additional 12 percent is met by imported coal.) This is not all, yet. The vulnerability of Japan's industrial economy to changing circumstances of oil-producing nations is even greater than the above figures suggest. A comparative study of energy demand structures reveals that, in Japan, business and industry take up approximately two-thirds of the total domestic energy requirement while the remaining one-third is consumed by transportation and households. This is a virtual reversal of the demand pattern in the United States (little over 40 percent for business and industry and the remainder for transportation and households). Other major industrial states fall somewhere between Japan and the United States in their energy-demand structures, albeit by and large closer to the latter than to the former.(17) This means that any disruption in oil supply would produce a proportionately far greater negative impact (for example, unemployment, a drop in GNP, agricultural production, recession, or depression) on Japan's economy much more quickly than on any other industrial state. The backbone of this economic giant is readily breakable.

TABLE 3.3

Structure of Energy Sources, 1974

	Oil	Coal	Natural Gas	Hydro-electric Power	Nuclear Power	Total
U.S.	44.7	20.2	29.2	4.2	1.7	100.0
Great Britain	54.8	28.3	12.9	0.5	3.6	100.0
West Germany	52.0	33.6	11.5	1.5	1.0	100.0
France	68.4	15.6	7.7	6.5	1.7	100.0
Italy	77.4	6.7	9.8	5.5	0.4	100.0
Canada	48.2	7.2	24.2	18.9	1.3	100.0
Japan	73.1	17.3	2.1	5.7	1.3	100.0
Japan 1977	74.6	14.8	3.7	4.8	2.0	100.0

Source: Takeo Takahashi, "Oil and Japan's 'Energy-Weak' Economy," Look Japan, June 10, 1979, p. 6.

In some of the nonpetroleum commodities to be imported, Japan's predicament is relatively better, but how long this comparatively benign condition will persist is problematic, as we shall soon see. Japan's sources of supply of metallic raw materials (for example, copper, iron ore, tin) are scattered geographically, from Chile and Peru in South America through the United States and Canada in North America, the Philippines and India in Asia, to South Africa. With the exception of Australia, which in 1977 supplied 31 percent of Japan's requirements, there was no single nation from which Japan imported more than 10 percent of the total.(18) These nations are not only geographically dispersed around the globe but also politically and culturally diverse, and, perhaps more important for Japan's immediate future, major suppliers among them are relatively stable and not threatened by immediate danger of serious internal upheaval, and their external conduct remains largely predictable.

Whether or not Japan can continue to import sufficient quantities of metallic raw materials from these nations depends, however, not only upon them but also upon its ability to pay for its purchases. Japan's ability to pay for its imports, in turn, depends upon these and other nations' willingness to import its products, plus the extent of oil price hikes in the meantime. There are signs that some of the major customers of Japan's products may not continue to purchase those products at the volume that would generate sufficient amounts of income for it to pay for industrial raw materials it needs. In 1977, for example, Japan exported $9.7 billion more in goods than it imported. This favorable balance of payments was generated at the expense of the United States and members of European Community (EC) who suffered $7.3 billion and $4.5 billion in deficits respectively in their bilateral trade with Japan.(19) By 1979 Japan's exports had grown barely in physical volume, although with higher prices for its exports, its income from exports had risen.(20) The economies of Japan on the one hand, and of the United States and the European Community, on the other, are not complementary enough to justify perpetuation of this rather lopsided pattern of balance of payments in favor of Japan, especially since these major customers of Japanese products, and the United States in particular, by far the largest customer, have been experiencing a serious balance-of-payments crunch that threatens the stability of their currencies and the worsening of their inflation and domestic economic conditions. They would not for long tolerate this adverse balance of trade with Japan, and they could readily take measures that would seriously curtail Japanese exports to them. (In the fall of 1980, the EC's foreign ministers' conference did present Japan with an unprecedentedly stiff demand for its restraint in export to Western Europe.)

In 1977, for which some figures have just been mentioned, Japan incurred in its trade with four major Persian Gulf oil-producing states a balance-of-payments deficit of $9.3 billion. When Indonesia, the largest non-Arab oil exporter to Japan, is included, Japan's deficits came to well over $12 billion. This last figure more or less equals that of a combined U.S.-EC deficit in trade with Japan.(21) In a sense, the United States and West European states financed over 60 percent of Japan's oil purchase from OPEC states (close to $20 billion) in that year. Japan's dependence on its major non-OPEC customers for revenues to pay for the OPEC oil would be sure to increase. Consider, for example, the possibility of an annual average oil price increase of, say, 10 percent: in 1978, Japan's oil payment to the Persian Gulf states alone amounted to approximately $20 billion. At an annual average of 10 percent increase in the oil price, by 1988 Japan would be paying over $52 billion for the same amount of oil from those Arab states alone. It would be unreasonable to expect the current major customers of Japanese goods to increase their imports proportionately, not only because of their unhappiness already mentioned but also because their own oil bills would rise at the same pace as Japan's would. Combined with the sure prospects of rises in prices of industrial raw materials and foodstuffs, this could have a serious impact on Japan's industrial economy. In a really desperate situation, the façt that Japan's economy is not complementary to that of many of the current major customers of its products renders it exceedingly vulnerable. Consider Japan's economic relationship with the United States, by far the largest of its trade partners (in 1978, over one-quarter of Japan's total export went to the United States). It is not entirely equal in its basic character.

Most Japanese exports to the United States compete with the latter's domestic manufacturers - automobiles, electronics, steel, industrial machinery, to cite a few major items - and, assuming other things to be equal for the moment, U.S. business and industry could be much better off without competition from Japanese products. On the other hand, major items that Japan imports from the United States are those it cannot do without since there are no domestic substitutes (for example, agricultural products, lumber, and mineral raw materials, which constituted nearly 60 percent of Japan's total imports from the United States in 1977). Nor could Japan readily find alternative sources of supply of these commodities. This inequality or disparity in the fundamental character of Japanese-U.S. economic relations would become glaringly manifest with vast consequences for Japan if the United States seriously began to pursue some of the radical short-term remedies for its deficit trade balance with Japan. Protectionist sentiments against Japanese products are said to be even stronger in European nations (which bought another 12 percent of Japan's exports in 1978). Should the United States and those other advanced industrial states undertake stringent measures with the view to reducing their trade imbalance with Japan, its ability to purchase not only oil but other essential raw materials would be severely curtailed and the precarious equilibrium of its intricate economic system would be gravely eroded on short order, which, in turn, would trigger spiral or multiplier effects in a direction that would be insurmountably difficult to reverse.

The impact of such a contingency on Japan's domestic socio-economic harmony and stability would be doubly serious because its economic system is structurally bifurcated in a way that would render the impact acutely differential and, as a consequence, permit that impact to destroy the very fundamental interpersonal and social relationship that has for generations made up that unique resilience of the nation's economy and society. The Japanese economy, awesome and dynamic as it may appear in statistical terms, is still a dual economy to an extent that might be surprising to foreigners. By dual economy here is meant a national economic system that is sharply dichotomized between an advanced, capital-intensive sector and a distinctly less advanced, more labor-intensive, small-scale-operation sector. In statistical terms, a great preponderance of economic enterprises in Japan are quite small. In 1975, for example, only 0.4 percent of the total number of Japanese firms had 500 or more employees and only 0.03 percent (288) of them employed 5,000 or more workers. Over two-thirds (67.5 percent) of all the firms had fewer than ten employees each. In terms of capital size, 0.05 percent of the firms controlled 48.5 percent of total capital investment in the country and 0.2 percent of the firms shared 63.7 percent of total corporate investment.(22) This lopsided bifurcation of the nation's economic structure is owing in the main to the policy of rapid economic growth of the past two decades and a half, the policy that deliberately favored high-growth industries fiscally and monetarily and in other forms of direct or indirect assistance. Fabulously capitalized giant corporations such as Toshiba, Hitachi, Matsushita, and many other internationally known ones have been made possible by a massive, multilayered, small-scale, labor-intensive support structure composed of hundreds of thousands of medium to precariously marginal firms scattered throughout the country and carrying out barely profitable subcontract works for them. A large number of these submerged firms subsist literally from hand to mouth, and they are at the mercy of those giant corporations that could grant or withhold subcontracts at will. It is these firms and their employees, who constitute the great majority of the nation's working population, that would be far more immediately and seriously affected by any kind of economic hardship or dislocation caused by changes in the nation's economic and trade relations with other nations, particularly OPEC states and the United States, since the modern upper sector would immediately shift the burden of dislocation to the lower sector composed of those fragile enterprises. Whatever potential socioeconomic friction that exists between the two dichotomous sectors of the national economy has thus far been largely glossed over or even obviated by a quarter century of continuous and rapid growth and prosperity and the essentially clientelist character of ties between those two disparate sectors; their differential resilience has thus far not been put to a really critical test. That test today is likely to be imminent, however. It might come sooner than later. In such a contingency, there is great danger that the objective gap between those two sectors of the economy would become subjectively painful, especially as the conventional expectation born of the era of rapid growth of well-being and security on the part of the managers and workers of the vast lower sector would lose its optimistic validity and be replaced by growing despair. The benign employer-employee relationship that in the past helped not only expand productivity but also maintain cohesion and harmony in the Japanese economic system would be rapidly eroded by the inexorable force of retrenchment, cutback, liquidation, and bankruptcy in large numbers of firms in the lower economic sector, critically depriving increasing proportions of workers of their whole existential security that they have always taken for granted and that has been the basis of sociopolitical stability of the nation. This would be bound to produce serious consequences for the viability of the nation's democracy, which has been judiciously fostered during the last generation.

A DELICATE GLASS TOWER

The economy, while it is the most immediate and most frequently discussed concern of government and people alike, is not the only dimension of Japan's fragility in the uncertain international environment. Among other relevant dimensions are physical, demographic, social, and military. The last of these dimensions will be discussed in Chapter 5 and this section will be confined to a brief comment on the others.

Compared to its internal and external condition before, say, World War II when it was universally regarded as an aggressive and powerful state, Japan today, its economic superpower status notwithstanding, is geometrically far more fragile than it was 40 years ago. Part of this fragility, of course, stems from its virtually total dependence upon foreign nations for its livelihood — energy, food, raw materials, and markets. In this regard alone, Japan may be by far the most fragile of the industrial nations, for it is externally dependent for a wider range of material requirements than any other. Japan is thus fragile in the face of political hostility by those on whom it depends for livelihood.

Japan is fragile in another sense, that is, fragile in the face of physical hostility from outside as well as from inside. In this regard, the fragility would become vastly magnified by certain factors that were largely absent 40 years ago, and this regardless of the level of military defense capability it may possess or attain. In fact, this particular dimension of fragility would really reduce the efficacy of that military capability.

One factor of this dimension is extreme demographic density and structural concentration. Japan is not only small, but with less than one-sixth of its land habitable, the degrees of density and concentration could be comprehended only by being there. To get a proximate picture of Japan's predicament in this regard, the reader only needs to visualize half of the U.S. population, together with half of its artificial structures, industries, and other life-support activities, all packed into the narrow coastal strip between, say, San Francisco and San Diego. In 1978 there were more than 40 cars, trucks, and busses for every single kilometer of negotiable road.(23) Despite the small size of the usable land, Japan for a number of years has been at the top among the world's nations in passenger kilometers served by its extremely well-developed and pervasive network of rail transportation. In 1976, for example, Japan's figure was 323 billion passenger kilometers, considerably higher than that of the vast and far more populous Soviet Union, which ranked second with 315 billion passenger kilometers. West Germany, a highly developed and rail-heavy nation with a population a bit larger than half that of Japan, compiled only 36 billion passenger kilometers.(24)

This enormously congested nation is sustained by an increasingly complex, sensitive, and sophisticated network of life-support infrastructures such as communication, transportation, utilities, circulation and distribution of goods and services, private and public administrative bureaucracies, all relying progressively upon delicate electronic technology. The whole nation is a mammoth exposed precision mechanism interconnected by sensitive joints and delicate links. Breakdown or disruption of any of its parts could have a devastating effect on the whole of it. Japan, as one analyst observed, is a huge glass tower.(25) Disruption, for example, in power supply caused by nature or human contrivance could create chaos in major population centers. A serious accident or work stoppage in, say, the national railroad system could quickly create shortages of perishable goods in any number of areas. Large-scale disruption in the life of the country would be relatively easy to cause. For example, it could be caused by an act of sabotage, for example, a simultaneous blow-up of major power-transmission facilities designed to paralyze a number of metropolises, a series of bombings or dynamitings of major national railroad tracks (half a dozen strategic points might suffice, especially bridges and tunnels), a similar attack on major petrochemical complexes (a few would do), or, as a recent popular suspense novel suggested, the explosion of a mammoth tanker in a narrow harbor in close proximity to a petrochemical complex, an industrial center, and residential districts. These are but a few of the more readily thinkable contingencies, some of which, incidentally, could materialize simultaneously. As one analyst noted, threats to the nation's physical security come from within as well: they are "ubiquitous."(26)

As for physical threats from outside, the extent of Japan's fragility is even more alarming. An enemy could easily cause paralysis of this huge and hugely exposed glass tower with savage effectiveness. He would not need to land troops, as such would seem superfluous militarily for its destruction or subduing. By a brief blitzkrieg of selective air and/or naval-missile strikes against several of the major nerve centers of this complex and sensitive network of delicate life-support infrastructures, he could effectively cripple the nation on short order. This combined with the ensuing chains of reaction and disorder among a panicked population could lead to total national paralysis. Troop landing would be essential later mainly for political and administrative purposes. This prospect is all the more real since no comprehensive plans for dealing with the kind of contingency suggested here has been made in the areas, for example, of civil defense, transport, communication, emergency stockpiles of food, medicine, and other essential commodities, urban evacuation, legal and political administration, and the like. Japan's lifelines beyond its territorial waters in the Western Pacific are most vulnerable to naval, especially submarine, attack. Its collapse as an industrial state could be brought about by their sustained disruption.

The prospect of national paralysis is all the more real especially because of certain sociocultural trends that have emerged during the past decade or so in Japan as one of the advanced industrial societies, phenomena that were discussed in Chapter 20. The almost familial sense of community that characterizes much of the labor-management relations in Japan today discussed earlier in this chapter, stands in particularly sharp contrast to the rapid decline of the tradition of mutual assistance and cooperation outside that particular nexus of interpersonal and social relations. The fast-paced demographic change accompanying the rapid economic recovery and growth within a span of less than a generation caused a sharp contextual demarcation between that particular employer-employee social nexus and the increasingly depersonalized urban life, with little existential link between the two. People by and large live hours away from their places of work, and the warmth and community of their places of work is the diametrical opposite of the increasingly impersonal "lonely crowd" atmosphere surrounding their places of residence. It is on these places of residence that the negative impact of any disruption of the nation's delicate life-support system would produce the most serious effect, for there remains little of a community to cushion it. Instead, the more and more impersonal "lonely crowd" atmosphere would give free rein to individual selfishness and cupidity in situations of anxiety and fear, compounding the panic and confusion that could in earlier times have been contained and defused. (The harbinger of this likelihood was the panic buying of certain household goods at the time of the "oil shock" of 1973-74, when the shelves of urban supermarkets and stores were quickly depleted.)

There is another critical aspect to the decline of community of Japan: As in other advanced industrial societies, people have become increasingly dependent upon the government for the management and solution of a wider range of problems and needs, and, as its corollary, they have become less and less reliant on themselves and on informal, private spheres of social and interpersonal relations. This fact, which, as noted in Chapter 2, put an enormous burden on the capability of the government even under "normal" circumstances, would exponentially complicate the task of the government. This would be further compounded by the significant decline of community, mutual help, self-help, and other traditional resilience-guarding virtues as the result of progress and prosperity. Management of the type of crisis discussed in this chapter, then, would be extraordinarily difficult; it may well prove to be impossible.

The fragility of Japan is multidimensional, and it arises in large measure from what other nations, as well as the Japanese themselves, view as its fortune: its spectacular growth into an economic superpower with all that it implies in demographic change, economic well-being, sociocultural tendency, and structural complexity, all taking place in a country that was compact in size and population density and bereft of natural resources to begin with. Four decades ago, Japan embarked on territorial expansion in search of permanent security through military superpowerdom only to be reduced and confined to its original tiny and overcrowded archipelago by devastating and traumatic military defeat. In recent decades, Japan has endeavored, backed by unanimous (albeit silent) national consensus, to seek an approximation of permanent security and stability through acquisition of an economic superpower status. It has succeeded all too well in its endeavor, only to find that the newly acquired status, so fervently coveted throughout all these years of diligent and single-minded endeavor, is riddled with unanticipated infirmities, unintended detriments, and unforeseen susceptibilities. In the face of this irony, the most critical task Japan now faces – the task that would call for as much care and deliberateness in planning, as much judiciousness and caution in implementing, and as much diligence and perseverance in awaiting its fruit as that in which it has achieved such success – is seeing that its multidimensional fragility be minimized and that the range of future contingencies threatening it be maximally reduced.

The stability of Japan cannot be contemplated without considering the security of the whole region of East Asia – and ultimately that of the whole world. It is only the limitations of time, scope, and competence that make it necessary to narrow our geographic focus to East Asia. In any event, it is abundantly clear that Japan's safety is predicated upon the stability of East Asia as a region, as a major source of its raw material supply, as the closest geographic space through which its trade with other regions of the world travels, and as its most proximate politicomilitary environment. This is the issue to which Japan now must begin to devote much of its national energy – political, intellectual, diplomatic, and economic – in much the same way it has during the postwar period devoted its energy to economic reconstruction and growth. In so doing, Japan could no longer afford to take as narrow and self-centered a view as it has done with respect to the task of economic growth. It must now act in ways that take into proper and integrated account the well-being and security of the region of East Asia as a whole. Only in so doing would Japan be able to influence the course of future events so that they might not threaten its stability. Otherwise, those events would come crushing down on the fragile glass tower.

NOTES

(1) For example, Herman Kahn, The Emerging Japanese Superstate (Englewood Cliffs, N.J.: Prentice-Hall, 1970); Norman Macrae, "Pacific Century, 1975-2075?" Economist, January 4-10, 1975; and Don Oberdorfer, "Japan: The Risen Sun," Washington Post, August 3-7, 1975.

(2) Yearbook of National Account Statistics 1978 (New York: Statistical Office of the United Nations, 1979), pp. 665 and 1386.

(3) Macrae, p. 16.

(4) Sorifu Tokei Kyoku, Nihon no Tokei (Statistics of Japan) (Tokyo: Okurasho Insatsukyoku, 1979), p.37.

(5) See, for example, Ryuken Ohashi, Nihon no Kaikyu Kosei (Japan's Class Structure) (Tokyo: Iwanami, 1972), pp. 138-40, and Howard Van Zandt, "Japanese Culture and the Business Boom" Foreign Affairs 48, no. 2 (January 1970): 347-48 and passim.

(6) Kokumin Seikatsu Kahusho (White Paper on People's Livelihood) (Tokyo: Keizai Kikakucho, 1971), p. 44.

(7) Showa 48 Nen Ban Kosei Hakusho (1973 Welfare White Paper) (Tokyo: Koseisho, 1973), p. 81, and Asahi Nenkan 1979 Bekkan (1979 Asahi Yearbook Supplement) (Tokyo: Asahi Shimbunsha, 1979), pp. 398-99.

(8) Robert Shaplen, "A Reporter At Large: From MacArthur to Miki – II" The New Yorker, August 11, 1975, p. 38.

(9) This refers to what might be called a "cultural distinctiveness approach" in the study of Japanese labor-management relations as the secret behind Japan's economic wonder. See, for example, James Abegglen, The Japanese Factory (Glencoe, Ill.: The Free Press, 1958). For an excellent work challenging this popular approach, see Robert Marsh and Hiroshi Mannari, Modernization and Japanese Factory (Princeton, N.J.: Princeton University Press, 1976).

(10) Chie Nakane, Japanese Society (Berkeley: University of California Press, 1970), p. 15.

(11) Ibid., pp. 3-5.

(12) For the behavior of Japanese labor unions, see, for example, Robert E. Cole, Japanese Blue Collar: The Changing Tradition (Berkeley: University of California Press, 1971), esp., Chapters 7-8.

(13) Nihon Kokusei Zue (Picture of the State of Japan) (Tokyo: Kokuseisha, 1979), p. 207, and Yasuhiko Yuize, "Taikoku no Shokuryo Senryaku to Nihon no Anzen Hosho" (Superpower Food Strategy and Japan's Security), Asahi Janaru, April 11, 1980, p. 33.

(14) Toki no Horei 959 (March 13, 1977): 43.

(15) Waga Gaiko no Kinkyo (Recent State of Our Diplomacy), p. 477.

(16) Japan Statistical Yearbook 1979 (Tokyo: Statistics Bureau, Prime Minister's Office, 1979), p. 296.

(17) Takeo Takahashi, "Oil and Japan's 'Energy-Weak' Economy," Look Japan, June 10, 1979, p. 7.

(18) Asahi Nenkan 1979 Bekkan, p. 340.

(19) Ibid., p. 339.

(20) Look Japan, December 10, 1979, pp. 12-13.

(21) Ibid.

(22) Computed from Japan Statistical Yearbook 1979, pp. 92-93.

(23) Computed from Nihon no Tokei, (Statistics of Japan) (Tokyo: Okurasho Insatsukyoku, 1979), pp. 121 and 126.

(24) Asahi Nenkan 1979 Bekkan, p. 317.

(25) Mineo Nakajima, "Boei Senrayaku to Nihon Gaiko" (Defense Strategy and Japanese Diplomacy), Chuokoron, January 1979, p. 91.

(26) Junnosuke Kishida, "Senshin Shakai no Sogo Anzen Hosho Towa Nanika" (What Is Comprehensive Security of an Advanced Society?), Chuokoron, January 1979, p. 97.

4
East Asian Relations: International Politics in Search of a Modus Operandi

DIPLOMATIC PROBLEMS OF POLITICAL UNDERDEVELOPMENT

The immediate geographic concern of the present volume is East Asia, which consists of what are commonly called Northeast Asia and Southeast Asia in the Western Pacific. East Asia thus defined is only a geographic expression, not a regional international system in the sense, say, that Western Europe or the North Atlantic are regional international systems. It is still much too inchoate in its internal relations to be viewed as a system, for a system implies regularized patterns of interaction among its component parts, including certain practices of issue management and problem solving. East Asia, in short, has yet to find how to live with itself.

The fact that East Asia is not a regional international system means that it is unstable and volatile. This is an obvious fact, for there have been violent conflicts among states within the region: the Korean War early in the 1950s, small and big wars in Indochina from the end of World War II until now, border skirmishes between China and the Soviet Union in the 1960s and 1970s, confrontation between Indonesia and Malaysia in the early 1960s, the war between China and Vietnam in 1979, and battles between Thai and Vietnamese forces over the Thai-Cambodian border in 1980. These violent incidences, among other phenomena, reflect the fact that most of the nations of East Asia are new, with the newness implying certain ramifications in their mutual relations. Only three of the region's nations were independent prior to World War II: China, Japan, and Thailand, and none of these three had developed the type of pattern of mutual intraregional relations that would be consistent with the pursuit of regional stability and harmony, that is, the emergence of a stable regional international system. After its national consolidation in the last third of the nineteenth century, Japan had pursued a general policy of imperialist expansion and regional domination. During the same period China had been incapacitated by a succession of internal turmoils and, as a consequence, was preyed upon by Western and then Japanese imperialists, remaining victim to events in its environment and unable to influence them so as to determine the character of their outcome. Thailand had essentailly been an inward-looking state, an attitude that had evolved through its century-long preoccupation with a careful balancing act in order to avoid subjugation and colonization by an imperialist Western power or powers. For all practical purposes, therefore, East Asian nations after 1945, old as well as new, were novices to the task of establishing cooperative and stable international relations.

To put the matter more concretely, the nations of East Asia lacked and still lack to a significant extent some of the most important bases for stable mutual interaction. Among these bases that could collectively make for a stable pattern of mutual relations - an international modus operandi - are: incrementalism as the normal expectation in mutual efforts for resolving a critical problem, the necessity to deal only with issues that lend themselves to mutually acceptable or tolerable management or resolution and to eschew the forcing of any issue that for the moment seems intractable or that the adversary cannot afford to deal with for a variety of reasons, the desirability of always allowing for compromise, and the wisdom of not limiting the adversary's choice to a desperate fight or abject capitulation. This list, of course, is far from exhaustive, but the items all pertain to what one analyst calls the "taboo line" in international interaction.(1) What we have listed here are among the more obvious ones. One of the most crucial among them is the acceptance, reluctant though it must invariably be in most cases, by the nations concerned not only of the desirability but also of the ultimate feasibility of mutual compromise and the eschewal of "all or nothing" expectations. Now, feasibility of mutual compromise, that is, mutual concession, which is the same as effective issue management and problem solving, is a matter of subjective perception of the parties concerned. If the parties concerned fail to perceive such feasibility, their behavior toward each other is likely to become contentious and strident, and the likelihood of concession and compromise recedes further.

The matter of positive perception in this regard is in important part a function of the routinization of mutual interaction over time, and such routinization, in turn, is the result of common experience over time. Clearly there are many other factors that help give rise to such positive perceptions of the feasibility of issue management and problem solving. Among them are: common historical and cultural tradition (for example, religion, race, ethnicity, language): common or similar economic systems and developmental patterns, or similarity in political systems; similarity in general political or ideological orientation; and/or elite compatibility through a tradition of routinized and intimate personal interaction and/or similar political preference and ideological orientations, common educational backgrounds, patterns of life experience, and intellectual ethos. These elements are, of course, variable in terms of intensity and range. Some nations share most or even all of these elements more widely and more intensely than others, making for what the Americans and the British would like to call "a special relationship." Some others share fewer of those elements but more intensely, and so on. In any event, it seems reasonable to say that English-speaking, largely Anglo-Saxon nations share a sufficient range of those elements with such a degree of intensity that their pattern of mutual interaction has become routinized to the extent that violent confrontation among them over any issue is improbable. West European states are becoming similar to these English-speaking nations in this regard. Where this condition prevails, mutual perception and behavior of parties concerned are likely to be stable, continuous, and predictable. In an important sense, the Atlantic Alliance and the European Community may be viewed as quintessential results/examples of a tradition of such a pattern of mutual interaction among the nations concerned. Of course, revolutionary change in a key state within any such group of nations could upset this pattern, as could extremely serious political or economic problems, for the capacity of this routinized pattern of mutual issue management and problem solving is finite at any given moment, and the level of capability of this patern does not remain constant, for it is continually affected by internal stress and strain within each party concerned as well as by the magnitude of external problems the parties face individually or collectively. For a regional international system to remain more or less stable, however, a certain viable pattern of stable mutual interaction must be present. Such a pattern of mutual interaction can exist among ideologically divergent nations or between ideologically opposed groups of nations, however pregnant that pattern may be with potentials of disruption. The Nuclear Test Ban Treaty, SALT I, and SALT II, for example, would have been impossible without the existence or cultivation of some such pattern.

East Asian nations still lack a strong tradition of this pattern of mutual interaction not only because they are generally "new" as actors in the regional international arena but also because of their mutual divergence in culture and history. Whatever modus operandi there may exist between any two nations in the region or among several nations is fundamentally fragile in character and precarious in duration. Inasmuch as a relevant tradition exists among Western nations rendering their conduct predictable and stable, each East Asian state tends to deal with them in accordance with the parameters of their modus operandi, much in the same sense that Japan, from the Restoration up to the late 1920s, had attempted to deal with those Western nations according to their diplomatic practices, in order to gain acceptance as a modern state in their eyes. When it comes to interaction among themselves, however, East Asian nations still seem uneasy with one another, uncertain that they would deal with one another in the same manner that they individually deal with, say, the United States, France, or Britain. Positive mutual perceptions of feasibility of compromise and the desirability of mutual concession in case of a serious disagreement are still difficult to come by because East Asian nations are far more diverse among themselves in culture, history, economy, ethnicity, language, and the like than Western nations are and, as a consequence, lack a relevant tradition of mutual interaction, that is, issue management and problem solving. They are still in search of an appropriate modus operandi. Rigidity of attitude, abiding mutual distrust, and fear of deception and betrayal remain powerful forces behind the behavior of Asian states, rendering the management of issues and resolution of problems plaguing the region extremely difficult.

Beyond considerations of culture and history, there is the matter of the structure of interaction. One of the important sources of the mutual interaction tradition that promotes effective issue management and problem solving is cultivation of multiple levels and contexts of mutual intercourse, hence communication, among nations concerned, ranging from the topmost official level down to the level of ordinary citizens. Multiplicity of communication levels and interactional contexts helps reduce or assuage mutual prejudices, preconceived notions, misinformation and misunderstanding, hence fear and mistrust. In this respect, too, relations among East Asian nations continue to suffer considerably. It is quite obvious that, being mostly poor and geographically widely scattered, and separated from one another by widely differential economic conditions, political inhibitions, and cultural differences, ordinary East Asians cannot and do not visit one another's countries. For those relative few who do travel, there is a far greater (often insurmountable) problem of communication than among Europeans: they have to resort to the use of an extraregional third language, usually English, which moreover, most of them speak poorly. This is a persistent problem even among intellectuals and scholars. When they meet, say in a symposium or a conference, their exchanges are more often than not formal, addressing one another from painstakingly prepared English texts, and generally unable or reluctant to follow through what is formally said in intimate and candid skull sessions in order to explore implications and nuances and to develop new ideas and further understanding and appreciation. Formal exchanges and speeches are generally sterile of substance and predictable in content. Most of those conferences, symposia, and colloquia, which are held in increasing numbers these days, provide only those select few intellectuals and scholars with occasions for luxurious junkets and little else. In a strict sense, they don't talk with one another.

What is more relevant within the context of our concern here, however, is the insufficient development of unofficial and private channels of political communication and discussion among the governments of East Asian nations.   Interaction between any two governments tends to take place mostly at one level, that is, the level of officials in their formal capacities, and this creates a number of problems. When any serious issue is dealt with at that level (and especially when it does not seem to lend itself to ready solution), the governments concerned tend to engage in public posturing and exchanges of demands, counterdemands, and epithets since neither side wishes to seem to be making concessions. Initial tension, instead of being contained or reduced, is likely to escalate, and the resolution of the issue becomes that much more difficult. Nations interacting on the basis of an appropriate tradition of mutual intercourse tend to maintain, as a matter of course as well as prudence, multiple channels of government communication so that, in the first place, mutual feeling-out and search for consensus or areas of potential agreement could be quietly undertaken without public notice, and careful preparatory groundwork may be made through unofficial, even secret negotiations. By the time the issue is officially dealt with at the formal government level, therefore, its management or resolution would have a reasonable chance of success.   Unnecessary stridency and counterproductive posturing could then be minimized or avoided.   Maintenance of mutual communication through a multiplicity of informal channels between two nations enables the sifting of issues that at the moment do not lend themselves to effective resolution without permitting them to reach the formal governmental or diplomatic level where there is clear danger of failure.   In the second place, the existence of multiple channels of interaction between the two nations or among nations concerned enables the continuation of discussion and negotiation in search of eventual solution even if the issue at hand creates tension at the official level. The Cuban missile crisis was resolved precisely because Moscow and Washington had by then established these multiple channels of communication, which they were willing to utilize fully.   Consequences of what would have happened had there not been those channels of informal and secret mutual feeling-out and communication are terrifying to contemplate.

Inadequate development of an appropriate modus operandi among East Asian states, including multiple channels of communication and interaction, can be only partly attributed to their newness as nations and their historical and cultural diversity. To a considerable extent, it is owing to the basic instability of their respective political systems and regimes. For purposes of narrative convenience, two of the fundamental problems of this instability may be briefly discussed: governmental process and political elites.

The governmental process of East Asian states is typically unstable, discontinuous, at times even haphazard.   It is not sufficiently institutionalized.   Put slightly differently, processes of policy initiation, deliberation formulation, legitimation, and execution are often ad hoc, intermittent, even capricious. Power tends to be arbitrarily exercised and accountability is often a matter of

arbitrary attribution, with the consequence that government person
nel are insecure, demoralized, mutually mistrustful, factionalized,
hence often corrupt. Instability of governmental process in turn
suggests a low level of legitimacy of the regimes concerned, for
legitimacy, while a matter of subjective perception of the populace
influenced variously by their particular history, tradition, and level
of development, nevertheless requires certain common ingredients
on the part of the regime that seeks it: stability, coherence,
continuity, and predictability in process and behavior (these are
among the vital elements of institutionalism, whatever specific
form of government a nation may in fact adopt).

That many, or perhaps most, East Asian governments suffer from
low levels of institutionalization, hence legitimacy, cannot be
blamed solely on the corruption and cupidity of their leaders.
Lacking a tradition of nationhood and fragmented by regional,
ethnic, communal, religious, and/or other particularistic cleavages,
there are extremely potent centrifugal tendencies in each of these
nations that its successive regimes have found virtually intractable.
Political response to this problem has been the emergence of
authoritarian regimes to repress centrifugal forces and all that they
imply for the development of these nations. However, the very fact
of the existence of these powerful forces has rendered institutionalization of governmental process extremely difficult even under
authoritarian rule. For one thing, inasmuch as even a highly
repressive authoritarian regime requires support for its survival, let
alone stability, recruitment of officials as well as patterns and
contents of policy making have tended to be particularistic and
contingent upon expediency for the survival of its incumbents, thus
circumventing the requirements of autonomy of government organizations, coherence of their respective procedures, and integrity of
decisional processes. In the end, government becomes the personal
fief of the incumbent rulers, with no guarantee of continuity,
predictability, or stability of policy once they suffer demise or even
during their indeterminate and insecure tenure. Government remains fundamentally unstable.

The political stability of a nation requires continuity of its
political elite or leadership. Such continuity, in turn, requires
several considerations regarding recruitment. Leadership recruitment patterns for this purpose should be popularly acceptable,
continuous, and predictable in terms, for example, of education,
training, apprenticeship, and selection. In addition, the pattern of
policy, policy making, and behavior of the leadership should also be
predictable and continuous as well as adaptable, in terms of
decisional parameters, direction, and national interest. Personnel
change in leadership as such should not result in radical policy
change. These are all problems that could be subsumed under the
general rubric of the problem of succession. Political leadership is
discontinuous, unstable, and unpredictable when its incumbents are
products, not of a well-established recruitment pattern supported by

a minimally consensual structure of relevant values shared by the population at large, but of a conspiracy of a group or groups promoting their own narrow particularistic interests, or of a chance congeries of disparate forces whose interests are actually or latently mutually incompatible. Such leadership may remain in power for a considerable length of time, but its behavior and policy as well as policy process are likely to be discontinuous and unpredictable because, in order to remain in power, it is compelled to act in a manner that would help insure its survival rather than continuity of its policy, and because the very centrifugal tendencies within the nation create potent imperatives for that leadership to behave according to contingencies of internal political fluctuation. In the end, leadership policy direction and behavior are functions of variable personal ambitions and interests of its incumbents. Politics, in short, personalistic.

Given the fact of instability both of governmental process and political leadership among most of the nations concerned, it is no wonder that the development of a stable pattern of international relations within the region of East Asia has been seriously inhibited. "Personalism in politics means personalism in diplomacy," observe some analysts. "In the absence of a well - developed foreign affairs bureaucracy. . . , it becomes difficult for governments to maintain the continuity, form, and substance of foreign policy when leadership changes hands."(2) Nations cannot count on one another's stability in conduct. It is apparent that this fact of governmental and leadership instability has prevented the sufficient development of multiple channels of effective communication and interaction among those nations. Instability and concomitant unpredictability of regimes and their incumbent leaders render foreign affairs personnel of these nations reluctant to become identified and enmeshed with their respective regimes' current orientation and policy more than is minimally necessary for job security, for fear that they might suffer persecution in case of regime changes. They are equally reluctant to cultivate personal ties with one another because they cannot be certain of one another's tenure security and policy consistency. This is not all, however. The very instability of governmental process and leadership renders these nations vulnerable to interference by outside powers that are more stable but intent on exploiting this inability to their own national benefit. Centrifugal forces within East Asian states can be covertly or overtly aided and abetted at various levels by propaganda, bribery, organizational or material assistance, and other forms of external manipulation. The very personalist character of regime and leadership lends itself to external meddling and manipulation in recruitment and selection and inducement for change in personnel and policy.(3) This fact of vulnerability to external interference further inhibits the development of such a modus operandi among East Asian nations as would stabilize the pattern of interaction among them.

Individual East Asian states have had far less frequent and intimate relations with one another than with extraregional nations: Japan, the Philippines, Thailand, and South Korea with the United States; China and North Korea with the Soviet-bloc nations; Vietnam with France and the Soviet Union; Malaysia and Singapore with the United Kingdom and the United States; and Indonesia variously with the United States, the Soviet Union, and Holland. Throughout much of the postwar period, they have been more concerned about their respective relations with those extraregional states than with one another. Compelling common regional identity has not really emerged among East Asian nations. Past attempts by these nations at intraregional cooperation and at establishing a stable pattern of mutual interaction were sporadic, haphazard, and mostly failures precisely because of the absence of sufficiently compelling sense of commonality of interest and destiny.(4) Lacking a tradition of extensive mutual interaction facilitated by common civilization, history, and culture, East Asian nations could hope to establish a stable pattern of mutual interaction among themselves only through an act of will. Without it, they would be unable to seek security in their region and they would run the sure risk of permitting their region to become, as some observers fear, "something of a crucible."(5)

EAST ASIA: A NEW VORTEX OF CONFLICT?

Both in character and consequence, major international developments in East Asia during the last decade were extraordinarily salient. Most of them, in fact, could not have been seriously contemplated even a decade earlier. Perhaps the most dramatic among those developments were Sino-American rapprochement in 1972 and their final normalization of relations in 1979; Sino-Japanese normalization of relations in 1972 and their consolidation by a treaty of peace and friendship in 1978; and the complete withdrawal of the United States from Vietnam by the mid-1970s. Less dramatic but no less salient from the perspective of the issue of regional security were the prompt unification of Vietnam by Hanoi in 1975, the growth of a Sino-Vietnamese rift shortly thereafter, the escalating conflict between a Soviet-backed Hanoi and Peking – aligned Phnom Penh and subsequent Vietnamese invasion and virtual occupation (not yet complete at the time of this writing) of Cambodia starting late in 1978 preceded by the formation of a virtual Hanoi-Moscow alliance through a treaty of friendship and cooperation in the fall of the same year, the Sino – Vietnamese war early in 1979, and the establishment of Vietnamese dominance over the whole of Indochina in the meantime, including Laos. In terms of direct superpower balance in the region, the decade of the 1970s also witnessed not only the withdrawal of over 0.5 million U.S.

ground troops from Indochina, but also a reversal, at least in numerical terms of the U.S.-Soviet balance in naval and air capabilities in the region.

What are some of the consequences of these events? How are they likely to influence the course of events in the new decade? What are some of the feasible directions in which Japan might move in order to help share that course of events so as to determine its outcome?

New Diplomatic Ties and Their Implications

Both the Sino-Japanese Treaty of Peace and Friendship (indicating a consolidation of relations normalized in 1972) of 1978 and the full normalization of Peking-Washington relations in 1979 came to add new dimensions to the problem of East Asian security and, as a necessary corollary, Japan's national defense. The initial popular presumption to the contrary notwithstanding, these two highly heralded diplomatic events complicated the problem far more than assuaged it. The most immediate consequence regarding the problem of regional security was that these events "markedly activated the Soviets' Asian strategy."(6) The long-simmering Sino-Soviet conflict came to assume new magnitude not only because of Moscow's suspicion of a Sino-U.S. or Sino-U.S.-Japanese anti-Soviet collusion but, more importantly for East Asian security, because Moscow's response to those recent diplomatic developments involving China was an acceleration of military expansion in Asia and an attempt to extend its power and influence in China's southern flank, for example, Indochina. The conjoining of those diplomatic events and Moscow's response to them now means that Japan and the United States will be, in spite of themselves, be in direct danger of being implicated in and seriously affected by the course of events in Sino-Soviet relations in the years to come. It also suggests that both Soviet-U.S. and Soviet-Japanese relations are now strained more than before.

Even prior to the conclusion of the Sino-Japanese Treaty of Peace and Friendship and full Sino-U.S. normalization, the Soviet Union had been quite vocal and explicit in its warning against anything that it could construe as a politicomilitary collusion between China on the one hand and Japan and/or the United States on the other. The Soviet ambassador to Tokyo, for example, had spoken of Moscow's readiness to introduce "certain correctives into its policy toward Japan" if the treaty were concluded.(7) This fact added to the context of the Soviet military-base buildup on three of the islands that Japan had always claimed as its own and the deployment of new generations of naval and air combat craft in East Asia. Later, Moscow made public expressions of suspicion of a potential Sino-Japanese security tie, accused Tokyo of pursing the kind of relationship with Peking that would be anti-Soviet in character and objective, and stated, "Such a policy inevitably results in making Japan an accomplice in Chinese adventures that endanger peace. Whether Tokyo's ruling circles want to or not, in doing so they are playing dangerously with fire."(8) Given this Soviet suspicion, which some diplomats in Tokyo tend to believe real, the Japanese prime minister's caveat to the Chinese, "Japan will not extend cooperation in the military field to any country – China constitutes no exception,"(9) was unlikely to be taken on its face value, especially since there was an increase in the number of conversations and visits between leaders of the People's Liberation Army (PLA) and their Japanese Self-Defense Forces counterparts and politicians. The closer Sino-Japanese relations became in trade, and in economic and technological cooperation, therefore, the greater the likelihood of Soviet politicomilitary pressure against Japan. In fact, Japanese-Soviet relations since the conclusion of the Sino-Japanese Treaty of Peace and Friendship have been strained more than ever before and compounded by later Soviet actions in Afghanistan. Soviet dealings with Japan have become more stubborn and contentious. One of the areas in which this is apparent is the annual Russo-Japanese fishery negotiations, with the Soviets further restricting access by Japanese fishermen to Russian waters and curtailing the amount of catch permitted them. Another is the Soviet military buildup on three of the disputed northern islands. True, Moscow had long maintained small installations on them, but, since 1978, it has vastly expanded those installations and deployed divisional-strength forces on the islands. A third area of Russo-Japanese relations in which Soviet retaliation may be observed is the issue of Moscow-Tokyo cooperation in the development of Siberia and Sakhalin, on which Japan once entertained considerable anticipation as a new source of energy supply. Moscow's dealing with Japanese interests on the matter, never very smooth or comforting to the Japanese, became harder and, when Tokyo deplored the Soviet invasion of Afghanistan, the Soviet ambassador pointedly warned the Japanese that his country was entirely capable of undertaking the development without foreign participation. Observers variously noted the Soviet tendency to use "an economic carrot and a military stick" and "coercive tactics, backed by military intimidation" in its dealings with Japan.(10) Others pointed to Soviet attempts to cause domestic anxiety in Japan "through such means as playing upon anti-Chinese forces in Japan, normalizing relations with the Japan Communist Party, and providing support for pro-Soviet factions within the Japan Socialist Party. . . ."(11)

To the extent that the United States views the new China either as a buffer against the Soviet Union in Asia or as an implicit ally in its own competition with the Soviet Union, China would seem to present a difficult security problem for Washington. Potentially powerful though it may be, China's PLA as a factor in the military equation in East Asia today is no match for the Soviet military in the region. The basis of PLA strength is solely in human numbers. By its origin, training, equipment, and experience, the PLA may be eminently suited to the Mao-type indigenous mass-based guerrilla warfare against foreign invaders. The Korean War notwithstanding, it is not suited either to protracted operations outside the country or to prosecution of modern warfare against a powerful external foe. The "punitive lesson" it wanted to teach the Vietnamese proved to be extremely costly to the PLA, and its forces suffered at least as much casualty and damage as it inflicted on the largely nonregular Vietnamese militia forces. The Maoist mass-line and all that it implied in terms of organization, training, and tactics during the late 1950s and the decade of the 1960s gravely inhibited the growth of the PLA as a modern, professional, technologically sophisticated military force. It is precisely for this reason that the military is one of the four principal areas of focus for China's current modernization program.

The actual character of Sino-U.S. security relations is yet obscure, for officially they do not exist, any more than they do between the United States and, say, Yugoslavia or Egypt, and Peking and Washington have both been judicious in avoiding any statement or discussion (at least any official one) that could be construed as suggestive of an emerging security relationship between them. Given the military weakness of China, however, there cannot but be serious mutual security concern over it. Official silence notwithstanding, the practical question remains: What would the United States do should an open military conflict break out between China and the Soviet Union? A Soviet air attack, including the use of nuclear missiles, would be more likely than either a Soviet land invasion of China or China's invasion of the Soviet Union.(12) China's missiles are few in number, unknown in accuracy but largely known and stationary in location, and thus constitute a relatively easy target for a Soviet preemptive attack. The Chinese do count on the existing U.S. nuclear umbrella over Japan on Russia's eastern flank as a deterrent against such a contingency and, to that extent, the U.S. security posture in East Asia becomes necessarily complicated even if Washington has no desire to get involved in a possible Sino-Soviet military conflict. Neither of the two clear alternatives for the United States in such an eventuality would seem attractive and each would carry with it serious implications and repercussions for the security of East Asia and that of Japan. In the meantime, China's new relations with Japan and the United States seem to add little to the issue of regional security or to the restoration of a stable balance of power there. It is in this sense that a prominent American observer of East Asian politics notes that the fact of these new Chinese relations "greatly increases American military responsibilities without corresponding gains in collective military strength" in the region.(13)

How and to what extent the Sino-Soviet conflict would worsen would most directly depend, among other things, on the two nations' respective internal courses of events, with consequent impact on relations with the United States (and Japan), and/or the character and severity of events in Indochina.

How events will unfold in China is extremely difficult to predict, for its current four-modernizations program involves dangers of severe trials and unanticipated tribulations. The very vastness of the land and population, the tradition of factionalism and the persistent center-periphery friction, the absence of adequate social overhead and infrastructure, the difficulty of consistently generating sufficient flows of developmental capital (China is still 80 percent agrarian and its rural sector has shown much lower levels of productivity increase in the past and is much poorer per capita than the urban sector), the shortage of sophisticated technical and managerial manpower, the consequently low capacity effectively to absorb and integrate whatever capital and technology may be imported, and the resultant magnitude of integration and coordination would singly and in combination create a range of extraordinarily complicated problems for the nation's modernizing leadership. Any one or any number of these problems could give rise to forces and trends that could dislodge the current leadership and change its policy direction. Despite the current dominance in Peking of pragmatic and nationalist followers of Liu Shaoxi, Zhou Enlai, and Deng Xiaoping and the purge of the Gang of Four,(14) there are numerous others (nearly one-half of the current party members) who achieved their positions and statuses by virtue of the Cultural Revolution and its aftermath and who still entertain serious misgiving about the course that the current leadership has set for the nation internally and/or externally. Depending upon the character and magnitude of the turn of domestic events, Peking's leadership might change hands as quickly as it has several times in the past, and China's relations with Japan and/or the United States could deteriorate as suddenly as they improved nearly a decade ago. On the other hand, the tension generated by various difficulties of the current modernization program and the resultant threat to the current leadership might dispose Peking to gamble dangerously on unifying the population behind it through an external venture against the Soviet Union (in the form of a border incident, for example) with the knowledge, correct or incorrect, that the United States would not stand idle in case of severe Soviet retaliation.

As for internal events in the Soviet Union, the most crucial would be the problem of succession within the Kremlin and how it would be affected by a range of domestic and external problems. Among those problems are: ethnic and national minorities, a stagnant economy that some observers believe is already experiencing a negative growth, the continuing low agricultural productivity, the persistent friction between hawks and doves, the strained condition of detente, the Afghanistan quagmire, the imminent need of oil imports, and potentially centrifugal forces in Eastern Europe.(15) To the extent that the Soviets fear a war with China, especially China with a vastly improved PLA and nuclear capability, there might emerge strong temptation within the Kremlin to strike, depending upon how those problems just mentioned would be reflected in and influence the struggle for succession in the Communist Party of the Soviet Union. Such a strike would most likely be designed to destroy China's nuclear arsenal and set back its modernization program but at the same time with such a limited duration as would make it extremely difficult for the United States militarily to intervene, particularly given the likelihood of resistance by its NATO and Japanese allies against a superpower confrontation.

Developments in Indochina could also trigger intensification of the Sino-Soviet conflict. Soviet success, for example, in turning Vietnam into a more closely Moscow-bound state would be perceived by Peking as posing a grave security threat from the south and an increased danger of Southeast Asia falling into the Soviet sphere of influence. We shall, however, put off a discussion of Indochina until later. Suffice it at this point to note that Indochina since 1975 has become an arena of intense Sino-Soviet competition in large measure owing to the Soviet Union's active Asian strategy.

Possibilities of a greatly intensified Sino-Soviet conflict notwithstanding, prospects for deescalation are by no means absent. The Chinese realize that some kind of resolution of the existing tension with the Soviet Union is necessary so that they may be able to concentrate on their domestic modernization. Moscow, too, finds it in its interest to keep China from developing too close relations with the United States (and Japan), especially since detente is in danger of unraveling. It would not be the first time for Peking to agree to shelve a territorial dispute. After all, it had in the mid-1950s deferred the refractory issue of disputed Sino-Indian border claims by shelving it and signing an agreement on the Five Principles of Peaceful Coexistence with India. (Four years later, China seized the disputed territory after secretly constructing a road through it and claimed the existence of the Chinese road proved Peking's ownership of the land.) It also had let its claim to the Paracel Islands lie dormant for nearly 20 years before seizing them from Vietnam with a brief but effective military strike.(16) Peking also decided to leave the issue of Senkaku Islands defused with Japan for, in Deng Xiaoping's words, "tactical reasons" in normalizing relations(17) with Japan and later signing a peace and friendship treaty. In fact, before the Soviet occupation of Afghanistan, Moscow and Peking had evinced some signs of mutual willingness to negotiate. It would not be improbable at all, therefore, that China might sooner than later choose to take a similar tactical stance vis-à-vis Moscow on the territorial dispute between them in order to assuage security pressure from the north and even to diversify sources of technological and economic assistance for its internal modernization.(18) Few observers believe that China would ever attempt to restore the kind of relationship with the Soviet Union that had existed before 1956,(19) but many are inclined to the view that it would be inevitable, against the background of China's internal programs for modernization and Russia's external and domestic problems, that they would make some move toward each other with the view to reducing the current tension that, after all, inconveniences both. How China's relations with Japan and the United States would be affected in such an event would depend very much upon its character and long-range objectives in the perception of Peking and Moscow. It is obvious that China has been tilting toward the United States and Japan since the death of Mao and the purge of the Gang of Four, and the pattern of accommodation between Peking and Moscow would be critically affected by events within China and Russia. Nonetheless, some kind of mutual Sino-Soviet accommodation cannot be ruled out. Indeed, China, recognizing its vast military inferiority vis-à-vis the Soviet Union, might choose to assume the role of a balancer in East Asia between the two nuclear superpowers so that it might acquire the power of initiative as well as mediation in the affairs of the region, a prospect that, as we shall see shortly, is not altogether comforting to some of the region's nations.

Expansion of Soviet Influence, Indochina, and Southeast Asia

Expanded Soviet presence in East Asia is a key factor that cannot but critically influence the course of events in the region in the new decade, for the shaping of that course will be determined by the way in which other nations concerned respond to it. The expansion of the Soviet presence was precipitated by two major sequences of events during the last decade: a shift in military balance between the Soviet Union and the United States within the region, and events in Indochina after the U.S. withdrawal.

Apart from the U.S. deployment of ground troops in South Vietnam in support of a series of Saigon regimes from the mid-1960s to the mid-1970s, it had always been its naval capability that constituted the bulwark of its military presence in East Asia throughout much of the post-Korean War period. The U.S. naval force, however, was radically reduced in the region during the last decade. Twenty years ago, the Seventh Fleet maintained 125 ships and 60,000 sailors in the region. These figures increased to 225 ships and 87,000 sailors at the height of the war in Vietnam. By 1978, however, the fleet had been reduced to only 50 ships and 28,000 sailors.(20) Only the crises that suddenly emerged in the Persian Gulf region and Southwest Asia late in 1979 caused the fleet strength to be upped to 58 ships (approximately 600,000 tons),(21)

but it was still about half, at best, of what it had been two decades
earlier. The U.S. naval presence in East Asia, however, was much
more reduced than the change in its force size suggested. The
Seventh Fleet had, even before 1979, been called upon to cover not
only the Western Pacific but also the Indian Ocean and the Persian
Gulf waters – a combined area of 50 million square miles of ocean.
The fleet came to be stretched very thin, thus further reducing its
capability in East Asia, so much so that U.S. officials, civilian and
military, were compelled to admit that their navy could not protect
Western Pacific sealanes should a serious military contingency arise
in Europe or the Middle East.

The decline of the U.S. naval capability – the most visible
component of the U.S. security commitment in East Asia – is more
significant when we realize the vast expansion the Soviet Union in
the meantime undertook of its Pacific Fleet. Two decades ago the
Soviet Pacific Fleet consisted of a total complement of some
300,000 tons.(22) By 1978 it had increased to more than 1.3 million
tons, with well over 500 ships manned by 130,000 sailors, and came
to outnumber the U.S. Seventh Fleet in all categories of major
combat craft except for the aircraft carrier.(23) According to the
1980 Defense White Paper published by the Japanese government,
the Soviet Pacific Fleet at this writing consists of a total of over 1.5
million tons, with 785 ships,(24) among which are some 130 submarines, nearly half of them nuclear-powered and 24 of them armed
with submarine launched ballistic missiles (SLBMs).(25) Once confined largely to the Sea of Japan and the Okhotsk Sea, since the
mid-1970s it came to be increasingly extensively deployed throughout the Western Pacific all the way down to the Indian Ocean and
waters adjacent to the Persian Gulf area, operating out of Cam
Ranh Bay, Da Nang, and Haiphong in Vietnam, Dohlak Island
(Ethiopia) in the Red Sea, and South Yemen, thus posing an
increasing threat to sealanes through which the bulk of trade by
East Asian nations takes place.

A similar expansion has been evidenced in the Soviet air capability in East Asia, albeit confined to Northeast Asia. Between 1968
and 1980, it rose from fewer than 1,000 tactical aircraft to over
2,000, which now include highly regarded Backfire bombers, while
the United States cut its air strength in the region down to about
400.(26) The Soviets also began deploying SS-20 intermediate-range
ballistic missiles in the region.(27) At least in quantitative terms,
the crucial air and naval balance between the two superpowers in
the region immediately surrounding Japan underwent a palpable
reversal.

Simple numerical comparisons could be misleading, of course.
For example, a senior American military expert in Tokyo pointed
out to the author that the Soviet Pacific Fleet was qualitatively
inferior to the U.S. Seventh Fleet, and Japanese defense officials
contended that the Soviet fleet in the area was only 60 percent

combat-effective while the U.S. fleet was nearly 100 percent combat-effective. Indeed, some experts suspect that the Soviet military capability in the region is quite exaggerated and that it is not nearly as potent as feared.(28) Still, the change in the posture and deployment of Soviet and U.S. naval and air capabilities in the last decade seems to give a strong credence to the observation of one prominent specialist on military affairs that, "considered as a whole, American resources in the Pacific do not now possess the deterrent power that the Administration perceives."(29)

In a speech in Washington in the spring of 1980, the U.S. senior State Department official in charge of East Asian affairs observed that "the rivalry among communists" had become "the basic cause of tension" in the region.(30) Banal as it might sound today, the observation nonetheless pointed to the remarkable sequence of events that had taken place in and over Indochina after the U.S. withdrawal from the peninsula in the mid-1970s, the sequence of events that came in the meantime greatly to aggravate and expand the theretofore simmering differences between two communist giants – China and the Soviet Union. Initial disagreements between Vietnam and Cambodia over some of their mutual border areas and Phnom Penh's treatment of Vietnamese residents on its premises, no doubt compounded by their traditional mutual animosity, quickly expanded into virulent confrontational conflict between the two brother communist states, which in turn drew their respective big brothers – China and the Soviet Union – into a direct mutual competition for influence over the entire Indochina region, each big brother acutely fearing the ultimate intentions of the other. Today, the struggle within and over Indochina among these communist states constitutes a seemingly insoluble danger to the security and stability of East Asia in general and Southeast Asia in particular.

As of mid-1980, Indochina is under virtual domination of Vietnam, with only the stubborn remnants of the ousted Pol Pot regime engaged in a protracted and apparently successful resistance against the Vietnamese occupying forces along and near the Thai-Cambodian border. The Sino-Soviet competition for influence over Indochina has so far gone clearly in Moscow's favor. To what extent the Soviet Union may be able to consolidate its position of influence in the peninsula remains to be seen, however, because it will depend upon the character of the Hanoi-Moscow relationship, its future development, and China's response to it – all of which are still largely matters of speculation.

It seems quite clear that the Soviet Union wishes to establish and expand its influence in East Asia, and that the relationship with Vietnam it has been seeking to consolidate is part of its "Asian strategy." There is, to be sure, considerable disagreement in interpretations of Soviet behavior in the region, ranging, as one analyst points out, from the view that "Soviet intentions are essentially benign, reflecting the natural evolution of the U.S.S.R.'s global concern, to the view that there is an evolving strategic design to establish the U.S.S.R. as a major Pacific power."(31) Some Japanese officials seem to persist in the notion that Soviet conduct in East Asia, as elsewhere in the world, is motivated by what they view as Russia's traditional sense of inferiority and insecurity vis-à-vis the West, which, some of them argue, was greatly reinforced by its distressing experience in the Cuban missile crisis in which it was compelled by its military inferiority vis-à-vis the United States abjectly to retreat. According to this view, the Soviets are seeking political and military parity with the United States as a genuine global power, which status alone would assuage their historic sense of insecurity and inferiority. This view, of course, is not universally shared in Japan, nor by the Americans. Some academic observers in Japan as well as American diplomats believe that the Soviet Union is seeking, not equality or parity with, but superiority over the United States in East Asia and elsewhere. This belief, incidentally, is consistent with the authoritative Soviet statement on Moscow's external policy objectives made by none other than that perennial Kremlin stalwart, Foreign Minister Andrei Gromyko, in 1975: "The Communist Party subordinates all its theoretical and practical activity in the sphere of international relations to the task of strengthening the positions of socialism, and the interests of further developing and deepening the world revolutionary process."(32) It may well be that the Soviet Union has not yet formulated a sufficiently systematic and internally coherent program of multi-regional expansion, but its behavior in the past seems to indicate that it seeks to exploit instability and vulnerability of any nation or any region in order to bring it under its sphere of influence for the purpose of establishing "strategic beachheads."(33) Vietnam (and ultimately the whole of Indochina) seems to be one of those strategic beachheads, "this Cuba in Asia" in the words of the Chinese.(34)

There is a strong consensus among Asian observers and officials that Hanoi is no more willing to be dominated by Moscow than it would be by Peking, and that its current tie with Moscow (formalized, in more senses than one, by the 1978 treaty of friendship and cooperation), is nothing but a temporary expedient dictated by the urgent and immediate contingencies with which Vietnam had found itself saddled,(35) and there is of course little doubt that the Vietnamese are fiercely nationalistic. The crucial question here, however, is not so much whether, as one analyst suggests, "Vietnam has abandoned its long-standing principle of 'independence' in the conduct of foreign affairs"(36) as whether or not it will be able to reassert such independence vis-à-vis the Soviet Union. It is difficult, for example, to imagine Cuba as a willing toady of Moscow, offering itself as a tool for the Soviet scheme in Africa or Latin America. Cuba behaves as it does in the international political and military arena, it can be argued, not because it does not want to act independently but because the particular manner in which its relationship with the Soviet Union has evolved in the last two decades permits it no independent options that would be palatable to Moscow. The Vietnamese, their nationalism and desire for independence notwithstanding, could, as the Cubans apparently have, find themselves increasingly dependent on, beholden to, and/or tied to the Soviet Union under the exigencies over which they are temporarily or permanently unable to exert control of their own.(37) There are many aspects in their domestic condition that could easily render the Vietnamese increasingly vulnerable to Soviet pressure and manipulation.(38) In this connection, it may be well to note a certain pattern in Soviet external conduct in the postwar period that seems to have demonstrated a remarkable consistency in objective and, more often than not, result.

As one seasoned observer points out, Moscow has used "treaties of friendship and cooperation" as effective devices for extending and consolidating its power and influence, and, wherever logistically feasible, undertaking military intervention in nations over which it wishes to establish or maintain dominance.(39) A Soviet "treaty of friendship and cooperation" typically includes a provision that obliges each signatory not to permit the use of its territory "for any actions, which could prejudice the security of the other party" and to "refrain from any actions encouraging any third party to take aggressive actions against either of them."(40) It also contains a clause for mutual consultation, cooperation, and assistance in order to safeguard security, independence, and territorial integrity of each party.(41) The Soviet Union, during the early postwar years, had concluded such a bilateral treaty with each of the East European states and Finland, and it was these clauses that provided Moscow with the formal pretext for military intervention (for example, Hungary in 1956, Czechoslovakia in 1968) or threat of such intervention (for example, Finland in 1958 and 1961) in order to insure these nations' compliance with or submission to its wishes and to protect what it viewed as its vital interests. During the last decade, the Soviet Union concluded similar treaties with India and Egypt in 1971 (the latter unilaterally abrogated by Sadat in 1976); Iraq in 1972; Somalia in 1974 (unilaterally abrogated by Somalia in 1977); Angola in 1976; Mozambique in 1977; Ethiopia, Afghanistan, and Vietnam in 1978; and South Yemen in 1979. The recent Soviet military intervention in Afghanistan, then, was formally justified by those relevant clauses in the Kabul-Moscow treaty of friendship and cooperation.

Whether and to what extent Moscow can effectively invoke those treaty clauses to undertake political and/or military intervention against its "friends" would clearly be influenced or determined by a number of factors which, thus far in any event, geographic proximity seems most crucial. Thus, it has failed in Egypt and Somalia while it succeeded vis-à-vis Finland, East European states, and Afghanistan. The Soviet hold on Cuba, however, suggests that perhaps there are compensatory factors that could work in Moscow's favor, such as severe economic crises (consider Cuba toward the end of the decade of the 1960s, at which time the Havana-Moscow ties, which had previously been strained, suddenly became closer; and Vietnam in 1977-78 when, precipitated in part by China's withdrawal of its aid programs, Hanoi found itself in a desperate economic situation) and leadership instability and/or political confusion (for example, Angola, Mozambique, Ethiopia). It is indeed this consistent aspect of all Soviet treaties of friendship and cooperation that, as soon as the Hanoi-Moscow pact was revealed, prompted another observer to warn that "the Soviet Union has now acquired a mechanism for further manipulation of Vietnam."(42) This warning, it appears, has at least partially been vindicated. Before the treaty, Hanoi's Premier Pham Van Dong had repeatedly stated: "Leasing a military base to a foreign state even temporarily is out of the question, be that state the Soviet Union, China, or the United States,"(43) but since then, Cam Ranh Bay and Da Nang, as well as Haiphong have become de facto bases for the Soviet Pacific Fleet, providing strategic ports of call between Vladivostok in the Soviet Maritime Province on the Sea of Japan and those newly acquired bases of Soviet naval operation in the Red Sea.

The probability that Vietnam may become further vulnerable to Soviet pressure and manipulation is all the more disturbing inasmuch as Vietnam is the strongest and most experienced military power in Southeast Asia and adheres to its declared policy of "revolutionary mission. . . .to form a greater federation of Indochina."(44) Vietnam's military capability and "revolutionary mission" would serve as useful surrogates for Moscow's power and policy for expansion in the region to the extent that the Soviets are able to maintain effective influence over Hanoi. Indeed, Vietnam has already succeeded in establishing a "greater Indochinese federation" of sorts through its virtual control of Laos and much of Cambodia. Perhaps in consideration for Hanoi's failure thus far to establish sufficient order and stability and the danger of Khmer Rouge attacks, the Soviet presence in Cambodia has been relatively unobtrusive, but in Laos it has been increasingly evident since 1978, including military aircraft, books, and films.(45) Neither Vietnam as a Soviet "strategic beachhead" nor Indochina as "a greater federation" has thus far been consolidated, however, and military danger to neighboring Southeast Asian states emanating from the Hanoi-Moscow axis as such would not be acute or immediate so long as neither is sufficiently consolidated. It may be sooner than later, however, that that danger would materialize, and when that happens, it will have an immediate impact not only on other Southeast Asian states but also on China.

One of the major events caused by postunification Vietnam was the massive exodus of Vietnamese "refugees." Whether by deliberate premeditation or not, the forced exodus has had the effect of serving three purposes, all compatible with Moscow's expansionist policy and Hanoi's immediate interest. These are: the expulsion of a class of Vietnamese citizens most resistant to assimilation into a socialist socioeconomic order, the straining of precarious race relations within some of the Southeast Asian states, and the inhibiting of closer relations between those Southeast Asian states and China.

Those hundreds of thousands of Vietnamese expellees, whom Hanoi viewed as "unadaptable to socialism,"(46) were mainly ethnic Chinese – pillars of Vietnam's middle class and victims of Hanoi's animosity toward Peking for supporting the Pol Pot regime in Cambodia and for withdrawing economic and technical assistance for Vietnamese reconstruction, and of Hanoi's failure in its domestic economic policy.(47) In a sense, they were the results of Hanoi's political, social, economic, and racial "purification" campaign to eliminate the last obstacles to the transformation of the nation into a disciplined, more homogeneous, hence stable, socialist state. Second, against the background of persistent "Chinese problems" in the Association of Southeast Asian Nations (ASEAN) such as Malaysia, Indonesia, and, to a lesser extent, Thailand, the Chinese refugees from Vietnam could not but affect and at times exacerbate the precarious pattern of ethnic relations in these nations, where ethnic Chinese constitute much of what middle class there exists and are the backbone of an indigenous modern economic sector. Because of these facts, they are the object of simmering antipathy by the native majorities that, as in Malaysia and Indonesia, intermittently flares up in the form of anti-Chinese riots and other forms of popular, sometimes thinly disguised, official persecution. Massive infusion of those refugees into these states also would have some impact on relations between these states and Singapore, the predominantly Chinese city state, the most prosperous, advanced, and stable member of ASEAN. Third, the aggravation of these "Chinese problems" would affect relations between these ASEAN states and China because of their traditional suspicion of Peking's influence over overseas Chinese, which Hanoi had attempted "to exploit," pointing out to these nations that "China's policies toward (their) Chinese communities pose a threat (to their security)."(48) The fundamental instability of most of the ASEAN states would render their respective external conduct, especially vis-à-vis China, vulnerable to the sort of internal tension caused by the refugee problem. It is in these senses that one leading ASEAN leader suspected an underlying motive of Moscow-backed Hanoi in expelling the ethnic Chinese from Vietnam: "The more pressure on these ASEAN countries" by the influx of those refugees, argued Singaporean Prime Minister Lee Kuan Yew, "the more balance is upset, the more anti-ethnic Chinese they become the more anti-China they become, which means eventually the more pro-Soviet they may become."(49)

Perhaps predictably, responses of ASEAN states were indicative of internal instability as well as mutual anxiety. Observers in Tokyo and Washington in the spring of 1980 were inclined to the view that the conflict in and over Indochina after the U.S. withdrawal had generated an unprecedented sense of mutual cohesion among the ASEAN states. This view was derived in large measure from the seeming public unity that the ASEAN members had demonstrated in an unaccustomed frequency of meetings of their leaders (they had not held a summit meeting of their national leaders until the tenth year of their organization's existence), in the explicit demands they presented for the cessation of hostility on the peninsula and for the withdrawal of Vietnamese forces from Cambodia, and in their declaration that any spread of the intra-Indochinese struggle into Thailand would be viewed as a direct threat to the entire ASEAN region, which would cause ASEAN to invoke "the right to protect its members threatened by attacks from outside."(50) These alleged demonstrations of ASEAN unity were remarkable, however, only in contrast to the group's previous lack of any significant sign of political and diplomatic cohesion, and they really did not go much beyond the level of statements of principles and rhetorical generalities. Below this seeming unity, ASEAN was and still is divided on a variety of issues of common concern and lacks critical political consensus regarding the struggle in and over Indochina and the problem of Soviet expansion.

ASEAN's lack of relevant political consensus seems to be the function of several cross-cutting cleavages among its member states. In the first place, there is this matter of differential geopolitical proximity to Indochina. Thus, Thailand, Malaysia, and Singapore share a more acute and immediate concern with the possibility of escalation of conflict there than Indonesia and the Philippines. Second, there is some sharp difference among ASEAN states in terms of how to deal with Hanoi for the purpose of restoring stability in Indochina. In this respect, perhaps the sharpest contrast may be seen between Singapore and Indonesia. Singapore (together with Thailand) is the preeminent hardliner vis-à-vis Hanoi, demanding that it withdraw its forces from Cambodia altogether to permit the latter self-determination, which, for Hanoi, would amount to relinquishing all the gains it had thus far made in Cambodia, and possible repercussions in Laos. Indonesia, on the other hand, is inclined to an opposite view that Hanoi could not be expected to do what its pride and nationalism would not permit it to do, that is, immediate and complete withdrawal from Cambodia, and that to demand what it would not do would only render it more recalcitrant and hostile. These contrasting views in part reflect Singapore's and Indonesia's national experiences. Singapore is predominantly Chinese in population and thus feels close affinity with and empathy for its ethnic brethren who have been expelled from Vietnam en masse. It is also extremely sensitive to the potentially dangerous impact on it of any Vietnam-induced anti-Chinese sentiment in Southeast Asia. The Indonesians, on the other hand, feel a different kind of affinity with the Vietnamese: Indonesia and Vietnam are the only two Asian nations that won independence through armed struggle,(51), and, moreover, both have had intermittent problems with their respective Chinese minorities. Third, there exists the problem of differential perception of threat posed by the Soviet Union in the region. Here, the Philippines began in 1980 to show a marked departure from the officially nonaligned ASEAN, precipitated in part by the Soviet invasion of Afghanistan. In that year, the Philippines not only decided to boycott the Moscow Olympics but also announced the need for closer defense coopera-tion with the United States on the ground that ASEAN was an "economic organization" and that, as such, it lacked an ability to insure peace on its premises.(52) Singapore declared that "the Kampuchean and Afghanistan crises are interlinked in the Soviet Union's global strategy."(53) This difference in ASEAN views of Moscow has its obverse side, that is, varying perceptions of the actual or potential policy of China. The Philippines, with the smallest Chinese minority among the ASEAN states, have little fear of Chinese influence on their domestic politics and they and Singapore have always been avowedly anti-Soviet; but Indonesia, especially because of its 1965 GESTAPU (the communist-led at-tempted coup and its bloody suppression by the military) experience and the fact of the continuing presence of exile PKI (Indonesian Communist Party) headquarters in Peking, is the most suspicious of China among the ASEAN members. Indonesia, in fact, views a modernized China in 10 to 15 years hence as presenting the greatest security threat to the region.(54) Thailand, on the other hand, considers China as the primary inhibiting force against Vietnam's or greater Indochinese federation's potential territorial or political ambition against it. Apart from differences in matters pertaining to regional security, there are other less obvious but nonetheless significant dissonances within ASEAN. Malaysia and Indonesia are members of the increasingly active and vocal Conference of Islamic Nations and they are coincidentally the only "have" nations within ASEAN in terms of oil, while the other three ASEAN states are "have-nots." Malaysia's province of Sabah has become a virtual sanctuary for the minority Islamic guerrillas in the Philippines, and there is a strong feeling of disenchantment (especially in the Philippines and Thailand) that, despite the 1978 agreement on intra-ASEAN cooperation in energy supply, Indonesia and Malaysia have not been fully cooperative.(55)

It is these patterns of discord, apparent as well as subtle, among the ASEAN members, combined with the fundamental governmental and leadership instability that is endemic among them (with the exception perhaps of Singapore), that inhibit the emergence of critical political and diplomatic consensus that would be indispensable in order for these nations to take an effective joint approach to the problems of security presented by the struggle in and over Indochina and the expanded Soviet politicomilitary presence in the region. The ASEAN declaration of its right to resist any serious military threat to the territorial integrity and security of Thailand, dramatic as it may have sounded at the time against the background of the organization's previous lack of cohesion, therefore lacks substantive content and most likely would not in itself intimidate or deter Vietnam or the Hanoi-Moscow axis.(56) The only immediate deterrence against any Vietnamese or Hanoi-Moscow venture against Thailand under the pretext of, say, hot pursuit of anti-Vietnamese Cambodian guerrillas, would be the Chinese, who have stated their intention of coming to Thailand's rescue.(57) Whether and to what extent this putative deterrence in fact continues to be effective, however, remains to be seen.

The Korean Peninsula: Is Renewal of Violence Unlikely?

To say that Korea is one of the most immediate danger spots in East Asia today might sound excessively alarmist, for there has been an increasingly widespread impression over the past several years that the situation on the peninsula, is, in the words of one American diplomat,* "potentially dangerous but practically stable." The impression is the result of several developments over the last decade. For example, there has been no overt saber-rattling by either Korea against the other; since 1972, there have been sporadic, albeit invariably unsuccessful, attempts at bilateral talks between Pyongyang and Seoul; there have been reports of a softening of attitude on the part of North Korea not only toward Seoul, but also toward Washington,(58) and of a growing disinclination of China (toward whom Pyongyang has tilted away from Moscow in recent years) to see an eruption of tension in Korea.(59) Indeed, on the occasion of the Japanese prime minister's visit to Peking in December 1979, his Chinese counterpart promised to help create a favorable international atmosphere for peaceful resolution of the Korean issue and the latter, on his visit to Tokyo in 1980, assured the Japanese that North Korea would not exploit the political instability in South Korea for aggressive purposes. Additionally, there has been some evidence that Moscow, too, would wish more than ever to avoid military conflict on the peninsula (for example, drastic reduction of Soviet military aid to Pyongyang after 1974, the first visit to the Soviet Union by an incumbent South Korean cabinet minister in 1978, the quick release in 1979 of a South Korean civilian airliner, together with its crew and

---

*Unidentified sources of quotes are individuals whose conversations with the author were assured of confidentiality.

passengers, which had inadvertently wandered into Soviet air space and been forced down by Soviet military planes).

The situation on the Korean peninsula, however, may be far more complicated than the optimistic picture generated by those developments might suggest. In the first place, the political arrangement in each Korea is pregnant with instability, hence unpredictability. North Korea, with its aging dictator nearing the end of his reign, will soon be facing the travail of power transition, for the official designation of the dictator's son as his successor in itself would not fully assuage an intraelite power struggle in Pyongyang. The disparity in economic conditions between the two Koreas, which has been widening in favor of the South, could affect the post-Kim power struggle in a way that would tempt North to strike South while there still are chances of winning. The noticeable recent expansion in the North's military power(60) adds an element of danger to the uncertainty over the Korean peninsula.

The course of events in South Korea since the assassination of Park Chung Hee in the fall of 1979 has only worsened the prospects of a viable North-South rapprochement. Early U.S. and Japanese assessments of the South Korean military in the immediate post-Park era were all optimistic about its direction and behavior: those South Korean military leaders were professional, politically mature and restrained, generally uncorrupt and, in the words of one American Korea watcher, provided "a model for other military establishments in Asia." Later events, however, cast serious doubt and apprehension upon Seoul's military rulers. President Chun Doo Hwan appears to be a latter-day Park Chung Hee, intent on suppressing domestic opposition into silence and insuring the survival of his newly achieved autocratic power and position. Behavior of Chun and his supporters thus far would have the effect of hardening Pyongyang's view of Seoul if North Korea had indeed looked forward to a post-Park South Korea as likely to provide a better opportunity for meaningful North-South contact. Post-Park political democratization in South Korea presumably would, according to one Japanese Foreign Ministry official, "encourage North to be more flexible" and thus enhance the changes of promoting a North-South dialogue. The repressive militarist turn of events in the South, then, could be said to have reduced them. As well there may be this danger of the South Korean regime succumbing to the temptation of diverting internal tension externally, much in the same sense that a post-Kim leadership in Pyongyang would contain it. At this writing, therefore, future conduct of both Pyongyang and Seoul remains uncertain, domestically as well as externally, hence unpredictable.

Uncertainty and unpredictability are compounded by the very fact that neither Korea seems to be amenable to restraining pressures from its traditional ally or allies. Pyongyang is neither Moscow's nor Peking's puppet; in fact, it is, as one Japanese diplomat observed, "a very difficult friend" to both and is not likely to hesitate to go its own way according to its own perception of need and expediency. Seoul, on the other hand, has since Park's days been increasingly resistant to U.S. pressures and wishes and pursued domestic policies that have been unpalatable to Washington. Its new strongman, President Chun, in fact took his initial decisive step as a junior Korean general toward his present position by blatantly violating the U.S.-South Korean joint military command structure, unilaterally deploying forces for his purposes without consultation and approval by the senior American general in command. This experience could not but be a cause for considerable apprehension about the future.

The current instability in South Korea, the emerging struggle for succession in the North, and their individual or collective impact on the North-South tension could invite miscalculation and over-reaction that in turn could erode inhibitions on military response to real or imagined provocation. What would be the response in such an event by the United States, China, and/or the Soviet Union? How would it affect Sino-U.S., Sino-Soviet, and Soviet-U.S. relations? Could the military conflict be contained at the peninsular level? For Japan, the threat posed by such an eventuality would not be only military, but political, social, and economic as well. For example, there is a high probability, perhaps a certainty, that a large number of refugees would head for Japan from South Korea, or even from the North. How would Japan handle this problem, given its persistent problems with fewer than 1 million Korean residents throughout the postwar period? The number of refugees could number in the tens of thousands, perhaps in the millions, according to one Korean estimate, depending upon the duration, severity, and outcome of the conflict. What would be the social, economic, and political impact of so many refugees on a fundamentally exclusivist, demographically compressed society such as Japan?

The most serious military contingency for Japan in the event of a renewed military conflict on the Korean peninsula would be a confrontation, however reluctant or limited, between the United States and the Soviet Union. One would be inclined to view it as highly unlikely, since neither of the superpowers would wish to risk an all-out war over Korea. However, Indochina experiences suggest that minor or medium states could drag reluctant big powers into their own conflict, and this danger would even rise when one of the superpowers has become less and less restrained in its external conduct and the other has already suffered a series of setbacks in its competitive struggle. Should a major conflict break out between the superpowers, Japan's position would be quite untenable. The nuclear umbrella provided by the Japan-U.S. security pact would be of little value. The U.S. nuclear umbrella cannot protect Japan in case of a major war; it can protect it only to the extent that it is able to prevent the outbreak of such a war.

IMBALANCE OF POWER IN EAST ASIA

Quite unlike Europe, where two clear-cut and structurally coherent groups of nations face and countervail each other, each with an institutionalized mode of internal coordination and external operation as an alliance, East Asia is characterized by the absence of clear lines of operative international groupings capable of checking and countervailing destabilizing conduct within the region. True, alliances of sorts exist in the form of a number of bilateral military pacts (for example, Japanese-U.S., U.S.-South Korean, U.S.-Philippine, U.S.-Thai), treaties of peace and friendship (for example, Sino-Japanese), treaties of cooperation (Hanoi-Moscow), and a regional association (ASEAN). They do not constitute anything that might remotely resemble a balance-of-power system or stable regional international arrangement, however, for they are fragmented. They are fragmented because they represent a multiplicity of overlapping conflicts and interests and, as a consequence, tend to perpetuate, even compound, particularistic orientations of each East Asian party to each alliance, which further inhibits the emergence of a relevant consensus required for the stabilization of intraregional relations. In part, at least, the problem is perpetuated by the very lack of relevant traditions of mutual interaction among the region's nations. Under the circumstances, the politically and militarily vigorous and expansionist Soviet Union and its "cooperation" partner, Vietnam, represent "the most powerful alliance in the region,"(61) because this alliance has objectives that go far beyond mere security and territorial integrity of its signatories. As events of the past few years indicate, other nations concerned with affairs of the region have done little more than be overtaken by, and then reacting more less haphazardly to, events created by these two nations.

Curtailing, not to mention reversing, this trend would inevitably call for participation of a big power as an effectively countervailing power against the Hanoi-Moscow axis. China, the largest and perhaps the most powerful of the region's historic states, is variously handicapped in this regard: it is poor, underdeveloped, militarily ill-equipped, and not entirely trusted by noncommunist Asian states, especially ASEAN nations whose fear of its potentially domineering tendency is both caused and reinforced by their own internal "Chinese" problems. There is also fear that China might resolve its differences with the Soviet Union and move toward close relations with it. ASEAN, the only regional grouping to be found in the region, is neither politically cohesive nor militarily significant enough to constitute even a feeble check against the power of the Russo-Vietnamese alliance, and their respective internal weaknesses would distract ASEAN states from the task of effectively cultivating their cohesion as a subregional collectivity. Under these circumstances, this leaves only the United States as the immediately available source of counterbalance against the Soviet or Soviet-Vietnamese power in the region. While they remain officially reticent, there is, in fact, a virtual unanimity of views among officials and observers the author had the opportunity to interview that the United States would be, in the words of one Asian diplomat, "the only guarantor of security in the region," and that it must, therefore, play the primary military role in East Asia. Fear in the region, especially among ASEAN states, was that the United States, owing to the cumulative effects of its bitter experience in Vietnam and its domestic sociopolitical upheavals, might withdraw entirely from Southeast Asia and that, with the reduction of the U.S. military presence in East Asia in general, the Soviets would attempt to increase its influence, which, in turn, would provoke reaction from China, with the result that Southeast Asia, especially, might become implicated in the Sino-Soviet conflict.(62) As a practical problem, creation of an effective countervailing power against the Hanoi-Moscow axis would seem to call for two alternative means. One is unilateral U.S. action in the form of the return of its politicomilitary presence to the region; the other is in the form of a U.S. alliance with one or more of the region's nations for the explicit purpose of maintaining regional security.

The first alternative, that is unilateral U.S. return to the region, would appear simple and expedient and the author during the course of his travels in some of the region's nations and talks with their observers did sense an undercurrent of a desire for it. The desire was muted, however, because of an uncertainty as to whether and to what extent the United States might in fact be willing to undertake such an alternative, the uncertainty resulting from a perception of the U.S. preoccupation with strengthening NATO military capability and with the defense of the Persian Gulf region. There was also ambivalence regarding the level of the U.S. military presence appropriate for East Asia. Thus many observers talked about the "beyond the horizon" presence of the United States, for fear that any "overpresence" of the United States in the area in the words of one of them "tends to create an undesirable 'superpower-client' relationship" and "would also lure other great powers to increase their presence in this region and this would definitely result in new instabilities."(63)

The second alternative for the United States in dealing with the expansionist danger of Moscow and/or the Hanoi-Moscow axis would be a military or security alliance with one of the major nations in the region. The one such nation that promptly comes to mind, of course, is China. Many diplomats and observers in Asia believe this is what China wants. Such an alliance, however, would suffer several drawbacks, some of which have already been alluded to earlier. One is the prompt worsening of already tense Soviet-U.S. and Sino-Soviet relations, with implications that could not be readily contained within the region. A second serious drawback of such an arrangement is that China, instead of significantly adding to the security and stability of the region, would become a huge additional burden to the United States that would drastically expand its strategic commitment and responsibility and, as a consequence, cause serious strain in its relationship with its NATO allies and even Japan. Some Southeast Asians consider this option as a device also to contain or restrain China's expansionist potentials, but even they feel quite apprehensive about Soviet reaction to the arrangement itself. Others are clearly opposed to it because they fear big-power domination of the region and a more explicit confrontation between a China allied with the United States and the Soviet Union. As one analyst puts it, "it is more likely that the PRC (People's Republic of China) intends to use the United States in its struggle against the Soviet Union" and because such an alliance "could even inflate the Soviets' already intense paranoia vis-à-vis the PRC . . . . (stimulating) greater Soviet reactions, essentially military in nature, which in fact is the only effective instrument it has at its disposal. Such a reaction by the Soviet Union would leave no country unharmed, including ASEAN."(64) The same analyst, however, suggests that "the idea of a potential alliance between (the United States and the PRC) could become an effective deterrent for the Soviet Union to take adventurous action in the Asia-Pacific region,"(65) and that the deterrent value of the idea would remain effective so long as this option is not exercised. Last, but not least, a Sino-U.S. military alliance would inevitably be handicapped by the fact that the policy predictability and leadership stability of China, for reasons discussed earlier, remain to be established. A bilateral military alliance, particularly for purposes of seeking regional stability, rather than security of its signatories, requires consistency of policy and stability of leadership in both parties, for, without them, the alliance may be disrupted any day and such disruption would cause an instability greater than the one that the alliance was designed to cope with.

Inasmuch as most ASEAN states wish to remain nonaligned and instead seek to transform its premises into a "zone of peace, freedom, and neutrality" (ZOPFAN),(66) no security arrangement resembling SEATO would be probable. The very weakness and instability of individual states in the area would make such an arrangement unwise even if possible. This leaves only one feasible option and it may still prove controversial. That is, the strengthening of the existing Japanese-U.S. security arrangement in such a way as to increase the effective U.S. security capability across the region.

A decade ago such an alternative would have been unthinkable in Japan as well as among its neighbors. The events synoptically described above, among others, however, have made it not only thinkable but increasingly necessary; it is one of the major points to be discussed in detail later in the present volume. This alternative, of course, would warrant a steady increase in Japan's military capability, avoidance of the risk of giving rise to dangerous tendencies in Japan as well as resurrecting fear of a militarily powerful Japan among its neighbors, as well as certain new measures to be incorporated into Japanese-U.S. military cooperation so as to maximize the capability for tactical defense of Japan and Western Pacific sealanes in order qualitatively to enhance the U.S. total strategic capability for the maintenance of security across the region. How all this can be done will be discussed later. Suffice it at this point to suggest that Japan, whatever its domestic political constraints, psychological inhibitions, and economic considerations that throughout the postwar period have prevented it from pursuing serious regional security concerns, is the only nation in East Asia that meets some fundamental prerequisites for effective regional security partnership with the United States. Among those requirements are: basic political stability and continuity, sufficient economic capability, and high levels of managerial and technological sophistication. No other East Asian nation can adequately meet these requirements. In short, Japan is the only nation with sufficient national reliability to be able to partake of the task with the United States of insuring peace and security in East Asia in the foreseeable future. Another fact that should perhaps be mentioned here, with a promise of elaboration in later chapters, is a significant change taking place both in Japan and among its neighbors in the patterns of expectation regarding its role not only for its own defense but also for the maintenance of regional security.

It is indeed appropriate that such change is taking place – and perhaps also that the kind of proposal just hinted at and to be elaborated later in this volume should be made – because the world of the 1980s is radically different in character from that of the preceding postwar decades. The changed, and still changing, world calls for careful but nonetheless salient departure from the kind of approach, perspective, method of issue management, and problem solution that have dominated the thinking of the Japanese – as well as their neighbors and Americans – for an entire generation. Without such a departure, Japan as well as East Asia at large would continue to be ill-equipped to deal with their environment that is more than ever pregnant with chance, accident, and contingency.

NOTES

(1) Kenneth E. Boulding, Stable Peace (Austin: University of Texas Press, 1978), p. 15 and passim.
(2) Sudershan Chawla, Melvin Gurtov, and Alain-Gerard Marsot, "The View from Southeast Asia" in Southeast Asia under the New Balance of Power, ed. Chawla, Gurtov, and Marsot, (New York: Praeger, 1974), p. 107.

(3) "Invitations to foreign powers to intervene are usually as much to preserve personal power as to protect national security. Moreover, foreign policy strength and credibility. . . .depends on a domestic consensus. Constant rebellions, revolutions, communal riots, and palace coups not only gravely weaken leadership, they also create opportunities for small or large powers to become involved." Ibid.

(4) These attempts include the Association of Southeast Asia (ASA) of 1961 involving Malaya, the Philippines, and Thailand; MAPHILINDO of 1963 with Malaya, the Philippines, and Indonesia; the Asia and Pacific Council (ASPAC) of 1966 joined in by the region's anticommunist states. They disappeared without fanfare after brief and strained existences. The only exception thus far is the Association of Southeast Asian Nations (ASEAN) composed of Thailand, Malaysia, Singapore, Indonesia, and the Philippines. It came into being in 1967 but remained largely dormant until 1976, about which more will be said later.

(5) Douglas Pike, "Communist vs. Communist in Southeast Asia," International Security 4, No. 1 (Summer 1979); 22-23.

(6) Mineo Nakajima, "Taiheiyo o koeta Shinwaryoku" (Power of Friendshp over the Pacific), Chuokoron, February 1979, p. 86.

(7) Quoted in Hiroshi Kimura, "Japan-Soviet Relations: Framework, Developments, Prospects," Asian Survey 20, no. 7 (July 1980): 716.

(8) Igor Latyshev's editorial in Pravda, May 21, 1979, p. 5, as reprinted in Current Digest of the Soviet Press, 31, no. 20 (June 13, 1979); 15.

(9) Prime Minister Masayoshi Ohira's speech in Peking on December 7, 1979, as translated by the Japanese Foreign Ministry, p. 8, n.d.

(10) Robert A. Scalapino, "Asia at the End of the 1970s," Foreign Affairs 58 (April 1980): 705; and Kimura, p. 713.

(11) Ajia 15 (June 1979): 21.

(12) The Soviets have in recent years deployed not only large numbers of ground troops but also nuclear forces in very substantial numbers along the Sino-Soviet border and their nuclear missiles are said to have been targeted on Chinese industrial and military installations. See, for example, Harrison Salisbury, "How a Nuclear War Can Start in East Asia," Bulletin of the Atomic Scientists 35, no. 4 (April 1979): 22.

(13) Scalapino, p. 737.

(14) It was reported that during the war with Vietnam in 1979, the word "Marxism" was not once used in government pronouncements and statements. China News Analysis 1154 (May 11, 1979): 1.

(15) For some of these critical problems, see, for example, Hiromasa Nakayama, "Soren Shakaishungi Bocho no Genkai" (Limits of Soviet Socialist Expansion), Asahi Janaru, April 25, 1980, pp. 10-16; Osamu Nakanishi, "Afugan Jiken mittsu no Kyokun" (Three

Lessons of the Afghan Event), ibid., pp. 16-20; and Yoshisuke Niizuma, "Seisaku Kettei Kiko to Posto Burejinefu" (Policy Decision Structure and the Post-Brezhnev Era), ibid., pp. 21-26.

(16) Wolf Mendl, Issues in Japan's China Policy (London: Royal Institute of International Affairs, 1978), p. 108.

(17) Allen S. Whiting and Robert F. Dernberger, China's Future: Foreign Policy and Economic Development in the Post-Mao China (New York: McGraw-Hill, 1977), p. 66.

(18) This latter point was suggested to the author by knowledgeable Japanese officials who noted that Western and U.S. technology is much too sophisticated and expensive for the Chinese and that two-thirds of the existing Chinese plants and equipment were Russian or East European and were in need of spare parts.

(19) For the views of those who seem to discern a much greater degree of compatibility between the Chinese and the Soviets, see, for example, Tomoyuki Kojima, "Chuso Wakai to Tairitsu no Kozu" (Structures of Sino-Soviet Reconciliation and Confrontation), Asahi Janaru, April 27, 1979, pp. 92-97, and Keitaro Hasegawa, "Chuso ga Wakai suru Hi" (The Day China and the Soviet Union Will Achieve Reconciliation), Bungei Shunju, May 1979, pp. 260-91.

(20) Barry M. Blechman and Robert P. Berman, eds. Guide to Far Eastern Navies (Annapolis: Naval Institute Press, 1978), pp. 16-17.

(21) Asahi Shimbun, February 6, 1980, p. 4.

(22) Takuya Kubo, "Kaijo Boei to Kaijo Kotsu no Kakuho" (Maritime Defense and Security of Maritime Traffic), Kokusai Mondai 217 (April 1978): 44.

(23) Blechman and Berman, pp. 29, 50-51.

(24) Showa 55 Nen Ban Boei Kakusho (1980 Defense White Paper) (Tokyo: Okurasho Insatsukyoku, 1980), p. 231.

(25) Asahi Shimbun, August 22, 1980, p. 3.

(26) United States-Japan Security Relationship – The Key to East Asian Security and Stability, Report of the Pacific Study Group to the Committee on Armed Services, U.S. Senate (Washington, D.C.: U.S. Government Printing Office, March 22, 1979), p. 7; Showa 55 Nen Ban Boei Hakusho, p. 231; and Tomohisa Sakanaka, "Military Threats and Japan's Defense Capability," Asian Survey 20, no. 7 (July 1980): 766.

(27) Asahi Shimbun, February 6, 1980, p. and August 6, 1980, pp. 1 and 4.

(28) See, for example, Tomohisa Sakanaka, " 'Soren no Kyoi' no Kento" (A Study of the "Soviet Threat"), Kokusai Mondai 247 (October 1980).

(29) Drew Middleton in the New York Times, February 25, 1979, p. E1.

(30) Assistant Secretary of State Richard Holbrooke in an address before the Women's National Democratic Club entitled "U.S. Posture in the Pacific in 1980" as published in Current Policy 154

(U.S. Department of State Bureau of Public Affairs, March 27, 1980): 1.

(31) Melvin Gurtov, "The Soviet Presence in Southeast Asia: Growth and Implications" in Conflict and Stability in Southeast Asia, ed. Mark W. Zacher and R. Stephen Milne (Garden City, N.Y.: Doubleday, 1974), p. 275. Also see pp. 291-92.

(32) Quoted in Robert Conquest, Present Danger: Toward a Foreign Policy (Stanford, Calif.: Hoover Institution Press, 1979), p. 32.

(33) Yoshio Morimoto, "Ajia no Shinjosei to Soren Gaiko" (New Asian Situation and Soviet Diplomacy), Sekai, March 1979, p. 111.

(34) Peking Review, April 10, 1979, p. 26.

(35) For good descriptions and analyses of the relevant sequence of events leading up to the Hanoi-Moscow treaty and the Sino-Soviet war, see, for example, J. L. S. Girling, "Politics in Southeast Asia: A Year of Conflict," in Southeast Asian Affairs 1979 (Singapore: Institute of Southeast Asian Studies, 1979), pp. 3-12, and Strategic Survey 1978 (London: International Institute for Strategic Studies, 1979), pp. 73-81.

(36) Pike, p. 30.

(37) For indications of Hanoi's search for independence in its external policy before the Hanoi-Moscow treaty, see Asia Research Bulletin, December 31, 1978, pp. 502-15, and Chin Kin Wah, "The Great Powers and Southeast Asia: A Year of Diplomatic Effervescence" in Southeast Asian Affiars 1979, pp. 52-55.

(38) Apart from the issue of governmental and leadership instability that was discussed earlier, see the domestic economic and political conditions in Vietnam in, for example, Time, June 2, 1980, pp. 46-47.

(39) This section draws on observations by Tetsuya Tsukamoto "Nisso Zenrin Joyaku no Wana" (The Trap in a Russo-Japanese Treaty of Good Neighborhood), Bungei Shunju, April 1980, pp. 92-111.

(40) Articles 3 and 4 of the "Draft Treaty of Goodneighborhood and Cooperation between USSR and Japan," which Moscow proposed to Japan in 1978 and which Tokyo rejected. Reprinted in Roger Swearingen, The Soviet Union and Postwar Japan: Escalating Challenge and Response (Stanford, Calif.: Hoover Institution Press, 1978), pp. 289-91. According to Tsukamoto, these phrases are identical to those in Moscow's bilateral treaties with East European states, Finland, Vietnam, Afghanistan, and so on.

(41) In the case of the draft treaty with Japan, a relevant article stated in part: "Should a situation arise, which in the opinion of both sides is dangerous for maintaining peace, or if peace is violated, the sides shall immediately contact each other with the aim of exchanging views on the question of what can be done for improving the situation." Ibid., p. 290.

(42) Noboru Yano, "Soren Betonamu Joyaku no Kikendo" (Dangerous Potentials of the Soviet-Vietnamese Treaty), Chuokoron, January 1979, p. 109.
(43) Quoted in Ajia 15 (June 1979): 20.
(44) Asia Research Bulletin, September 30, 1978, p. 502.
(45) Asia Research Bulletin, January 31, 1979, p. 524.
(46) Tetsusaburo Kimura, "Indochina Higeki no Kozo" (Structure of Indochinese Tragedy), Sekai, September 1979, p. 15.
(47) For this failure and its consequences, see, for example, Koichi Kondo, "Betonamu Shakaishugi no Satetsu" (Fiasco of Vietnamese Socialism), Chuokoron, September 1979, pp. 66-90.
(48) Khaw Guat Hoon, "Recent Development in China-ASEAN Relations" in Southeast Asian Affairs 1979, p. 65.
(49) Quoted in Asia Research Bulletin, June 30, 1979, p. 572.
(50) Ibid., p. 579, and Asahi Shimbun, September 18, 1979, p. 2.
(51) On the Indonesian sympathy for Vietnam, see, for example, Leo Suryandinata, "Indonesia: A Year of Continuing Challenge," in Southeast Asian Affairs 1979, p. 117, and Indonesia Gaikyo (Indonesia Outline) (Jakarta: Japanese Embassy, January, 1980, mimeo.), pp. 5-6.
(52) Asahi Shimbun, April 1, 1980, p. 7. Also see Hisayo Shirai, "Mosukuwa de miru Taikoku no pawa gemu" (Superpower Game Viewed from Moscow), Asahi Janaru, January 16, 1979, pp. 30-35.
(53) Asia Research Bulletin 10, no. 4 (September 30, 1980): 722.
(54) See, for example, Jusuf Wanandi, Security Dimensions of the Asia-Pacific Region in the 1980s (Jakarta: Center for Strategic and International Studies, 1979), pp. 35-36.
(55) Asahi Shimbun, April 1, 1980, p. 7.
(56) As of 1979, combined total strength of ASEAN military forces was less than half that of Vietnam: 472,500 troops versus 1 million and, while ASEAN and Vietnam were fairly close to even the number of combat aircraft (448 versus 495), the Vietnamese air force was far superior in equipment and combat capability. Beyond a simple numerical comparison, there is this crucial element of discipline and combat experience that would give Vietnam additional advantage over ASEAN. See Military Balance 1979-1980 (London: International Institute for Strategic Studies, 1979), pp. 63-73.
(57) Asia Research Bulletin, April 30, 1970, p. 560.
(58) For example, see Ron Richardson's report in the Far Eastern Economic Review, May 18, 1979, pp. 43-50; New York Times, July 1, 1979, pp. 1 and 12; and Gareth Porter, "Time to Talk with North Korea," Foreign Policy 34 (Spring 1979): 52-73.
(59) For example, The United States, China and Japan: A Report to the Committee on Foreign Relations, United States Senate (Washington, D.C.: U.S. Government Printing Office, 1979), p. 17.
(60) Intelligence reported that, by 1979, North's army had grown to a total of 40 divisions and 600,000 troops from 24 divisions and 430,000 several years earlier. Compare Shimbun Geppo, 408 (November 1980): 58-59.

(61) Middleton, p. E1.

(62) See Tatsumi Okabe, Tonan Ajia to Nihon no Shinro: "Hannichi" no Kozo to Chugoku no Yakuwari (Southeast Asia and Japan's Road: Structure of "Anti-Japanism" and the Role of China) (Tokyo: Nihon Keizai Shimbunsha, 1976), p. 12.

(63) Jusuf Wanandi, A View from ASEAN on the Interest and Role of the United States in Southeast Asia (Jakarta: Institute for Strategic and International Studies, n.d.), mimeo, p. 8.

(64) Ibid., p. 10.

(65) Ibid., pp. 9-10.

(66) Originally proposed by Malaysia with the endorsement of its ASEAN partners at the 5th Conference of Nonaligned Nations held in Colombo in 1976 (rejected by the Indochinese states on the grounds that U.S. bases still remained in the region) and subsequently reiterated repeatedly by ASEAN. See Sekai, April 1979, p. 115.

5
Status of Defense of Japan and U.S.-Japanese Relations

JAPAN'S DEFENSE POLICY

The current Japanese defense policy is based on two major government decisions: the Basic Policies for National Defense of 1957 and the National Defense Program Outline of 1976. The Basic Policies for National Defense stated:

> The objective of national defense is to prevent direct and indirect aggression, and once invaded, to repel such aggression, thereby preserving the independence and peace of Japan founded upon democratic principles.
>
> To achieve this objective, the Government of Japan hereby establishes the following principles:
>
> 1. To support the activities of the United Nations, and promote international cooperation, thereby contributing to the realization of world peace.
> 2. To stabilize the public welfare and enhance the people's love for country, thereby establishing the sound basis essential to Japan's security.
> 3. To develop progressively the effective defense capabilities necessary for self-defense, with due regard to the nation's resources and the prevailing domestic situation.
> 4. To deal with external aggression on the basis of the Japanese-U.S. security arrangements, pending more effective functioning of the United Nations in the future in deterring and repelling such aggression.(1)

In the fall of 1976 the National Defense Council proposed and the cabinet approved the National Defense Program Outline. The Outline was intended to provide greater flexibility for administration, upgrading, and operation of the Japan Self-Defense Forces (JSDF) in responding to any major changes in the domestic or international situation and to provide for "a smooth transition to a heightened state of defense preparedness in such an event."(2) Japan's defense policy today is called kiban teki boeiryoku koso (the basic defense policy or, more literally, the standard defense capability plan).(3) "Basic" is in reference to the JSDF as constituting the "basis" of national defense, with the security arrangements with the United States under the Japanese-U.S. security pact "supplementing" it.(4) Presumably, this would contrast to an earlier Japanese understanding that the JSDF were to play a function that would be "supplementary" to U.S. forces in the event of a military conflict involving the nation's security. Under the current policy, Japan would cope, on its own, with an indirect aggression and a small-scale limited aggression, while repelling a large-scale aggression in cooperation with U.S. forces.(5) Specifically, the basic objective here is to raise the cost for such an aggression against Japan by maintaining its "rejective power" (kyohiryoku), and, in case of a large-scale aggression, to hold off the enemy until U.S. forces come to its aid.(6) Supporters of the current policy have viewed this "basic" aspect as signaling a departure from virtually total dependence on the United States and Japan's assumption of a greater responsibility for its own defense. Some even found in it "an unprecedented realism and rationality in Japan's defense thinking."(7) A closer look at the policy has suggested, however, that the difference or departure was more rhetorical than substantive and that it left the question of the level of defense requirements largely unanswered and the problem of traditional constraints on effective defense intact.

Among others, there were during the past decades five types of putative constraints inhibiting the strengthening of the JSDF to the level that many defense experts and other security-minded Japanese (and Americans) regarded as minimally imperative for effective self-defense. They were: the spirit of the peace Constitution, the "exclusively defensive purposes" of the JSDF, the Three Antinuclear Principles, the ceiling of 1 percent of the GNP for defense expenditure, and the popular consensus.

Whether or not the JSDF were constitutional was once a highly emotional political issue and, while the inevitable generational metabolism of the population plus a series of definitive court rulings eventually led to a popular acceptance of the JSDF, there persists a strong feeling in Japan that the Constitution with its so-called no-war clause is a unique historical document. Those opposing the JSDF or their expansion argued that the nation must remain faithful to its spirit of pacifism, for it is this spirit that makes Japan unique among nations. Thus, one American analyst observed that Article 9 of the Constitution (the no-war clause) "gave legal sanctity and symbolic dignity to pacifism within the country and placed Japan in a sui generis category internationally."(8) This remains a powerfully inhibiting factor against the expansion of JSDF capability.

The "exclusively defensive purposes" principle is the empirical correlate of this pacifist spirit, although doctrinaire pacifists have always argued that the principle is not pacifist enough. It has compelled the nation to be very wary of even appearing to increase its military capability lest it cause anxiety and fear among its neighbors and incite domestic mass opposition, so much so that it forced the government to strip the F-4s (the mainstay of the Air Self-Defense Force during the past decade acquired at enormous costs and now being gradually replaced by F-15s) of their key operational features (bombing and mid-air refueling capabilities) in order to keep them "exclusively defensive" in purpose. The same principle has also kept out bombers, cruisers, battleships, aircraft carriers, and everything else that could be construed as possessing offensive capacity.

The Three Antinuclear Principles enunciated in 1967 by the then prime minister in response to pacifist demands and popular fear precipitated by China's nuclear explosion and the escalation of war in Vietnam, pledged that Japan, as a matter of deliberate policy, would neither produce, nor obtain, nor permit the deployment of nuclear weapons on its soil. The principles are part of the current policy, though it should be noted that no Japanese government has ever agreed that nuclear weapons as such are unconstitutional.

A fourth constraint on an effective defense buildup has been the longstanding budgetary practice of limiting defense spending to a maximum of 1 percent of GNP. This limitation came about by happenstance entirely unrelated to security considerations. There is no evidence that the first "below 1 percent" defense budget (1959) was deliberate. At the same time, the fact that the rate of annual economic growth in the 1960s and into the early years of the 1970s generally exceeded 10 percent in real terms automatically guaranteed that 1 percent or even less of the GNP was sufficient to generate consistent increases in the JSDF budget (it rose three times from 1957 to 1977 in constant price).(9) This, of course, was a statistical accident, with little relation to serious and comprehensive planning and deliberation of security requirements. In any event, the 1 percent limit soon became a standard operating rule in the nation's bureaucratic budgetary politics, a rule that all other sectors of the government bureaucracy, together with their lateral policy counterparts within the ruling party, and their clienteles in society quite understandably found compatible with their self-interests in their competition for preferential access to budgetary resources. In fact, at the time of the adoption of the National Defense Program Outline (NDPO) in 1976, the government officially endorsed this 1 percent practice, adding to the NDPO a provision that "in maintaining the armed strength, the total amount of defense expenditure in each fiscal year shall not exceed, for the time being, an amount equivalent to 1/100 of the gross national product of the said fiscal year."(10)

Last but not least, the requirement of consensus in any significant policy change in Japanese democracy has rendered the government extremely resistant to undertaking any drastic departure in policy in so sensitive an area as national security. Even those officials and politicians who desire much enhanced defense capability have considered popular support indispensable and contended that "however powerful JSDF may become and no matter what sophisticated weaponry they may acquire, they could not constitute a genuinely effective defense capability unless they enjoyed the people's understanding, support, and cooperation."(11) As we shall see shortly, critical popular consensus for serious attempts at improving the nation's defense capability is still lacking, despite the fact that the popular support for the JSDF as such has increased considerably.

These are among the constraints that have been discussed by officials and observers alike as inhibitive of an expeditious expansion of the JSDF. They constitute especially nettlesome obstacles to national security because they have derived from domestic sources and have little relevance to security requirements that are determined by the character and contingency of the nation's external environment. Nevertheless, they have in effect provided officials, politicians, and people alike with exceedingly convenient pretexts for avoiding difficult decisions that ought to be made. Nobody disagrees that diplomacy is the first and foremost means of insuring national existence and security, but the inescapable problem, as one former defense official argued, is: What to do when diplomacy, however carefully and competently conducted, turns out, as it often does, to be ineffective or insufficient in preventing danger to the nation?(12) Doctrinaire pacifists would not admit the problem, insisting that diplomacy should work. The external environment and contingencies that its change engenders cannot be defined or willed by domestic ideological aspirations, psychological propensities, or political preferences.

CAPABILITY OF THE JAPAN SELF-DEFENSE FORCES

The JSDF may look quite impressive in simple numerical comparison to military forces of most of the nations of the world. In military expenditures, Japan ranked eighth in the world and second only to the massive People's Republic of China in East Asia in 1980. While the Ground Self-Defense Force (GSDF) was smaller than its counterparts of the five highly militarized and battle-anticipating nations in the region (China, North and South Korea, Taiwan, and Vietnam), in the more crucial naval and air power, Japan was perhaps superior overall to any nation of the region except for China.

The GSDF consisted of approximately 160,000 personnel divided into infantry and mechanized divisions; tank, airborne, and artillery brigades; and antiaircraft groups. The Maritime Self-Defense Force (MSDF) was made up of over 90 surface ships, 14 submarines, and 200 aircraft. The Air Self-Defense Force (ASDF) was composed of some 450 planes and five ground-to-air missile groups.(13) Major equipment for the JSDF included, among other, domestically developed tanks, howitzers, antitank guided missiles, submarines, destroyers, antisubmarine aircraft, supersonic trainers, and was augmented by such U.S.-developed weapons as F-4s (now being replaced by F-15s as the ASDF mainstay), Nike ground-to-air missiles, domestically manufactured under U.S. license. Especially given the high level of its technological capability, Japan, on paper at least, was and is indeed a considerable military power, armed with highly modern ground, air, and naval forces. How effective the JSDF in fact are or would prove to be in a serious contingency, however, could not be deduced from mere statistics. Statistical and other hard data available do not tell enough about actual JSDF capability regarding the kind of contingency for which it should be prepared.

One of the more relevant aspects of any military force is its personnel structure. There are approximately 240,000 JSDF personnel today. They may or may not be adequate in themselves, but one of their characteristics is top-heaviness. The officer-NCO (noncommissioned officer) ratio is 1:3, and for every non-NCO enlistee, there are 1.5 NCOs.(14) One retired JSDF general noted that, relative to the total size of the military personnel, there are more generals and admirals in Japan than in any other modern state.(15) The JSDF's non-NCO enlisted personnel are more than one-quarter below the required or authorized numerical strength.(16) This problem is particularly acute for the GSDF. Platoon-and company-level exercise maneuvers are reported seldom to have their full personnel complements.(17) While some observers contend that this top-heaviness would enable a rapid force expansion should Japan decide on it, a combination of recruitment difficulty (evidenced by the very understrength personnel), an extremely small number of reservists, and a low level of public interest in enlisting for the JSDF would seem to render such a rapid force expansion quite problematic.(18) Such neutral nations as Sweden and Switzerland, which many Japanese consider models of pacifism and noninvolvement in international conflict, maintain relatively small forces on active duty (65,000 in Sweden and 18,500 in Switzerland) but are prepared to mobilize large forces on short notice – 750,000 within 72 hours in Sweden and 625,000 during the first 48 hours in Switzerland;(19) Japan's armed forces, in contrast, have fewer than 40,000 reservists to draw on in case of emergency. Recognizing the problem, the Japanese government began studying the possibility of increasing the size of the reserve force to 180,000,(20) but when the actual size of total JSDF personnel on active duty is barely 240,000, it would take years to generate more than 140,000 additional reservists. (Reservists are former JSDF personnel who volunteered to remain in the reserve.) Particularly worrisome is the fact that, of those fewer than 40,000 reservists, only some 600 are MSDF and but a handful ASDF.(21) Given the critical importance of air and naval defense of the nation, the personnel situation here remains disturbing.

The JSDF have a seemingly impressive array of modern defense equipment, as briefly alluded to earlier, but this could be very misleading in assessing their capability. There is little depth to their arsenal. Their ammunition inventory, for instance, is reported to be extremely low. Two decades ago the three branches of the JSDF maintained a total of 140,000 tons of ammunition. By 1978 the amount was halved to 70,000 tons, and this in the face of size increases in the GSDF from 140,000 to 160,000 persons, in the MSDF from 78,000 tons to 180,000 tons of ships, and in the ASDF from 260 aircraft to over 400.(22) Although the Japan Defense Agency (JDA) never disclosed the exact numbers of bullets and shells available to the JSDF, one study estimated it at 700 bullets per combat trooper and 300 shells per artillery piece for the GSDF. These figures were viewed as barely adequate for two weeks in a small localized battle.(23) In case of a more serious contingency, the GSDF would, according to one former senior officer, exhaust its ammunition supply in ten minutes.(24) An authoritative 1980 study reported that a majority of GSDF equipment was over two decades old and reiterated the critical shortage of ammunition.(25) As for the ASDF, it was discovered toward the end of the last decade that its inventory of air-to-air missiles was adequate only for one sortie or at the most two per combat plane and that, when the missiles were spent, the most deadly weapon at the disposal of ASDF fighter and interceptor pilots would be 20-mm cannons.(26) Until the summer of 1980, the combat aircraft were not permitted to carry missiles on patrol duty, in deference to the "pacifist spirit" of the nation's Constitution. The radar sites, so vital to air defense, remain unprotected at this writing. The MSDF is in no better condition. In 1980 the JDA altered its traditional "no torpedoes policy" to permit MSDF ships and antisubmarine aircraft to carry their torpedoes on routine patrol, but it admitted that it would take some time before all relevant ships and planes are even partially so armed.(27) Earlier, one study reported that there was only as much naval ammunition as the existing combat vessels could carry, most of which, of course, was stored at their bases.(28) Only five of the 32 destroyers (the largest surface combatants of the MSDF) and none of the other ships are equipped with antiaircraft missile systems, leaving most of the MSDF complement totally vulnerable to enemy air attack.(29) Thus, should a serious military emergency arise today or in the very near future, the JSDF could be incapacitated within a matter of hours or at the most a few days even if the enemy failed to destroy them.

The principal reason for this dangerous state of JSDF prepared-ness, of course, was and continues to be budgetary. In recent years, over two-thirds of the JSDF budget went to salaries, benefits, food, clothing, recreation, and the like and less than one-fifth was spent on actual arms procurement.(30) In 1978, for example, Japan's defense industry manufactured 25 units of the Sparrow air-to-air missiles (one of the three types of such missiles used by the ASDF) and 1.7 million rifle bullets per month, to cite but two major items.(31) Twenty-five missiles would be adequate for one sortie each but six interceptors, and 1.7 million bullets would mean something like ten bullets per GSDF soldier. This, among others, was the direct result of the consistently small allocation out of the total defense budget for weapons procurement − about 17 percent in 1979 and 20 percent in 1980,(32) proportionately about half of what other modern military forces spend for such purposes.(33) The problem for the JSDF is even more acute because unit costs of weapons and ammunition production in Japan are said to be signifi-cantly higher (as much as three times on some items) than in other modern states.(34) As some JDA sources argue, ammunition produc-tion could be increased fairly rapidly once additional funds became available. True, but what about a sudden emergency?

In the longer run, there is more serious trouble arising out of inadequate defense spending, the inadequacy that the Japanese government has come to admit publicly, and that has to do with research and development. Here, the question is not so much about Japan's developing just "new" weapons. If it needed only new weapons, it could buy them, say, from the United States. In view of its geography and topography, which, as many observers note, make defense against lateral penetration extremely difficult,(35) and the most likely contingencies, Japan should concentrate on research and development of particular types of weapons specifically suited for its physical and military predicament. To an extent, it has been doing precisely that. Military technologists are engaged in research and development, among other items, of a short-range surface-to-air guided missile, a medium-range air-to-ship missile, and an electronic detection system.(36) The extent of efforts, however, seems to leave much to be desired. By the JDA's own estimate, only 0.9 percent of the defense budget was devoted to research and development from 1975 to 1978 (approximately $67 million in 1978),(37) and, in 1980, the amount barely reached 1 percent.(38) Comparable figures in other nations in 1979, for example, were 10.6 percent for the United States, 13.6 percent for Britain, 12.1 percent for France, and 5.0 percent for West Germany.(39) It would seem clear that relatively little effort was being expended in Japan in the area of military technology. This is a cause for concern because military technology elsewhere has been advancing rapidly. Japan, as a nation committed to nonaggression and peaceful diplomacy, eschews the development or possession of strategic arms although it is perfectly capable of developing them, including nuclear arms, on short order. As a sovereign state, Japan has in effect renounced the option of strategic defense and its military capability is consequently much narrower in range than that of other nations. This is all the more reason that Japan should redouble its effort for the development of specifically appropriate tactical weapons to meet its unique security requirements.

The JSDF are a fighting force, organized and maintained to engage in combat against attacks. The proof of its combat capability is in fighting but, quite unlike the proverbial pudding, the nation cannot afford to wait for the proof to ascertain if its defense force can in fact adequately do the job it is expected to do. We have already taken a glimpse at some of the crucial dimensions relating to JSDF capability, but there are more immediate and serious problems.

Effectiveness of any combat force depends critically upon the extent and quality of its training. Aside from the problem of low ammunition inventory, the JSDF are seriously hampered in this regard by a number of constraints imposed upon their training and combat preparation.

Japan, as was noted in Chapter 3, is extraordinarily high in human and structural density, so much so that there is little space available for large-scale, sustained military training and maneuvers. Some of the equipment available is quite sophisticated, but relevant military personnel are handicapped by lack of sufficient opportunities to engage in effective and rigorous combat training with it. Newer GSDF tanks, for example, are in many ways superb in their operational features, but those features could not be adequately exploited because there are few areas in the country where their crews could freely and thoroughly train. Artillery firing ranges are both few in number and limited in size. The ASDF is particularly limited in its combat training. The economic growth and prosperity of the nation has created a vast and increasingly congested network of civilian and commercial air corridors over and around the country; and this has resulted in forcing combat pilots to train farther and farther away from their bases, compelling them to spend much of their crafts' fuel in getting to and returning from areas where combat training can take place. As a consequence, they could spend but a few minutes in actual combat training on their outing, which is less than sufficiently frequent because of the rising fuel cost and the low ammunition supply. The MSDF, while able to use open seas for training, also suffers from adequate combat training owing to the insufficient ammunition.

JSDF training is further handicapped by administrative jurisdictional constraints, constraints deriving at least in part from the still lingering antimilitary predilection of the nation at large. The GSDF, for example, must request permission from relevant Regional Forestry Offices of the Ministry of Agriculture, Forestry, and

Fishery in order to secure troops' passage through national forests and parks to their exercise grounds, permission that GSDF commanders often complain is not readily forthcoming. Ministry bureaucrats admit that the influence of leftist labor unions in certain regions causes local Forestry officials to be cautious in handling GSDF requests. Transportation of troops, equipment, and supplies through roads and highways and local administrative entities requires prior approval by a range of relevant civilian authorities outside of the JDA. For GSDF troops, all this makes it extremely difficult to acquire thorough familiarity with the geography and topography of areas where combat might take place in the future, let alone engage in the kind of rigorous training required of the maintenance of a first-rate combat force. Regarding the use of air space by ASDF squadrons, the authoritative decisional power rests with the Civil Aviation Bureau of the Ministry of Transport, whose operative motto, ASDF commanders complain, is "safety of civilian aviation over defense requirements,"(40) giving higher priority to satisfying civilian and commercial air traffic needs and preferences. These constraints upon JSDF training, especially for the GSDF and the ASDF, have made it necessary to seek critical training of some of their personnel in the United States. However, the fact that the proportion of JSDF combat personnel sent to the United States for training is very small suggests that the effect of such U.S. training on the total combat effectiveness of these forces would be marginal at best.

The state of combat readiness of the JSDF is further complicated by the absence of legal provisions that would enable the JSDF promptly to respond to a sudden or surprise enemy attack. According to the existing law governing the JSDF, no elements of the military may be deployed for or engage in combat for national defense until the prime minister, as supreme commander, issues an explicit order upon Diet approval. Given Japan's prewar experience with its military and the necessity of maintaining civilian supremacy over the JSDF, this seems entirely proper, and, besides, in case of emergency, the prime minister is empowered to issue the order to the JSDF without the Diet's prior approval. Yet there is a serious problem under the present circumstances that cannot be left unresolved. Even if the prime minister were to issue an appropriate order for combat to the JSDF in an emergency without Diet approval, there might not (and many critics argue would not) be sufficient lead time for prompt and effective response by the JSDF. With no JSDF officers on the prime minister's staff and no military liaison between him and the Joint Staff Council, communication between the JSDF and the supreme commander is through civilian bureaucratic channels. Passage of any length of time, owing to communications problems (for example, the prime minister may be out playing golf or the JDA director-general who must inform him could be attending a private meeting), decisional hesitation on the

part of the prime minister or (inasmuch as the current interpretation of law still warrants its concurrence)(41) his cabinet before the
issuance of a proper order could fatally tip the scale of combat
against the nation, not to mention the likelihood of death and
destruction, military and civilian, that could otherwise be avoided or
minimized. Thus, even if the JSDF were themselves 100 percent
combat-ready and capable of repelling a surprise attack, the
potential lack of dispatch in the action of civilian authorities cold
reduce, even nullify, whatever level of effectiveness they might in
fact possess. It is precisely this particular predicament of national
defense that in the summer of 1978 prompted the chairman of the
Joint Staff Council to suggest that, in case of an emergency,
frontline commanders might have to act "supralegally" in order to
defend the nation, a suggestion that immediately led to his dismissal
and forced retirement for having challenged the principle of civilian
control of the military.(42) This problem of prompt response to
security contingencies has proved more difficult to deal with than
one might imagine. The Japanese are understandably sensitive
about the principle of civilian control of the military, and the
parliamentary opposition in particular fears that legislation enabling
the JSDF expeditiously to respond to those contingencies might
start some dangerous trend toward the erosion of the principle and
toward the revival of militarism. Because of the potentially
emotional character of the problem, the government has been
extremely cautious in dealing with it for fear that any critical
debate on it, let alone any focused attempt to seek necessary
legislation, might undermine the popular acceptance of the JSDF,
which had been so carefully cultivated during the postwar period. In
the meantime, the problem remains unresolved.

The JSDF as a fighting force do not seem to provide much
comfort to those concerned with the security of the nation. Even
ten years ago, when they were in more senses than one in a better
condition relative to the level of potential threat posed against the
nation, officials and knowledgeable observers were already pointing
out that, in case of a serious contingency, the ASDF would be
annihilated within one hour, the MSDF in a few days at most, and
that the GSDF would immediately have to resort to guerrilla
warfare in case of enemy troop landing.(43) A Soviet diplomat was
reported recently to have told a Japanese journalist that an invasion
of Japan would "take only several tens of minutes if we did it in real
earnest."(44) Clearly, he was not over exaggerating, for many
experts' assessments of the JSDF's capability today are even
gloomier than ten years ago,(45) and the general pessimism was
publicly shared by none other than the chairman of the Joint Staff
Council, who told in a speech in 1980 that the JSDF would lack a
capability to repel even a small-scale, limited aggression even if
their current five-year (1980-84) military buildup program (called
the "midterm service estimate") were fully implemented.(46)

Should these views sound excessively pessimistic, it might be useful to recall the so-called MiG-25 incident. When a Soviet Air Force lieutenant defected to Japan in September 1976 aboard his ultramodern MiG-25, the ASDF, with its full complement of electronic surveillance and detection systems and supersonic F-4s, proved incapable of intercepting the intruder as it approached and entered the nation's air space, and well before it finally located the MiG's whereabouts, the Soviet plane had safely landed at a civilian airport only minutes away from a major ASDF base.(47) Clearly, it would not be fair to judge the overall ASDF or JSDF capability from any single incident, but the particular incident was especially salient in its character and implications because it took place in Hokkaido, which was and still is the focus of the most concentrated and intense security efforts by the JSDF. The incident, therefore, suggested not one single local or isolated gap in national defense but some fundamental defect in the overall security system of the nation. Defense experts in the past were reported to hold that the combat objective of the JSDF, whose purpose is strictly defensive, was to inflict a 30 percent loss on the attacking enemy force.(48) Why a 30 percent loss would cause the enemy to relent has never been clear, but the more fundamental question now is whether or not the JSDF could in fact inflict on the enemy any loss at all, let alone a 30 percent loss, and how much greater a loss they themselves, and the nation, would have to suffer in the meantime. A recent authoritative study of Japan's security reported that none of the specific steps enumerated in the National Defense Program Outline for the upgrading of the nation's defense capability had been carried into execution.(49) In the final analysis, it may well be that the JSDF, in their basic posture and capability, remain little more than "a parapolice force," as once characterized by a Japanese analyst.(50)

U.S.-JAPANESE RELATIONS AND SECURITY CONCERNS IN JAPAN

Lack of Mutuality

The foundation of Japan's defense and security has been and continues to be its relations with the United States. The existing Japanese-U.S. security arrangements originally came into being with the 1951 Security Treaty between the United States and Japan, which was concluded simultaneously with the San Francisco Peace Treaty that restored Japan's independence and sovereignty. Japan had been disarmed at the end of World War II and, since then, had been without a military force, except for a small Police Reserve organized in 1950 under order from the U.S. occupation administration to augment internal security against potential communist-instigated disorder. Japan's restoration to the status of an independent state also restored the right to self-defense as well as to collective self-defense. Since Japan was then deemed unable promptly to develop means to exercise this right, the United States sought to fill the gap. The 1951 Security Treaty stated in part:

> The United States of America, in the interest of peace and security, is presently willing to maintain certain of its armed forces in and about Japan, in the expectation, however, that Japan will itself increasingly assume responsibility for its own defense against direct and indirect aggression, always avoiding any armament which could be of an offensive threat or serve other than to promote peace and security in accordance with the purposes and principles of the United Nations Charter.

The treaty obligated the United States to use its armed forces to insure "the international peace and security in the Far East" as well as the security of Japan. According to treaty provisions regarding Japan's responsibility, the Police Reserve quickly developed into the JSDF consisting of ground, air, and maritime self-defense forces by 1953. The treaty, which was to be in force until such time as the United Nations had acquired adequate ability to guarantee peace and security or some alternative arrangements for the same purpose could be provided "in the Japan area," was negotiated by Tokyo and Washington in 1958 and 1959 and was superceded in 1960 by a Treaty of Mutual Cooperation and Security between the United States and Japan. This revised security pact stated:

> Considering that (the two nations) have a common concern in the maintenance of international peace and security in the Far East, ... The Parties, individually and in cooperation with each other, by means of continuous and effective self-help and mutual aid, will maintain and develop, subject to their constitutional provision, their capacities to resist armed attack.

Quite unlike its predecessor, the 1960 treaty permitted either party, after ten years, to terminate it by giving notice to the other. A subsequent exchange of notes between the two governments established for the United States an obligation of "prior consultation" with the Japanese government whenever it desired to make a major change in the deployment of its forces into or out of Japan, in their equipment and use of facilities and areas in Japan, or in combat operations to be undertaken from Japan for purposes other than the repelling of an armed attack against Japan itself or U.S. interest in Japan.

Its prescribed "mutuality" notwithstanding, the Treaty of Mutual Cooperation and Security was conspicuous in its lack of such mutuality. It obligated the United States to help defend Japan but did not require a reciprocal obligation on the part of Japan to help defend the United States: It stipulated only that Japan help defend U.S. interests on its premises. Even in the defense of Japan, the ultimate responsibility seemed one-sided; inasmuch as Japan had in effect renounced possession of strategic weapons and the JSDF were little more than "a parapolice force," it clearly would be the United States, not Japan, that would have to assume major combat responsibilities in all cases but the most insignificant and inept enemy attack. Interestingly enough, however, this absence of mutuality in their security arrangements was more or less taken for granted by both nations, because of a unique relationship that had during earlier postwar years developed between them, which had the effect of powerfully defining the pattern of interaction between them thereafter.

Whatever its psychological or cultural origin, the United States had developed what might be termed a Pygmalion complex toward Japan almost as soon as it had subdued it. General MacArthur was the personification of this attitude, Cold War calculations aside. He was not so much a conquering Caesar as a Dr. Higgins to the Eliza Doolittle that was Japan – an errant, misguided, untutored, but promising youth (the general compared Japan to a "twelve-year old") who only needed careful and patient tutoring in democratic manners and virtues of free enterprise, to be remade in his image. The United States, in a sense, had taken Japan as its special ward. Japan, on its part, soon began to view the United States (initially through MacArthur) with an attitude of amae, a peculiarly pronounced psychological trait of the Japanese that predisposes an individual to depend on and presume on another's indulgence.(51) This attitude often characterizes a child's relationship with its mother, a little brother's with his big brother, a kobun's (follower) with oyabun (boss), and so on. In an important sense, therefore, there soon emerged a subtle but potent emotional content in the relationship between Japan and the United States during the early postwar years that would persist after Japan regained its independence. In the area of mutual security arrangements, the United States would for more than two decades effectively assume the role of a patron, a protector, providing Japan with a powerful military shield behind which it could engage in single-minded pursuit of capitalist economic growth, a pursuit in whose virtues the United States had eagerly tutored it and for which it would promptly demonstrate an extraordinary aptitude that the United States found gratifying. Japan, on its part, would assume the role as well as "the psychology of the junior partner,"(52) taking it for granted that the senior partner – the patron – would continue to shoulder the burden of all substantive responsibility for their "mutual" enterprise and protect it from all dangers, even though from time to time the patron might let out his annoyance at the junior's failure to carry its share of the burden. It was thus that the security arrangements between the United States and Japan remained largely a one-sided affair in which Japan, basking in peace and safety provided by the U.S. military shield, made little substantive and inherently hard efforts to increase the level of its effective self-defense capability relative to those that the United States maintained in its behalf. Japan, then, was not a security partner, but rather a holder of "an American insurance policy — with remarkably reasonable annual premiums."(53)

The arrangements, however, were bound to be affected by changes in circumstances in each of the two nations and their respective external environments, as well as by concomitant changes in these two nations' mutual perceptions.(54) The U.S. attitude toward Japan and its contribution to the mutual security treaty began to shift ascertainably, starting at the end of the 1960s. This shift was caused by a combination of certain external and domestic developments. One of the most crucial of these, of course, was the decline of the bipolar stability discussed in Chapter 2 of this volume that need not be reiterated here. Another important external event impinging upon the U.S. attitude toward Japan was the war in Vietnam, which engaged much of the U.S. military capability available outside of the NATO region. Not only was the war enormously costly for the United States, but it was also extremely frustrating because of its intractability and, as became apparent soon, unwinnability, thus causing the United States to reassess its traditional policy of opposing any foe and helping any friend anywhere in the world, including East Asia. One result of this reassessment was the Nixon Doctrine of 1969, which, while professing U.S. faithfulness to its treaty commitments and proclaiming its readiness to use its nuclear capability to protect any ally threatened by the Soviet nuclear power, pointedly stated that "in cases involving other types of aggression, we shall furnish military and economic assistance when requested in accordance with our treaty commitments. But we shall look to the nation directly threatened to assume the primary responsibility of providing the manpower for its defense."(55) The Nixon Doctrine contained another significant note: "We are not involved in the world because we have commitments; we have commitments because we are involved. Our interests must shape our commitments, rather than the other way around."(56) A third external or international development that had a critical impact on the U.S. view of Japan and its self-defense efforts was Japan's spectacular growth into the third largest economic power in the world, the growth that even the most nationalistic Japanese admit would have been unthinkable without the military security provided by the United States.(57) As one Washington official would later put it, the United States had been proud of Japan for being such an excellent pupil in learning from and emulating it and its economic system and lifestyle but had not conceived of it overtaking the United States in the very metier that had always been its national forte. The recognition that Japan had been able to make this achievement because the United States had allowed itself to be maneuvered by her amae attitude – "a form of emotional judo"(58) – into underwriting its security at enormous costs to itself and letting it evade responsibility for its own defense would become stronger as years elapsed in the 1970s.

Some of the domestic developments within the United States also contributed powerfully to the shift in the U.S. attitude toward Japan and the security arrangements with it. Starting in the decade of the 1960s, what we earlier referred to as the revolution of rising entitlements had gained increasing momentum in U.S. politics, placing growing stress and strain on the fiscal and political resources of the country for the maintenance of domestic stability. This revolution was quickly joined by a rapidly expanding antimilitary sentiment prompted by the frustration, disillusionment, and dubious legitimacy of the unsuccessful and protracted prosecution by the United States of the war in Vietnam. The combination of these two domestic developments, among others, would soon lead to a diffuse popular demand for reductions in military expenditure in favor of an expanded spending on social and human services and avoidance of entanglement, especially military involvement, in events around the world (Europe excepted, perhaps). In regard to Japan in particular, various sectors of the U.S. economy began to feel an increasingly acute pressure of Japanese economic competition, a competition that was allegedly unfair because it was widely believed that the Japanese invasion of U.S. domestic markets was powerfully subsidized by Tokyo's discriminatory protectionist policies in collusion with dubious pricing and other practices of the Japanese industries concerned. Japan, in more senses than one, came to be viewed, not as a loyal ally or friend, but rather as an opportunistic ingrate, an unprincipled and avaricious economic animal, unabashedly continuing to expect the United States to provide it with protection against external danger and simultaneously threatening its workers' jobs and industries' survival with an increasingly massive and unscrupulous economic invasion.

In the eyes of more and more Americans, therefore, Japan ceased to be their special ward or protégé and instead became an increasing "burden." The traditional Japanese insistence that special legal, constitutional, political, and economic constraints prevent them from expanding defense efforts ceased to be credible to the United States. However polite the diplomatic language used, Japan came to be viewed by the Americans as enjoying a "free ride" on their military power, and the security treaty appeared, as one Foreign Ministry official admitted, "more and more one-sided" as "a U.S. obligation." The one-sidedness of the treaty was a matter of fact from the beginning, but because of the change in the U.S. predicament and Japan's capability, it began to assume a critical political and military dimension to the United States. Thus it became palpably unconscionable in the eyes of Americans that Japan, with a per capita income virtually equalling theirs, had been spending less than one percent of its GNP on defense while other industrial states had been expending at least 3 percent and the United States, with its commitment to the defense of Japan, had been devoting over 5 percent despite its worsening economic condition (much of which was attributed to Japan's aggressive economic aggrandizement) and domestic sociopolitical problems requiring consistently expanding nondefense spending. As one State Department official put it rather bluntly to the author, fairness would dictate equity and reciprocity in U.S.-Japanese security relations.

Security Concern in Japan

As recently as a few years ago, an observer lamented: "There exists a view in Japan that to think (about the issue of national defense) in military and security terms is criminal or immoral."(59) This was no mere hyperbole. Throughout most of the postwar period, there was an "atmosphere" in Japan variously attributed to the ideological influence of the "pacifist" Constitution and the subsequent popular "antimilitary allergy" that inhibited candor and seriousness in discussing national defense and security requirements. The causes of this atmosphere were more complicated, as we shall discuss in Chapter 6, but the inhibitive atmosphere was nevertheless real. The debate on defense and security, therefore, was characterized by what one American analyst called "the moral cast . . . defining the security issue in such completely moral terms"(60) as the incontrovertible virtue of pacifism, the palpable evil of war and destruction, and the uniqueness of Japan's constitutional commitment to peaceful resolution of international disputes. One consequence was national reluctance to undertake authentic appraisal of defense needs and security requirements. At the same time, an almost ritualistically pious incantation of those moral principles may be said to have produced a false popular sense of security that, so long as Japan remained faithful to those principles, especially to the pacifist spirit of the Constitution, other nations would respect its sincerity and refrain from harming it. A cross-national survey in 1974 showed the Japanese to be most optimistic about the avoidance of World War III among national samples (64 percent, in contrast, for example, to 48 percent of the British, 52 percent of the French, and 37 percent among the Swiss).(61) A 1974 survey of "opinion leaders" in Japan indicated a similarly optimistic trend. To the question, "What will be the world military situation within . . .?" responses (in percentages) were as follows:(62)

	Within Next 5-10 Years	Within Next 10-20 Years	Within Next 20-30 Years
About same as now	61.2	0.0	0.0
Partially disarmed	26.2	61.9	34.4
Totally disarmed	0.0	6.3	31.3
Militarily expanded	8.7	11.2	5.0
World War III	0.0	0.0	2.5

In 1978 with the international situation becoming increasingly unstable, a plurality of Japanese (36 percent) believed there was no risk of their nation being provoked to or involved in war and only one in five felt the risk existed, and one out of every three who believed there was no risk cited the pacifist Constitution as the reason.(63)

All these findings reflected the passive optimism characteristic of the Japanese people (about which, see Chapter 6), but there was another dimension to those findings, and that is, to quote one concerned Japanese scholar, the Japanese as a nation had become "lulled by peace" (heiwa boke) by their existence behind the shield of U.S. military power in the previous three decades into a false feeling that "security is free, like air and water." It was this false feeling, which initially predisposed many Japanese in government and out, in the opinion of some observers, to viewing the Soviet naval expansion and military-base buildup around Japan with rather extraordinary equanimity and inclined them to attribute these Soviet military moves to what one Foreign Ministry official termed as Moscow's "historical" sense of inferiority and insecurity. The late Masayoshi Ohira, widely regarded by liberals as possessing a wholesome view of international politics, in an interview immediately upon his election as prime minister in the fall of 1978 had reflected this feeling when he observed, "Fundamentally, Soviet security policy is very prudent. My view is that it is defensive. The Soviet Union has conducted excellent diplomacy very steadily. I do not think Soviet defense policy and diplomacy are bellicose."(64) Public opinion remained largely indifferent to the JSDF as an instrument of national defense and security. Until toward the end of the 1970s, the role most frequently assigned by popular perception to the JSDF was "rescue and relief operations" (that is, in case of natural disaster, accident, and so on, by 38 percent of the people in 1972 and 34 percent in 1975), and those who felt that national defense was the primary function of the JSDF were relatively small in number (24 percent in 1972 and 30 percent in 1975). Others identified such missions as "civic programs" and "domestic security" as principal JSDF functions.(65) As late as 1978, only 18 percent of the Japanese felt any need to strengthen the JSDF, as opposed to 61 percent who believed the existing level of JSDF strength was adequate.(66)

Political reluctance seriously to deal with the issue of defense and security and the lack of compelling public concern with it were long reflected in a rather remarkable apparent equanimity within the ruling party about the nation's military needs. One top Defense Agency official told the author as recently as 1979 that only about ten members of the party (out of some 400 in the Diet) had been active in pondering and discussing national security. A few years earlier, a team of investigative reporters had discovered that the National Defense Division (kokubo bukai), one of the 16 senior standing policy committees of the ruling Liberal Democratic Party (LDP), had only 32 MPs (members of parliament) as members, that few of them attended its sessions, and that most LDPers were not interested in the issue of national security because, quite unlike the issues of price support for rice (Agriculture and Forestry Division with over 100 members) and highway construction (Construction Division with as many members), it did not generate electoral support for them.(67) A Defense Agency division director complained to the author that neither the people nor the party had sufficiently serious interest in or concern about security matters. One upper-house MP observed that it was not only opposition parties but also the ruling party and its government that had put national security under taboo.(68)

Against the background of these peculiar political orientations and psychological proclivities, it is no wonder that the security debate until recently was largely sterile in substantive content, ambiguous as to direction, and devoid of critical relevance to both the existing security environment and future contingencies. It was throughout most of the postwar period conducted at a level of vague generalities and rhetorical obfuscation. The two key documents (Basic Policies for National Defense and National Defense Program Outline) cited earlier in this chapter as the bases of the current defense policy were, in more ways than one, quintessential manifestations of these orientations and they did not provoke or generate any compelling security assessment or strategic policy for national defense. As an American observer noted, "independent concern for matters of realpolitik" had consistently been "eschewed in principle as well as in fact by the government and opposition alike."(69) Instead, such seemingly plausible but substantively barren slogans as "exclusively defensive" policy, "the spirit of the Constitution," and "neither invading nor being invaded"(70) were treated as substitutes for hard thinking and critical scrutiny about national security and self-defense, leaving the nation without policy and without strategy.

The unfolding of disturbing events and developments, indeed the rapid and visible change in its external environment, in the latter half of the 1970s, however, was bound to cause an increasingly ascertainable, albeit frequently ambiguous, shift in the character and direction of security concern in Japan. Among them were: the violence and intracommunist rivalry in and over Indochina and the threat they posed against Southeast Asia in particular and East Asia in general, an accelerated Soviet military and political expansion in and through East Asia, the decline of the U.S. military presence in the region, an increasingly widespread anxiety about U.S. reliability, the growing perception of acute vulnerability of Japan's life-line, the MiG-25 incident, the effect of OPEC petropolitics, the instability in Korea, crises in the Persian Gulf region and Southwest Asia. The change became noticeable first in 1978 with a sudden increase in the number of magazine articles and books discussing the issue of national defense and security from a realistic perspective without a corresponding increase in the number of articles and books extolling the unalloyed virtue of pacifism or unarmed neutrality.(71) Simultaneously, the security debate in the formal political arena became unprecedentedly active, with the prime minister devoting for the first time in the postwar period a whole section of his annual policy address to the Diet to national defense and the parliamentary opposition adopting a subdued and inquisitive tone instead of the customary shrill idealistic pacifist rhetoric in subsequent interpollation. Government officials also began to talk about defense and security problems in an uncharacteristically candid (to some observers, dangerous) fashion. The Defense Agency director-general (a minister of state) exhorted JSDF officers that their capability should be such that potential adversaries would "fear" them, for a nation whose defense forces could not be feared would be unable to deter aggression.(72) The chairman of the Joint Staff Council in a widely debated article argued that only offensive capabilities would ultimately insure the nation's security.(73) In June, the Defense Agency revealed a "defense study" plan focusing on deployment and operation of the JSDF in "military emergencies,"(74) thus breaking the "taboo" that had been in effect since the controversial Three Arrows Plan of the early 1960s.(75) A month later, the chairman of the Joint Staff Council publicly suggested the necessity of JSDF commanders to act supralegally in the absence of relevant law enabling prompt military response to a sudden enemy attack, compelling his civilian superiors to dismiss him under pressure from the opposition charge of threat to the principle of civilian supremacy.

In the meantime, the 1978 Defense White Paper for the first time explicitly pointed to the Soviet forces in East Asia, especially the expanded naval and air power, as "a factor that cannot be ignored for regional security."(76) Shortly thereafter, the first "defense think-tank," the Research Institute for Peace and Security, was established and the prime minister instructed the Defense Agency to commence a feasibility study of legislation for times of emergency, and leaders of one opposition party held meetings with the three service chiefs to listen to the latter's emphatic urging for legal and logistic necessity to prepare the JSDF for a surprise enemy attack. The Defense Agency submitted a budget request designed to strengthen defense, especially in the northern part of the country.(77)

One result of the flurry of verbal activities in the area of national defense and security since 1978 was that it effectively ceased to be "immoral or criminal" to talk about national security in military terms. The major opposition party, the Socialists, which had been the champion of pacifism and unarmed neutrality and which could have put the brake on the new trend of security concern, suffered a serious political setback early in 1979 when China invaded Vietnam to teach a "punitive lesson." In the words of one Foreign Ministry official, "the Chinese have silenced the Socialist party opposition to the defense policies we favor."(78) The Chinese invasion of Vietnam proved to the Socialists, theretofore the most pro-Peking of the Japanese parties, that they had been "wrong to assume the unalloyed virtue of Socialism as demonstrated by China over decades since the Revolution."(79) A Defense Agency official was reported to have observed: "Our Socialist friends are no longer a worry. They can no longer act as an obstacle to realistic defense policies."(80) Indeed, by that time, virtually all opposition parties that had traditionally adhered to the literal "pacifist" interpretation of the Constitution's Article 9 had visibly shifted their respective stands in the direction of at least implicitly endorsing the JSDF. There began to emerge a growing consensus among the parties that the security debate was indeed a legitimate function of the formal political arena, the consensus that by early 1980 led to the establishment of a special committee for security in the House of Representatives (there had never been a parliamentary committee on defense or national security) and a cabinet council on national security. The issue of national defense had, to borrow the words of a foreign correspondent in Tokyo, "come out of the closet."(81)

The ascertainable shift in the character and direction of security concern in Japan, of course, was in no small measure owing to a noticeably heightened and persistent pressure from the United States. In terms of electoral politics, there indeed were "no significant domestic political pressures to adopt a more active foreign policy, especiallly one that would involve substantial risks of any kind."(82) The pressure from Washington during much of the 1970s had been sporadic, though increasingly frequent, but became sustained and intensified toward the end of the decade, as the United States became progressively alarmed by the decline of detente, the intractable crises in the Persian Gulf region and Afghanistan, and the increased danger to the safety of the Western Pacific, making it increasingly difficult for Japan to "evade" it, and gradually convincing the Japanese government that the United States would, in the words of one Tokyo official, "keep pressing this demand until it is actually met."(83) Not only was Washington increasing its demand that Japan devote more efforts to its own defense, but it greatly discomfited Tokyo in 1980 by explicitly stating that it did not believe the JSDF were capable of "even the basic minimum resistance against a small-scale limited aggression."(84) To many in the Japanese government, the increased U.S. pressure for an enlarged military spending and defense buildup was closely linked to the rising strain in trade relations between the two nations, and they were increasingly of the opinion that those trade relations would dangerously worsen unless Japan took part of the heat off by acceding to the U.S. demand regarding its military expenditure.(85) It was thus that the growth in tension between Japan and the United States in recent years played perhaps as significant a role as the change in Japan's security environment in causing the shift in the character and direction of Tokyo's security concern.

One salient (and, in the eyes of some sectors, dangerous) manifestation of the rise of an unprecedentedly serious security concern is what increasingly appears to be the government's effort to cultivate a public opinion that would be supportive or acquiescent of not only an expansion of the JSDF but also an expanded security role of the nation under the existing security arrangements with the United States. Recent Defense White Papers have become increasingly emphatic about "potential threats" to the nation's security emanating from the Soviet military expansion. Civilian leaders of the Defense Agency have become uncharacteristically vocal (clearly with the acquiescence of the cabinet) in their public discussions of the extent and specific contents of the continuing Soviet military expansion in East Asia and the decline of the U.S. forces in the region.(86) Even the late Prime Minister Ohira, reputed to have been one of the principal doves in his party, publicly acknowledged the inadequacy of the nation's defense spending as an "objective fact," urged that the nation's defense efforts should be commensurate with its ability, and stated that the 1980s would be the decade of trial for the nation's existence and security.(87) The Foreign Ministry traditionally had been frequently at odds with the Defense Agency and with the more national security-oriented elements within both party and government. It had viewed their concern about the threat of the Soviet military expansion as "excessive," and their urging about the necessity of legislation for times of emergency as provocative of unnecessary controversy. That changed. It instead became unprecedentedly outspoken (at times even more so than the Defense Agency) about the necessity of strengthening the Nation's defense capability on the grounds that Japan should be able to persuade potential aggressors that the cost of their mischief would be high and that only such persuasion would constitute effective deterrence. To the opposition charge that any increase in defense spending would be at the expense of social welfare outlays, the ministry's response was that the issue was not either security or welfare but rather that there could not be welfare without security, thus clearly giving national defense priority over social programs.(88) The government in 1980 made a significant disclosure: Its traditional argument, invariably made in response to the U.S. pressure to increase its defense budget, that its total defense spending had amounted, not to less than 1 percent of GNP, but to 1.5 percent if calculated under the so-called NATO formula (that is, including funds for pensions and annuities for retired military personnel and surviving families) was not accurate. The "correct figure was <u>not</u> 1.5 percent but 1.14 percent.(89) Shortly thereafter, the government announced that it would endeavor to undertake a "steady" increase in its defense spending, with a projected minimum annual increase by 5.7 percent in real terms, which would compare favorably with the anticipated defense outlay growth rate of 3 percent for NATO in the following fiscal year.(90) Even the Economic Planning Agency, traditionally preoccupied with domestic economic growth and business activities, came out urging that defense spending should be raised to well over 1 percent of GNP.(91)

Its pronouncements and observations during the last year or so also suggested that the government was attempting to steer the public opinion toward acceptance of an expanded security role for the nation under the security arrangements with the United States. The Foreign Ministry late in 1979 established a high-level "security policy planning committee" for the task of reassessing the nation's role in the Japanese-U.S. security arrangements within the broad context of the world military situation. This committee's first general policy proposal was disclosed in the summer of 1980, and the central thrust of the proposal was the necessity of the nation to seek effective implementation of the Japanese-U.S. mutual security pact and the strengthening of the nation's defense capability "on the basis of a global perspective."(92) The conjunction of the existing security pact with the United States and the call for a "global perspective" was significant for its ultimate implication of Japan as an ally cooperating with the United States in carrying out its global strategic responsibilities. Foreign Ministry officials began referring to their nation as "a member of the Western bloc ready to assist the United States" in dealing with the Soviet threat in crises.(93) This marked a significant departure from the traditional interpretation of the security arrangements with the United States that the mutual security pact applied only to the defense of Japan and U.S. interests in Japan and that Japan's participation in any collective security effort on behalf of another nation or nations would be inconsistent with the peace Constitution. Many in Japan began to fear that these developments would inexorably lead it into dangerous entanglement in U.S. security conflicts not directly involving its safety.

Such fear, of course, is not wholly unfounded. Indeed, lifting the taboo of the security issue quickly gave rise to calls for the type of policy change that would be dangerous for Japan and for the region of East Asia. For example, one former Chief Justice of the Supreme Court urged in his commencement speech at the Defense Academy and in the presence of the prime minister that Japan should have an independent defense capability and made a clear implication that the nation should also have nuclear weapons, for "Japan is in a miserable state, depending as it does on the Japanese-U.S. mutual security treaty."(94) The notion of an independent defense capability (the so-called autonomous defense thesis(95)) was not new but no responsible official or former official had ever argued for it on such a public occasion as the Defense Academy's commencement exercises. Moreover, the newly energized security concern led to proposals and demands that only take advantage of the concern for interests other than national defense and security. Some sectors of big business, for example, quickly became aggressive in their demand not only for an increase in defense spending (some urging 4 percent of the GNP) but also for the elimination of the existing official ban on arms export, and their underlying motive was thinly disguised, that is, the revitalization of their own industries through massive defense contracts and arms exports, a purpose increasingly favored by organized private-sector labor.(96) A recent survey of the Japan Junior Chamber of Commerce membership disclosed that a clear majority felt that Japan should possess nuclear arms, and the organization itself publicly proposed that the peace Constitution be amended to elimi-nate constraints on the JSDF.(97)

The issue of national defense and security acquired legitimacy at the very time when temptations to exploit it for particularistic special interests had never been so irresistible. Industries even marginally involved in defense contracts had formed an association (called the Keidanren Defense Production Committee) in the mid-1950s to promote a strong military, expanded weapons procure-ments, research and development, and arms export,(98) and some individual zaikai (big business) leaders had proposed, for example, 1.5 percent of the GNP for defense expenditures, opposed the ratification of the nuclear nonproliferation treaty,(99) or demanded the pursuit of "autonomous defense,"(100) to cite a few examples. These activities had had little discernible impact on the issue, however, because of the absence of a sufficiently broad consensus within zaikai at large. Zaikai had prospered in the postwar period in, or because of, the absence of heavy military spending and because it had not had to depend on Defense Agency procurements for any significant portion of its revenue (in fact, no major manufacturers derived more than a small fraction of their revenues from defense contracts),(101) thus had been content with the traditional national policy of virtually total reliance on the United States for national security and of limited defense expenditure. In short, making the security issue taboo, then, had been entirely compatible with the interest and inclination of zaikai at large. Apart from its emotional or nationalistic appeal to some individual zaikai leaders, the issue of security had not been attractive or critical to the industrial sector as an institution.

The downswing in economic growth initially precipitated by the "oil shock" of 1973 and progressively aggravated by the effect, among others, of OPEC petropolitics and consequent slackening economic trends in industrial nations at large eventually came to make it apparent to the Japanese that the era of continuous and rapid growth to which they had become accustomed was over. The differential impact of the effect of the new international and domestic economic predicament became particularly hard on certain segments of the modern sector. The pressure of business distress and its effect on an increasing number of private-sector unions converged with the emergence of the security issue from the closet of political taboos. The convergence of these two separate sets of developments led to the increasingly vocal demands for defense expansion and arms export. This phenomenon today contains considerable elements of danger to Japan's external conduct as well as to the maintenance of democracy at home. Some observers are worried that it might lead Japan on the path of becoming an international arsenal.(102) There is a potential danger that these demands, together with the Defense Agency and their new allies in the party and bureaucracy and elsewhere, might exceed the hazy boundary of probity and lead to the emergence of a self-aggrandizing military-industrial complex.

The heightened security concern within party, government, and certain sectors of society notwithstanding, the public opinion seems to remain ambivalent. A combination of the inevitable generational change in the population (well over one-half of the Japanese had been born after the war by the second half of the 1970s) and the change in the nation's security environment had of course eroded the once-potent "antimilitary allergy." However, whether and to what extent a positive and critical popular concern about national defense and security had risen as a result was not all that clear. At the end of the last decade, nearly nine out of every ten Japanese supported the maintenance of the JSDF, and the increase in support for the JSDF was especially pronounced among the young, students in particular (from 32 percent in 1972 to 74 percent in 1978), according to one observer.(103) The widespread general support for the JSDF, however, remained a bit ambiguous in its content, and it seemed to lack depth when it came to the question of whether and to what extent the JSDF should be strengthened. As recently as 1978, only 38 percent of the people viewed national defense as the principal mission of the JSDF, although this figure, in relative terms, constituted a noticeable increase over previous years (24 percent in 1972 and 30 percent in 1975), and national defense replaced "rescue and relief operation" as the function most frequently attributed to the JSDF.(104) A comparison of surveys conducted by the prestigious Asahi Shimbun indicated some changes in the popular view of the JSDF between 1978 and 1980: Among all party voters, the support for the strengthening of the JSDF had risen from 18 percent to 25 percent, including opposition-party voters, while those favoring the "present level of strength," "reduction," and "abolition" of the JSDF had all declined (from 61 to 58 percent, from 11 to 7 percent, and from 5 to 4 percent, respectively).(105) It also showed a notable growth of support for the strengthening of the JSDF among people in their twenties, thirties, and forties, the groups crucial in the near future of the nation. How significant these changes might be would be a matter of speculation, but any conclusion that there now emerged a "national consensus" for the expansion of the nation's defense capability would seem still premature. The popular support for the JSDF to function as the guardian of the nation's safety, not to mention for their strengthening to meet security requirements of the country, seemed still lukewarm and thin at best. To the extent that Japanese democracy must rest on a broad popular consensus for any significant policy change, those who argue that there is not yet such a consensus for an expanded defense effort might well be right. Popular concern for defense and security is obviously there, but it seems still to be diffuse and unfocused. In short, it is not yet critical.

This may well be at least one of the reasons for the fact that the heightened security concern within the government has yet to lead to a clear definition of the nation's security requirements, the determination of the specific level of capability the JSDF should endeavor to acquire, and the explicit formulation of methods of effective deployment of the JSDF consistent with those requirements. There remains considerable apprehension within the government that moving too rapidly and openly in the direction of an effective upgrading of the nation's defense capability might cause serious backlash from the opposition that is still wary of potentials of militarism and from the population that is either lukewarm or ambivalent about such upgrading. The failure of the Japanese government to increase its 1981 defense spending to the level that had been widely anticipated both in Japan and in the United States (instead of a 9.6 percent increase that the government had earlier proposed, the actual figure turned out to be 7.6 percent) may well have been caused, at least in part, by this apprehension.

Whatever trials and tribulations that may have surrounded the shift in the character and direction of security concern in Japan, it would seem that the shift is irreversible, by virtue of circumstances, the imperatives they have created, and their growing recognition by the Japanese government. One high Foreign Ministry official told the author that the government had remained passive in its external and defense policy because it had been preoccupied with sengo shori (dealing with and disposing of the effects and ramifications of the nation's war and defeat). The nation's amae attitude toward the United States, its "pacifist" foreign policy, and this sengo shori had, in an important sense, been the three mutually convergent and reinforcing aspects of the nation's unique, largely self-imposed international predicament during much of the postwar period. The predicament, however, had to change in recent years, and, with it, the nation's direction. The new direction came to require what another Foreign Ministry official called "a posture change from passive to positive security concern." What this posture change ultimately would warrant in terms of specific security measures will be discussed in Chapter 7. In the remaining pages of the present chapter, we will take a quick look at some of the recent signs of change in the Japanese-U.S. security arrangements in order to complete our quickly drawn sketch of the status of Japan's defense and security.

EVOLVING JAPANESE-U.S. SECURITY ARRANGEMENTS

Earlier in this chapter, we noted the conspicuous absence of "mutuality" in the Japan-U.S. mutual security pact during most of the postwar period. The term "mutual," of course, applied only to the defense of Japan and U.S. interests in Japan, and in this sense, it called only for mutuality of efforts between the two nations to that end. It was at this particular context that the absence of mutuality was noted. In the past few years, there was some noticeable awareness on the part of the Japanese government that the imbalance in efforts between the two nations would have to be remedied. This awareness was prompted by a multiplicity of motives, as was the shift in the character and direction of security concern just discussed. Indeed, it was part of that shift. By the same token, the shift in the character and direction of security concern in Japan inevitably would cause some important, albeit often subtle, change in the Japanese-U.S. security arrangements. In this section, we will comment on three recent aspects of an emerging change in the arrangements.

The status of force agreement between Japan and the United States under the security treaty required Japan to assume expenditures for providing the U.S. forces in Japan (USFJ) with bases and the United States to foot all other expenses for the operation and maintenance of those bases (for example, labor, housing, relocation, and so on). The agreement came into being in 1960 when Japan's GNP was only 9 percent of that of the United States. By the end of the 1970s, Japan's GNP has risen to approximately 50 percent of that of the United States. Clearly, fairness warranted that Japan increase its share of the costs of maintaining U.S. forces on its premises for its own defense, and there was considerable pressure from the United States to do so. In the meantime, there were pressures from Washington on Tokyo to increase its defense spending and to reduce the lopsided trade imbalance between the two nations. Starting in mid-1978, these pressures caused the Japanese government to increase its financial contribution to USFJ maintenance, and, for fiscal 1979, its share of USFJ maintenance rose by 50 percent over 1977 to approximately $750 million, and by 1980 Japan was contributing well over two-fifths of the cost of maintaining the USFJ consisting of 43,000 troops (23,000 army and 21,000 marine), some 200 aircraft, and support facilities. The Japanese government was endeavoring further to increase its share of the cost at this writing.(106)

The extent to which Japan should further increase its share of the cost of maintaining the USFJ would yet have to be determined, as well as the appropriate criteria of equity and mutuality. It is significant, in any event, that the Japanese government not only decided that its contribution to USFJ should be substantial but also was clearly determined to increase it further. Perhaps it was no mere accident that a highly respected critic of Japanese foreign and defense policy who had just published an article arguing that "with Japan's GNP now almost equal to that of the United States on a per capita basis, one reasonable measure to reduce tensions and share the cost of defense more fairly might be for Japan to assume a larger share of the burden of U.S. military expenditures incurred in the area of Japan and related to Japan's defense"(107) shortly afterward was appointed as foreign minister – one of the few cabinet ministers recruited from outside the ruling party's parliamentary membership in postwar history. Upon becoming foreign minister, he declared, "The time has come for the Japanese-U.S. relationship to be maintained and strengthened through Japan's more positive cooperation and contribution."(108) The man he chose as ambassador to Washington publicly urged that Japan must do its utmost "to help lessen the United States' defense burden within the framework of existing bilateral security arrangements."(109) These utterances quoted here were not isolated examples; their substance since then was repeated by government leaders including the prime ministers. Clearly there emerged a great concern on the part of the Japanese government for financial equity with the United States in the defense of the nation, something that could not have been expected several years earlier.

Another aspect of the emerging change in the Japanese-U.S. security arrangements relates to mutual coordination and cooperation between the JSDF and the USFJ. A serious concern about this matter emerged shortly after the U.S. withdrawal from Vietnam among defense officials of both nations and, as a result, a Japanese-U.S. Subcommittee for Defense Cooperation was quietly created in 1976 under the Security Consultative Committee (established at the time of the coming into being of the existing security pact in 1960) to study ways and means of more effective working relations between the JSDF and the USFJ. Two years later, this subcommittee completed "The Guidelines for Japan-United States Defense Cooperation," which was shortly thereafter approved by the Japanese and U.S. governments. "The Guidelines" stipulated manners by which to promote effective cooperation between the JSDF and the USFJ in "such areas as operations, intelligence, and logistics," and established, at least in principle, a specific division of labor and methods of operational coordination between the two security partners in case of an attack against Japan. "The Guidelines" added, according to one senior State Department official concerned with Japan and East Asia, "operational credibility and efficiency to our alliance with Japan."(110) How credible and efficient the security arrangements may in fact become still remains to be seen, however, because no document in itself is capable of translating itself into action, let alone effective action. Considering the differences in patterns and structure of decision making and in the character of constraints and inhibitions between the two partners, the JSDF and USFJ would seem to face considerable difficulties in operationalizing "The Guidelines." There are specific areas in which the partners would face particularly nettlesome problems and these include intelligence and command, among others.

"The Guidelines," for example, stipulate: "The JSDF and U.S. Forces will, through operations of their respective intelligence systems, conduct intelligence activities in close cooperation in order to contribute to the joint implementation of effective operations. To support this, the JSDF and U.S. Forces will coordinate intelligence activities closely at each stage of requirements, collection, production, and dissemination." This objective, however, would require a high degree of trust in the integrity, competence, reliability, and security of each other's intelligence personnel, process, and organizations. Japan is said to be "a paradise for spies,"(111) and the revelation in 1979 of Soviet espionage activities involving a retired JSDF general did nothing to dispel widespread doubt about the 'state of Japanese intelligence, and the government thus far has been reluctant to tighten security laws for fear of provoking opposition charges of "reactionary militarism."

Command coordination would be the most crucial aspect of joint defense efforts in the case of actual emergency, which, if the JSDF and the USFJ were really to work together at some stages of combat, would call for a series of instantaneous operational decisions in response to its not easily anticipatable development. There is a relatively small number of JSDF officers with sufficiently proficient English skills to engage in complex decision making on a genuinely equal footing with the American counterparts under circumstances that would inherently require precision of analysis, promptness of evaluation, economy of language, and connaturality of mental vibration. The number of American officers who could engage in a similar task with their Japanese counterparts using Japanese as the medium of communication is vastly smaller. Various problems presented by this phenomenon would not be solved overnight.

Another important aspect of JSDF-USFJ cooperation pertains to their joint training and exercise. Inasmuch as operational cooperation is an integral part of the total security arrangements for the defense of Japan, despite the formal division of labor between the two national forces, and since various possible contingencies would make actual combat cooperation unavoidable, joint training and exercise at various levels is imperative, even though "The Guidelines" lack specificity on this matter. Thus far, the extent of joint training and exercise has been at best peripheral both in breadth and depth. Part of the problem is the continuing reluctance on the part of the Japanese to engage in any kind of JSDF activity that might provoke the still residually pacifist opposition.(112) In order to raise the level of joint combat capability of the JSDF and the USFJ, however, serious attention would be warranted regarding this issue.

A third significant aspect of an evolving change in the Japanese-U.S. security arrangement has to do with the mutual popular perception between the two nations regarding the defense of Japan. It is underlain by a seeming paradox, but, in the end, it may suggest a growth in unsentimental realism on the part of both the Americans and the Japanese. In Japan, there was in recent years an increase in popular support for the U.S.-Japanese security treaty and a simultaneous decrease of popular confidence that the United States would honor the treaty in case of emergency. When the 1960 Treaty of Mutual Cooperation and Security came into being, more Japanese were opposed to it than were for it (though about one-third were undecided), in part because of the massive nationwide antitreaty agitation by socialists, organized labor, and other "progressive" elements in society. (This caused the cancellation of a scheduled visit by President Eisenhower in the summer of that year and the resignation of the prime minister who had negotiated the treaty.) The major cause of opposition to the treaty was said to be (we say "said to be" because, as we argue in the next chapter, the cause or causes were little related to the treaty as such) the fear that, allied with the United States, Japan might be dragged into war, perhaps in Korea, or with China or the Soviet Union. Judging from the then prevailing amae predisposition of the Japanese toward the United States, it perhaps would not be wide of the mark to say that most of those who opposed the treaty nevertheless took it for granted that the United States would protect Japan even without the formal treaty. As years elapsed, opposition to the treaty declined and, at the same time, the reason for the remaining opposition shifted from fear of being dragged into a U.S. war to anxiety that the treaty "stands in the way of diplomatic relations between Japan and China."(113) Interestingly enough, however, opposition to the treaty was never translated into any popular demand for the termination of the treaty in 1970 when the first ten-year period had ended. In part, at least, the rampage of the Cultural Revolution and its immediate aftermath in China had clearly dampened whatever level of fervor with which many Japanese had felt it necessary, for reasons of history, geography, and the like, for Japan to restore normal relations with China. In any event, this new basis of opposition to the security treaty was soon to be nullified by the Peking-Washington rapprochement and the normalization of Sino-Japanese diplomatic relations in 1972. As a consequence, opposition to the treaty thereafter declined rapidly and support rose correspondingly to the point where, by the end of the last decade, the later outpaced the former by better than 5 to 1.(114) The popular acceptance of the treaty had become definite.

Paradoxically, however, the rapid increase in recent years of support or approval of the security treaty was accompanied by a decrease of confidence in the United States as Japan's defender. In 1970, when the support-opposition ratio was virtually 1 to 1, nearly two out of every five Japanese believed that the United States would come to Japan's defense in case of military emergency while fewer than 30 percent of them doubted it would.(115) Eight years later, in 1978, only one out of every five Japanese felt that the United States would honor its treaty obligations and come to help defend Japan in case of such an emergency and nearly three out of every five felt it would not.(116)

This seeming paradox in Japanese public opinion regarding the security arrangements with the United States was perhaps the function of twin recognition in Japan of the critical importance of the arrangements in an increasingly unstable external environment on the one hand and of the range of domestic and external constraints that threaten the declined capability of the United States on the other. In an important sense, it could be argued that the Japanese did indeed become more realistic and unsentimental in their perception of their environment and of the United States as their ally.

The American public attitude toward Japan regarding the mutual security treaty also showed some seemingly paradoxical aspects. Before the issue of Japan's "free ride" became intensified during the second half of the last decade, the popular support in the United States for the use of U.S. military forces to defend Japan in case of an attack on that country by the Soviet Union (viewed as the most likely contingency by the Americans) had been relatively low (for example, 37 percent in 1970).(117) It began to rise noticeably, however, as the tension between the United States and Japan over the latter's meager defense spending became increasingly aggravated: to 42 percent in 1978 and then to 54 percent in 1979.(118) Again, the seeming paradox defies facile explanation, but its character might be similar to that of the paradox of the Japanese public opinion noted above. The Americans, it may be said, were becoming more realistic in their view of Japan, both as an extraordinarily potent economic power and as a nation of critical strategic value to their national interest.

Thus, despite tension and divergence of policies and preferences between the two nations, a new basis of relations may have begun to emerge, a basis that would be more consonant with the actual capabilities of each nation and, in the words of one Foreign Ministry official, "unencumbered by sentiment." At least on the part of Japan, the remarkable fact – remarkable in contrast to what would surely have been the case several years earlier – that the increase in the nation's contribution to the costs of the USFJ and the adoption of "The Guidelines" for defense cooperation, with all the public statements and candid official utterances surrounding them, as well as the shift in the whole character and direction of security concern elicited no significant political protest would seem to support this observation. Politically, Japan might at last be coming of age after three decades of U.S. protection from the trials and tribulations of realpolitik.

Whether, how, and to what extent the putative direction in which Japan now seems to have taken a hesitant though significant step would be followed still remains to be seen. Concrete measures in that direction would still have to be determined. Some of these measures will be discussed in Chapter 7, but there seems to be little doubt that the Japanese-U.S. security arrangements would not only have to but already have begun gradually to be redefined and restructured. Before a discussion of what specific as well as general measures Japan would have to take for its defense and security and how the security arrangements would be redefined and restructured, however, it is necessary for us to consider in the next chapter certain salient aspects of Japanese politics that in the past crucially affected the diplomatic and security conduct of the nation. We suggest this in order that we may avoid overexpectations as well as underestimations as to what Japan could and most likely would do. These aspects would exert considerable influence on its national will, and it is its national will, far more than its apparent economic capability, that would determine the course of its conduct.

NOTES

(1) Defense of Japan (Tokyo: Defense Agency, n.d.), p. 31.

(2) Defense Bulletin 3, no. 2 (October 1979): 14. For the full text of the Outline, see Showa 54 Nen Ban Boei Hakusho (1979 Defense White Paper) (Tokyo: Okurasho Insatsukyoku, 1979), pp. 227-32.

(3) For this policy and other alternative policies debated in Japan, see Taketsugu Tsurutani, "The Security Debate" in Defense Policy Formation: Towards Comparative Analysis, ed. James M. Roherty (Durham, N.C.: Carolina Academic Press, 1980).

(4) See, for example, Prime Minister Fukuda's statement in the House of Representatives Budget Committee on February 6, 1978, as reported in Asahi Shimbun, February 7, 1978, p. 2.

(5) 1978 Boei Nenkan (1978 Defense Yearbook) (Tokyo: Boei Nenkan Kankokai, 1978), p. 603.
(6) Sogo Anzen Hosho Kenkyu Gurupu, Sogo Anzen Hosho Senryaku (Strategy for Comprehensive Security) (Tokyo: Okurasho Insatsukyoku, 1980), pp. 51-52.
(7) Compare, for example, Makoto Momoi, "Basic Trends in Japanese Security Policies," in The Foreign Policy of Modern Japan, ed. Robert A. Scalapino (Berkeley: University of California Press, 1977), p. 359.
(8) Donald Hellmann, "Japanese Security and Postwar Japanese Foreign Policy," in ibid., p. 323.
(9) World Armaments and Disarmament: SIPRI Yearbook 1978 (Stockholm: Stockholm International Peace Research Institute, 1978), pp. 152-53.
(10) Quoted in Yoshiteru Oka, "Questioning the 1 percent of Japan's Defense Budget," Business Japan, July 1979, p. 57.
(11) 1978 Boei Nenkan, p. 281.
(12) Takuya Kubo, "Gemba kara no Boei Ron" (A View of Defense from the Field), Chuokoron, January 1979, p. 120.
(13) Defense of Japan, pp. 9-10.
(14) Ibid.,p. 12.
(15) Masatake Okumiya, Nihon Boei Ron (A View of Japanese Defense) (Tokyo: PHP, 1979), pp. 68-76.
(16) Defense of Japan, p. 12.
(17) Okumiya, pp. 64-65.
(18) Compare Thomas M. Brendle, "Recruitment and Training in the SDF," in The Modern Japanese Military System, ed. James H. Buck (Beverly Hills, Calif: Sage Publications, 1975), pp. 67-96, and Gekkan Yoron Chosa (Public Opinion Survey Monthly) May 1979, pp. 57-58.
(19) Military Balance 1978-79 (London: International Institute for Strategic Studies, 1978), pp. 31-32.
(20) Asahi Shimbun, April 30, 1979, p. 1.
(21) 1979 Boei Nenkan (1979 Defense Yearbook) (Tokyo: Boei Nenkan Kankokai, 1979), p. 421.
(22) Asahi Shimbun, December 16, 1978, p. 41.
(23) Ibid.
(24) Quoted in Okumiya, p. 41.
(25) Sogo Anzen Hosho Senryaku, p. 55.
(26) Asahi Shimbun, December 16, 1978, p. 4.
(27) Asahi Shimbun, August 20, 1980, p. 1, and August 24, 1980, p. 2.
(28) Asahi Shimbun, December 16, 1978, p.4.
(29) Sogo Anzen Hosho Senryaku, p. 55, and United States-Japan Security Relations: The Key to East Asian Security and Stability (Washington, D.C.: U.S. Government Printing Office, 1979), p. 12.
(30) Compare, for example, Showa 54 Nen Ban Boei Hakusho, pp. 233 and 238. This trend was particularly pronounced within the

GSDF in which 77.7 percent of its budget was expended on those noncombat items and only 10.7 percent was devoted to arms purchase. Shimpei Fujimaki and Yonosuke Nagai, "Gendai Shakai ni okeru Guntai to Gunjiryoku" (The Military and Military Power in Contemporary Society), Kokusai Mondai 247 (October 1980): 10.

(31) Asahi Shimbun, December 16, 1978, p. 4.

(32) Sogo Anzen Hoshyo Senryaku, p. 10.

(33) Oka, p. 57.

(34) Hiroomi Kurisu, Watakushi no Boei Ron (My View of National Defense) (Tokyo: Takagi Shobo, 1978), p. 178.

(35) Compare, for example, Tomohisa Sakanaka, "Military Threat and Japan's Defense Capability," Asian Survey 20, no. 7 (July 1980): 764.

(36) Showa 54 Nen Ban Boei Hakusho, pp. 244-45.

(37) Ibid., pp. 233 and 238.

(38) Sogo Anzen Hoshyo Senryaku, p. 56.

(39) Ibid., p. 60.

(40) Asahi Shimbun, December 21, 1978, p. 4

(41) Asahi Shimbun, February 7, 1980, p. 4. Defense Agency officials contend that it would take "several hours" before the prime minister could act. See ibid.

(42) Asahi Shimbun, July 26, 1978, pp. 1-3.

(43) Compare, for example, "Nihon no Senryoku" (Japan's War Potential), Sande Mainichi, August 27, 1972, p. 20, and Martin Weinstein, Japan's Postwar Defense Policy (New York: Columbia University Press, 1971), p. 114.

(44) Quoted in Far Eastern Economic Review, April 20, 1979, p. 29.

(45) See, for example, Sakanaka, p. 768.

(46) Nihon Keizai Shimbun, July 18, 1980, p. 1.

(47) For a detailed description and evaluation of the incident, see Kaoru Murakami, "MIG-25 Jiken kara nani o mananda ka" (What We have Learned from the MIG-25 Incident) in 1977 Jieitai Nenkan (1977 JSDF Yearbook) (Tokyo: Boei Sangyo Kyokai, 1977), pp. 31-49.

(48) See Osamu Kaihara, Nihon Boei Taisei no Uchimaku (Inside Japan's Defense System) (Tokyo: Jiji Tsushinsha, 1977), pp. 216-21.

(49) Sogo Anzen Hosho Senryaku, p. 53. For the specifics of JSDF upgrading planned in the outline, see Defense Bulletin 3, no. 2 (October 1979): 15, or Showa 54 Nen Ban Boei Kahusho.

(50) Momoi, p. 343.

(51) Takeo Doi, Amae no Kozo (The Structure of Dependence) (Tokyo: Kobun Do, 1975).

(52) I. M. Destler, Hideo Sato, Priscilla Clapp, and Haruhiro Fukui, Managing an Alliance: The Politics of U.S.-Japanese Relations (Washington, D.C.: The Brookings Institution, 1976), p. 2.

(53) Joint Working Group of the Atlantic Council of the United States and the Research Institute for Peace and Security, Tokyo,

The Common Security Interests of Japan, The United States and NATO (Washington, D.C.: and Tokyo: Atlantic Council of the United States, December 1980), p. 20.

(54) For a more detailed discussion of the postwar U.S. view of Japan and its recent change, see Taketsugu Tsurutani, "80 nen dai ni okeru Beikoku no Tainichi-kan to Nihon no Taio" (America's View of Japan in the 1980s and Japan's Response), Kokusai Mondai 250 (January 1981).

(55) U.S. Foreign Policy for the 1970s (Washington, D.C.: U.S. Government Printing Office, 1971), p. 14.

(56) Ibid., p. 13. Emphasis added.

(57) Shintaro Ishiwara, Susumu Hani, and Hirotatsu Fujiwara, Ikani Kuni o mamoru ka (How to Defend the Nation) (Tokyo: Nisshin Hodo Shuppan Sha, 1970), pp. 21-22.

(58) George De Vos, Socialization for Achievement: Essays on the Cultural Psychology of the Japanese (Berkeley: University of California Press, 1973), p. 49.

(59) Akihiko Ushiba in Kurisu, p. 129.

(60) Hellmann, p. 325.

(61) Sankei Shimbun, Nihon no Anzen (Japan's Security) (Tokyo: Sankei Shimbun Sha, 1976), Vol. 1, p. 128.

(62) Ibid., p. 144.

(63) Defense Bulletin 3, no. 1 (September 1979): 28 and 30.

(64) Quoted in Haruhiro Seki, "Hendo suru Ajia to Nihon Gaiko" (Changing Asia and Japanese Diplomacy), Sekai, February 1979, p. 29.

(65) Defense Bulletin 3, no. 1: 14-16.

(66) Asahi Shimbun, March 25, 1980, evening edition, p. 3.

(67) Sankei Shimbun, Nihon no Anzen, vol. 2, pp. 120-22. Endicott reported there were 43 members in the Defense Division in 1974. See John E. Endicott, Japan's Nuclear Option: Political, Technological, and Strategic Factors (New York: Praeger, 1974), p. 54.

(68) Yutaka Hata in "Ronso: Nihon o mamoru towa do yu kotoka" (Debate: What Is Meant by Defense of Japan), Chuokoron, January 1978, p. 84.

(69) Donald Hellmann, Japan and East Asia: The New International Order (New York: Praeger, 1972), p. 140.

(70) Defense Bulletin 3, no. 2: 14.

(71) For this new phenomenon, see Japan Echo 5, no. 4 (Winter 1978): 15-16.

(72) See Taro Akasaka, "Boei Rongi no kuruizaki" (Unseasonable Flowering of Defense Debate), Bungei Shunju, March 1978, p. 164.

(73) Asahi Shimbun, January 25, 1978, p. 2.

(74) Asahi Shimbun, June 22, 1978, p. 1.

(75) A secret military plan prepared by JSDF staff officers for a joint Japanese-U.S. operation in the event of a second Korean War. The existence of the plan was exposed by opposition parties in the

Diet and the prime minister was compelled to dismiss some 20 top JSDF officers. See Hiroshi Osanai, Nihon no Kakubuso (Japan's Nuclear Armament) (Tokyo: Diamondo Sha, 1975), p. 136, and Albert Axelbank, Black Star Over Japan (New York: Hill and Wang, 1972), p. 51.

(76) Showa 53 Nen Ban Boei Hakusho, p. 32.

(77) For these and other developments, see, for example, Asahi Shimbun, July 28, August 24 and 29 and October 19, 1978.

(78) Quoted in the New York Times, March 25, 1979, p. E3.

(79) Novelist Kobo Abe quoted in ibid.

(80) Quoted in ibid. Also see Oriental Economist 47, no. 822 (April 1979): 2.

(81) Far Eastern Economic Review, April 20, 1979, p. 28.

(82) The United States, China, and Japan (Washington D.C.: U.S. Government Printing Office, 1979), p. 25.

(83) Nobuhiko Ushiba as quoted in Japan Times Weekly, March 15, 1980, p. 8.

(84) Quoted in Nihon Keizai Shimbun, July 5, 1980, as reprinted in Shimbun Geppo 405 (August 1980): 66.

(85) See, for example, an article entitled "Bei tono Kankei akka osoresu" (Fearing the Worsening of Relations with the United States), Asahi Shimbun, May 16, 1980, p. 1.

(86) See, for example, Eiichi Sato, "Nihon ni okeru Boeiryoku Seibi Koso" (Defense Buildup Plans in Japan) Kokusai Mondai 247 (October 1980); Asahi Shimbun, August 6, 1980, p. 5 and February 6, 1980, p. 4.

(87) See Tokyo Shimbun, April 29, 1980, p. 1: Asahi Shimbun, April 30, 1980, p. 2 and May 15, 1980, p. 2.

(88) Asahi Shimbun, May 15, 1980, p. 2.,

(89) Japan Times Weekly, March 29, 1980, p. 1.

(90) Asahi Shimbun, April 21, 1980, p. 1.

(91) Asahi Shimbun, June 3, 1980, p. 2.

(92) For the content of the proposal, see Nihon Keizai Shimbun, July 28, 1980, and as reprinted in Shimbun Geppo 405: 69-70.

(93) Asahi Shimbun, September 21, 1980, p. 2.

(94) Kazuto Ishida as quoted in The New York Times, March 25, 1979, p. E3.

(95) For this and other policy options for defense suggested in the postwar period, see Tsurutani, "Security Debate," pp. 176-84.

(96) For these and other disturbing developments, see, for example, Susumu Kodama, "Zaikai-jin no Boei Hatsugen" (Proposals by Big-Business Leaders), Asahi Janaru, April 11, 1980, and Takehiko Kamo, " 'Gunkaku no Shiso' sasaeru Keizai Nashonarizumu" (Economic Nationalism That Sustains 'The Ideology of Military Expansion'), Asahi Janaru, May 2, 1980.

(97) Mainichi Shimbun, March 29, and July 27, 1980, and reprinted in Shimbun Geppo 401 (April 1980): 33-34, and 405 (August 1980): 68.

(98) See David R. Hopper, "Defense Policy and the Business Community: The Keidanren Defense Production Committee," in Buck.

(99) Hellman, Japan and East Asia, p. 224.

(100) John K. Emmerson, Arms, Yen and Power: The Japanese Dilemma (New York: Dunellen, 1971), pp. 147-48.

(101) In 1976, for example, the total JDA procurements, including such nonweaponry items as fuel, clothing, and food, amounted to slightly over $2 billion, accounting for only 0.4 percent of the GNP, well behind the share of the GNP by color-TV production. Asahi Shimbun, March 20, 1978, p. 1.

(102) See, for example, "Zaikai ni takamaru Boei Rongi" (Heightening Defense Debate within Zaikai), Asahi Janaru, April 4, 1980, p. 7.

(103) Taro Ominato, "Boei Mondai ni kansuru Kokumin Ishiki no Doko" (Trends of Popular Perception of Defense Issues), Kokubo 315 (May 1979): 36.

(104) Defense Bulletin 3, no. 1: 14-16.

(105) Asahi Shimbun, March 25, 1980, evening edition, p. 3.

(106) See, for example, Asahi Shimbun, March 24, 1980, pp. 1-2.

(107) Saburo Okita, "Japan, China and the United States: Economic Relations and Prospects," Foreign Affairs 57, no. 5 (Summer 1979): 1099.

(108) Asahi Shimbun, March 4, 1980, p. 1.

(109) Ambassador Okawara as quoted in Japan Times Weekly, March 22, 1980, p. 3.

(110) Assistant Secretary of State for East Asia and Pacific Affairs Richard Holbrooke, "U.S. Posture in the Pacific in 1980," Current Policy 154 (Washington, D.C.: Department of State, Bureau of Public Affairs, March 27, 1980), p. 2.

(111) Japan Times Weekly, February 9, 1980, p. 3.

(112) For past instances of joint training and exercise, see, for example, Asahi Shimbun, October 24, 1979, p. 1; Asahi Janaru, November 9, 1979, p. 102; and Tokyo Shimbun, May 1, 1980, p. 1.

(113) For a detailed study of the changing Japanese view of the treaty, see Akira Saito, "Changing Attitude on Security Treaty," Look Japan, March 10, 1980, pp. 4-5.

(114) See ibid., and Gekkan Yoron Chosa (Public Opinion Survey Monthly), May 1979, p. 61.

(115) Showa 53 Nen Ban Yoron Chosa Nenkan (1978 Yearbook of Public Opinion Surveys) (Tokyo: Okurasho Insatsukyokum 1979), p. 494.

(116) Asahi Shimbun, October 13, 1978, p. 2.

(117) Japan Times Weekly, March 29, 1980, p. 3.

(118) Jon Riley, "The American Mood: A Foreign Policy of Self-Interest," Foreign Policy 34 (Spring 1979): 81, and Japan Times Weekly, March 29, 1980, p. 3. Another set of polls, while slightly differing figures, nevertheless confirmed the trend cited here: 37

percent in 1974, 45 percent in 1976, and 50 percent in 1978. Gallup polls as quoted in "New Considerations on Security — Part 2: Will the U.S. Defend Japan?" an internal memo, Ministry of Foreign Affairs, April 1979, p. 3.

6
Sources of Japanese Conduct in the Postwar Period

The international environment is clearly fundamental to security policy making in Japan. The way in which it was perceived and approached in Japan during the postwar period, however, differed considerably from that in any other major nation and rendered Japan's external conduct reactive, desultory, and, in the end, exasperating to the United States in the area of defense and security and almost obsessive of economic pursuits. The consensual style of decision making characteristic of Japanese society and politics was certainly a factor, but its role in foreign and defense policy making was contributive rather than centrally causal. So was the "pacifist" Constitution, even though, as was indicated in Chapter 1, it has most frequently been viewed by knowledgeable analysts and observers as crucial to understanding postwar Japanese external conduct. The postwar Constitution is important to understanding Japan's external conduct in the past three decades only in the sense that it provided an extremely effective and plausible pretext for the pattern of conduct that had in itself nothing to do with its apparent pacifism. Major sources of postwar Japanese conduct reach much farther back than either August 1945 or the promulgation of the peace Constitution.

THE PSYCHOLOGY OF JAPANESE POLITICS

Japan's external conduct was underlain, among others, by two distinct, at times mutually incongruent psychological orientations (or, if you like, national characteristics). One of them was rooted in its long premodern history – the millennia-long national insularity from the rest of the world prior to its "opening" in the midnineteenth century. The other was historically more recent, a consequence of the nation's increasingly extensive exposure to the world since the Meiji Restoration, a largely alien world in which the nation had to search its identity and place. To a significant extent, these two orientations were the motivating forces underlying Japan's external conduct in its modern century. During the past hundred-some years, their presence in and determinant influence on Japanese conduct were consistent, including the postwar period; the nation's conduct, however, was not.

Passive Optimism

Throughout its long history prior to the nineteenth century, Japan was able to maintain its independence free from external threat largely because of its fortuitous geographic location. As a nation and society, it evolved and developed more or less naturally, at its own pace. With the exception of one brief period late in the thirteenth century, there was no invasion, not even an attempted invasion, from outside, no impingement by a domineering foreign culture or political system, and no incursion of alien population. Whatever elements of foreign culture and civilization Japan adopted, it did so entirely on its own terms, selectively and eclectically, always with modification to suit its conditions and preferences. In an important sense, particularly from the perspective of world history, the Japanese led an idyllic existence, innocent of war and destruction, untouched by foreign brutality and exploitation that consistently befell most of the world. This fortuity of historical circumstances came deeply to influence the collective as well as individual attitude of the Japanese.

The fortuitous external peace was combined, in its impact on Japanese culture and attitude, by the particular character of the nation's internal condition. Poor though it always was in resources, Japan, in the words of a prominent cultural historian, was "blessed with the climate, vegetation, etc. typical of the moderate, temperate regions. Her mountains, plains, and rivers similarly exhibit none of the forbidding extremes which one finds on the continent, but tend to the moderate, the delicate, the minute, and the approachable."(1) As a consequence, the Japanese were "passive and submissive to objective nature and lacking in the will to conquer it by means of rational and measured thinking."(2) The combination of uncontrived external security and natural internal temperateness thus produced an important psychological orientation, best exemplified in traditional folk Shinto (as opposed to the contrived "official Shinto" of the Imperial Dynasty or "state Shinto" of the modern century). Here, nature was essentially benevolent, the source of fertility and fortunes. In the literature, Shinto is always translated as "way of gods," but a more appropriate translation would be "ways of nature," for the origin and substance of this unique Japanese folk culture was nature worship. (Its anthropomorphosis was contrivance by powers that be at the various levels of the political system.) Men must live in a manner compatible with ways of nature; since nature was benign, it followed that it should not be tampered with. It was not to be conquered, but to be lived in and with. Trust in nature, for we shall all be well, if not at the present, then surely in the end.(3)

This particular orientation of the Japanese — trust in nature — was indeed vindicated when Japan faced the only serious external threat prior to the nineteenth century. In 1274, some 30,000 Mongolian forces of Kublai Khan attempted to invade Japan. The Mongols had already overthrown the Sun dynasty in China and established an empire extending from Korea in the east and the Indochinese peninsula in the south to parts of Russia, Poland, and Hungary in the north and west. These forces were far superior to the Japanese in both art and technology of war, and the defending Japanese forces in the southern island of Kyushu were in imminent danger of annihilation. Extremely inclement weather and heavy winds, however, forced the invading Mongols to retreat to Korean bases after a single night of engagement on the shore. In the Japanese eyes, nature thus protected them. The Mongols in the meantime remained intent on conquering Japan and, after their emissaries failed to secure submission of the Japanese government and were executed by the enraged Japanese, dispatched a total of 140,000 troops aboard 4,000 vessels in the summer of 1281. Even though the Japanese had in anticipation of the renewed attack prepared their defense in the area of enemy landing by building barriers to limit the invasion forces to a narrow beachhead and resisted enemy advances for nearly two months, the outcome of the engagement was uncertain. At this point, a fierce typhoon struck, destroying a large portion of enemy ships, stranding many enemy troops to be killed, and forcing the rest to retreat to Korea. The Mongols were never again to attempt to conquer Japan. The Japanese called the typhoon "the divine wind," attributing the fortunate development to nature's benevolence and protectiveness toward them. (It was after this typhoon that the kamikaze suicide air squadron that harassed the U.S. fleets toward the end of the Pacific War was named.)

Even after the opening of the country and the Meiji Restoration, a number of external events involving Japan's security would prove, in the eyes of the Japanese, to have reaffirmed their trust in nature. The Russo-Japanese War was one such event. Even though Japan was relentlessly pushing the Russian forces back in Manchuria and destroying the Czar's Baltic Fleet in the famous Battle of the Tsuhima Strait, costs of the war and the internal stress and strain it caused in the nation were enormous. Despite its surprising success in the military campaign, Japan was financially and physically on the verge of collapse by late spring of 1905. Had the Russian government been less corrupt and a bit more efficient, the course of the war might have been quite different. Japan would have been bled white on short order, in any event, had Theodore Roosevelt not offered his good offices for truce and peace negotiations. Japan's victory over Russia, from a more clinical viewpoint, was facilitated decisively first by the corruption of the Czarist regime and its military high command with all that it implied in terms of strategic, tactical, and logistical management and, at the most critical moment, by the intercession of the U.S. president. To the Japanese, however, it was another convincing instance of things somehow working out in their favor.

In some ways, the success of early Meiji modernization, too, was evidence of the truth of this trust in nature, for Japan had been vastly inferior to China, for example, in a variety of crucial dimensions relevant to modernization: internal political fragmentation into 200-odd feudatories, economic poverty aggravated by the recent war of restoration, technological backwardness caused by the past national seclusion, the lack of natural resources, the extreme precariousness and inexperience of the Restoration government, among others.(4) Yet, within a short period of one-third of a century, Japan emerged as a power to be reckoned with by defeating China in a contest of arms and then triumphing over Russia, the two largest nations in the world. There are, of course, a variety of dispassionate explanations for this success,(5) but to the Japanese of the time and even later, it was owing to the benevolence of nature of whose good fortune their nation had always partaken. This deep trust in nature as benign and benevolent to their nation was not an insignificant part of the motivation of the militarists and ultranationalists of later years in undertaking the ultimately disastrous wars of aggression in China, the Pacific, and Southeast Asia.

The passive trust in the natural course of events persisted even after World War II. How it was manifested in postwar Japan's external policy would be discussed later. In a sense, it was reinforced by the failure of the nation's activist and aggressive external policy of the 1930s and the 1940s, the policy that in hindsight appeared to have been deliberately contrived, hence against the course of nature. (In a sense, it can be said that there is considerable moral ambiguity in this trust in nature: Whatever works must be in accordance with nature; what fails is not; but this is beside the point here.) At this point, it may be well for us briefly to note that it affected Japan's domestic politics in general and the conduct of the ruling Liberal Democratic Party (LDP) in an interesting way. Japan's opposition parties, particularly Socialists, were constantly accused of lacking in political realism and of unrealistically capitalizing on ideological differences between themselves and the ruling Conservatives who proved enormously successful in promoting economic growth and prosperity. Indeed, this lack of realism was correctly cited as the major cause of their inability to challenge effectively the semipermanent monopoly of power by the LDP. Yet, in election after election, the Socialists, instead of providing meaningful and feasible alternatives to LDP policies, counted on some putative but undefined "trends" and "tendencies" (nariyuki) that, according to their leaders, would presumably favor them over the Conservatives in electoral outcomes.(6) The consistent result, of course, was their defeat in election after election, and they remained weak, unpopular, and as far away from capturing power as ever. The LDP, on the other hand, never really felt the compelling urgency of its own reform precisely because its members believed that, however they might be vilified by the press and public opinion for its corruption and convoluted ways of governing the nation, things would somehow continue to work for them. Apparently they were right, it was in part for this reason that they permitted their intraparty factionalism to continue unabated.

At the level of the citizenry, the trust in nature, in the realm of domestic politics, referred especially to the eventual outcome or final turn of events and, for this reason, temporary unhappiness was indeed frequently present. This was seen in public opinion polls. Asked about how they felt about their present living condition, for example, the Japanese would express their discontent with it (for example, "the living standard has not sufficiently improved" and "it is worse than last year"), but when queried about their expectations of "two years hence" or "the near future," a majority of the respondents would express their confidence that their condition "will improve" and that their socioeconomic status would go up.(7) The passivity of this optimism was apparent even among the young Japanese. They were more dissatisifed with their condition or "the way things were" than their foreign counterparts (for example, in one recent comparative survey, nearly three-fourths versus little over one-third of the Americans), but showed a significantly lower level of willingness to engage in political activities (for example, petition, demonstration, strike, and other means permitted by law for the purpose of bringing about change) than their opposite numbers in other industrialized democracies (for example, only one-quarter versus over three-fifths of the Americans), while looking to the future with more positive anticipation than other national samples (three-quarters versus two-fifths of the Americans).(8) Despite their very high level of education, they were also far less informed of domestic political issues than their opposite numbers in other advanced societies.(9) Their optimism was largely divorced from the notion of human intervention: it was passive.

Self-Uncertainty

If passive optimism was a trait that had evolved through centuries of external security and internal temperateness before the last century, self-uncertainty was an entirely modern phenomenon for the Japanese. With the unwelcome visit by Commodore Perry and his awesome black ships in the midnineteenth century and the development of subsequent domestic and external events, the Japanese were for the first time in their long history and in spite of themselves thrust into a larger and more hostile world dominated by alien civilizations, races, and cultures – in short, into the arena of international politics. The Japanese as a nation suddenly found that they could no longer live according to their own preference or define their national destiny solely by their wishes. The world from which they had remained secluded turned out to be ominously threatening, with Western powers and their technology, economy, and institutions far superior to Japan's vying for opportunities to engulf it – a contingency the Japanese had never encountered throughout their long history. That this sudden recognition genera-ted an acute sense of insecurity is entirely understandable, but it was not the only cause for self-uncertainty of the Japanese. The other side of this coin of sudden recognition was the suspicion that their ways of the past had been responsible for their new predica-ment, that they had somehow failed themselves. (Two of the Five Principles of the Charter Oath at the time of the Restoration specifically addressed "evil customs of the past" and the urgent need of seeking "knowledge . . . . throughout the world.")(10) All this generated a feeling of self-uncertainty as to how properly to cope with and get along with those superior powers of the West. This self-uncertainty would persist into the postwar period. Underlying this uncertainty at the time was a feeling of inferiority as a late starter and (inasmuch as Asia as a region was a late starter and much of it was being colonized by Western powers) as an Asian nation. Japan's external behavior since the Meiji Restoration came to be critically affected by this national self-uncertainty.

Immediately upon the Restoration, Japan launched an extremely ambitious modernization program to rapidly transform an antiquated feudal society into a modern state. The motivation was entirely other-directed and the sense of uncertainty just discussed rendered the effort not only feverish but also single-minded, under the slogan of "a rich nation and a strong army" (fukoku kyohei). Industriali-zation was viewed as the source of internal resilience of the nation and modern military forces the foundation of national security and territorial integrity. Combined, they would make the nation equal to those modern Western states. To an amazing extent, the effort was successful, but the success was not enough to assuage the sense of insecurity and uncertainty in the world still dominated by Western powers and Western civilization. Merely to become indus-trialized and to have strong military forces was inadequate for Japan to acquire a feeling of external safety and internal serenity or to recapture the kind of unharried sense of self-contentment and well-being it had once taken for granted. Thus, by the turn of the century, the continuing sense of insecurity would cause Japan to seek the status of a regional power in East Asia equal to or exceeding that of Britain, the United States, France, Germany, or Russia. In this endeavor, too, Japan soon achieved a measure of success, through the Sino-Japanese War, the Russo-Japanese War, a series of concessions forced out of the tottering China, and the incorporation of Korea into its empire. The chance participation in World War I even resulted, apart from Japan's acquisition of territorial and other German interests in China and the Pacific, in conferring upon it the status of a major power in the Versailles Conference and subsequent League of Nations.

These developments favoring Japan's quest for recognition in the international arena, however, failed to dispel its sense of insecurity and uncertainty. For one thing, those very same developments had rapidly thrust Japan into fuller and more extensive interactions with major Western powers that remained superior, particularly in its eyes, in the realms of modernity, progress, wealth, and actual or potential military power. For another, while those favorable developments (again, benign nature's ways) had apparently made it a power to be increasingly reckoned with by those Western states and others, Japan, precisely because of them, found itself an outsider in an essentially Western group of nations with whom it shared little by way of culture, civilization, and history, and by whom it felt it was still treated with a mixture of curiosity, condescension, and disdain. The perfunctory "major power" status Japan had achieved, therefore, only intensified its fundamental insecurity and uncertainty. The self-doubt could be permanently dispelled only if Japan attained a genuine world-power status equal to the British Empire and the U.S. dominion over the Western Hemisphere – in short, by dominion over the whole of Asia. (By its ultimate logical and psychological extension, this, of course, would compel the nation toward world domination as espoused by ultranationalists and as expressed in the prewar slogan of "The whole world under one roof" (hakko ichiu).) In the end, the policy of the "Greater East Asia Co-Prosperity Sphere" and the attack on Pearl Harbor, then, were the culminating and violent dash toward national catharsis.

The defeat in 1945 was devastating to Japan not only in the physical and military sense but also in the psychological. Subjugated and occupied by foreign powers for the first time in its history, it was overwhelmed by the recognition of failure of its past thought and conduct. Japan was reduced to utter dependence on its erstwhile adversaries' tender mercy and was stripped of that fragile self-confidence and precarious self-esteen that had been so painstakingly nurtured since the Meiji period, together with the growth in international standing. The principal effect of the defeat on Japan's national psyche, then, was self-rejection, for what it had once viewed as legitimate pride and self-confidence had now been proven to have been misplaced hubris. Much more than at the time of the Meiji Restoration, the ways of the immediate past seemed "evil" in 1945, an evil of which it should cleanse itself. Quite unlike the earlier time, there now was a deep feeling of shame, a shame of hubris and devastation that it had wrought throughout Asia, and of having mistakenly embarked on war, abjectly lost it, and become an international outcast. The popular literature of the early postwar years was thus characterized by a penchant for national self-flagellation, denouncing or denigrating anything and everything Japanese – tradition, culture, habit, custom, lifestyle, physiognomy, language – as reactionary, feudalistic, backward, or dangerous. (Conversely, virtually everything and anything Western, especially American, was glorified or praised, including cowboy movies, chewing gum, garish shirts, and Coca Cola.) Never had Japan been so low in national spirit. This was the basis of that extraordinary receptivity of the Japanese as a nation toward reforms imposed, proposed, or suggested by the U.S. occupiers.

Japan's single-minded pursuit of economic recovery, growth, and prosperity, which soon amazed the rest of the world as an "economic miracle," was in an important sense a collective attempt to sublimate its newly compounded sense of self-uncertainty; or, to put the matter slightly differently, its intense absorption in the pursuit was an escape from it, an attempt to repress it. As such, it was not different in motivation from its earlier single-minded pursuits such as those of rapid modernization in the early Meiji period, of a major-power status early in the present century, and of domination of East Asia in the 1930s and the 1940s. After the war, it took only a different form but kept the same psychological substance.

There was some difference as well, however, between Japan's conduct prior to 1945 and after that, and this difference arose from different ways in which passive optimism and self-uncertainty combined. To the extent that passive optimism in its essential character deemphasized the efficacy of human contrivance and intervention in the course of events, it would be largely apolitical in itself. Self-uncertainty, on the other hand, could lead either to inaction or hyperaction, to passivity or aggression. When self-uncertainty lead to hyperaction or aggression, passive optimism would tend to reinforce it, generating a belief that such action would succeed because nature or the universe was on its side. It was thus that Japan as a nation was aggressive both at home and abroad, passive optimism sustaining the aggressiveness. It sought to establish a garrison state at home and a massive colonial empire abroad. Domestically and externally, the nation projected an ever-explicit political profile and a forceful ideological posture with all that they implied in potentials of excess and violence. It was bent on prevailing, believing in its ultimate success, brooking no challenge, tolerating no opposition, and suffering no detraction. The ultimate result of this aggressive, hyperactive national posture, of course, was the sequence of repression at home, wars of aggression abroad, and total national defeat.

If, on the other hand, self-uncertainty, by virtue of perceived circumstances, inclined toward passivity or inaction, then passive optimism would combine with it to render it wary of contrivance and intervention in the course of events, that is, the notion that things would turn out well only if we patiently waited; and this was the case with postwar Japan. The circumstances surrounding the defeat impressed upon the Japanese that political aggressiveness as well as its concomitant, ideological contention, should be scrupulously avoided because it was they that had led the nation to the historic and devastating blunder. Thus, when self-uncertainty expresses itself in passivity, then passive optimism combines with it to induce what may be termed "politophobia."

The Politics of Politophobia

It was not surprising, then, that postwar Japanese politics turned out to be neuter in its basic thrust. It was passive both in domestic and external manifestations. It eschewed ideological disputation and political confrontation. It was largely devoid of drama, excitement, and moment. Indeed, ideologically vocal parties and political groups, of the right as well as the left, remained permanently weak institutional minorities, objects of annoyance, bemusement, or derision more than fear. The ruling Liberal Democratic Party in fact owed much of its staying power to its nonideological stance and its judicious, although not always successful, avoidance of political disputes. Concentrating on its apolitical policy of "high economic growth" (kodo keizai seicho), the LDP government almost invariably moved with the tides of popular inclination and bureaucratic preference that were virtually exclusively materialist in nature and objective. In its external relations, the nation opted for what one former foreign minister characterized as "value-free diplomacy" (issai no kachi handan o shinai gaiko – literally, diplomacy devoid of value judgment),(11) avoiding political conflict and skirting ideological friction, insisting on the "separation of economics from politics" (seikei bunri). This ideologically indifferent, politically colorless "value-free diplomacy," would officially be termed variously as "equidistant diplomacy," "multidirectional diplomacy," and "omnidirectional diplomacy." Outside of economic pursuits, therefore, this political eunuchry and ideological inertness predisposed the nation toward attentisme. The politophobia underlying this posture of the nation was precisely what determined the manner of treatment (or nontreatment) of the issue of defense and security and the moralistic invocation of the pacifist "no-war clause" of the postwar Constitution that prevented the nation from serious security concern. Article 9 (the "no-war clause") of the postwar Japanese Constitution reads:

> Aspiring sincerely to an international peace based on justice and order, the Japanese people forever renounce war as a sovereign right of the nation and the threat or use of force as means of settling international disputes.
> 2. In order to accomplish the aim of the preceding paragraph, land, sea, and air forces, as well as other war potential, will never be maintained. The right of belligerency of the state will not be recognized.

Article 9 has been viewed in relevant literature as the source of postwar Japanese "pacifism."   Thus, one Japanese diplomat contended "the pacifism ingrained in the Constitution quickly took hold, and has become the 'flesh and blood' of the nation."(12) A Japanese political scientist argued: "The pacifism represented and popularized by Article 9 rapidly developed into a popular cult. Pacifism became the object of fervent devotion among large numbers of Japanese. It became deeply instilled in their hearts . . . ."(13) Representative as they are of the relevant literature, these observations smack of hyerbole at best. The circumstances surrounding its inclusion in the Constitution suggested that the article was not rooted in any profound, let alone philosophic, "pacifism" but instead was prompted by a certain psychological exigency felt by great numbers of the Japanese during the immediate aftermath of the 1945 defeat. Put another way, the article, which, contrary to the common belief, was not proposed by the Americans, was a manifestation not of an abiding faith in the efficacy of pacifist resolution of international disputes (for the Japanese as people were no more nor less "pacifist" than any other people) but of a certain behavioral imperative dictated under the extraordinary circumstances by Japanese tradition.

Japan had just been defeated after wreaking havoc throughout East Asia and the Pacific, and the war-crimes trial was under way, in which the foremost political and military leaders of the wartime period whom the nation at large had supported stood in klieg lights of outraged world public opinion.   As we noted earlier in this chapter, there pervaded throughout the nation a deep sense of guilt and shame, and the popular literature was characterized by an almost manic penchant for national self-flagellation.   This phenomenon (which was much less in evidence in Germany at the time) had its official political corollary — that is, the new government's felt need to convince the world that the nation would henceforth be genuinely peace-loving and trustworthy — and both reflected a peculiarly Japanese obsession with expressing "sincerity" (magokoro or seii) of feelings, in this particular case, "sincere contrition." Crime or misdeed, in traditional Japanese culture, was forgivable (or, in any event, punishment for it would be greatly reduced or commuted) if the guilty party convincingly demonstrated his sincerity of remorse and repentance.   Conversely, the judge would impose a far stiffer penalty than might objectively be warranted if the guilty one showed insufficient signs of genuine contrition or defended himself vigorously. (In a sense, the traditional Japanese judicial system incorporated in itself a high degree of compassion for repentant criminals.) In any event, during the early postwar years, the Japanese as a nation were seeking, in a manner of speaking, forgiveness by the international community and, for this, "sincerity" of national contrition had to be demonstrated. A well-known ultranationalist and one of the accused at the war-crimes trial at the time urged, "We Japanese have the national duty of atoning for our sins to the allied powers."(14) The "no-war clause" was a product of the imperative of "sincere repentance."

The crucial article was proposed by none other than the first postwar civilian prime minister, Kijuro Shidehara, in a private meeting with General MacArthur in January 1946.(15) There was no transcript of this meeting because Shidehara, a prewar ambassador to Washington and then foreign minister, did not require an interpreter and also because the ostensible purpose of the meeting was personal (the prime minister wanted to thank the general for a personal favor done to him earlier). MacArthur later confirmed Shidehara as having been the source of the no-war clause.(16) Shidehara was a veteran diplomat and seasoned politician, conversant with the vagaries of politics among nations as well as at home, hardened by his abrasive experience with the militarists in the 1920s and 1930s but sharing the abiding anticommunism and fear of the Soviet Union that had in part motivated the rise of militarism, and deeply conservative as well as patriotic. He was no idealist reformer. He proposed the no-war clause (the fact that surprised MacArthur, who had not thought of it himself) because some such clause in the new Constitution would be the most public and official demonstration of the nation's sincerity in repudiating past militarist sins. In the Japanese eyes, it was imperative that the nation convince the world of its atonement. Shidehara did not tell his own cabinet, not even his own foreign minister, about his proposal to MacArthur, and, when his ministers found the no-war clause for the first time in the General Headquarters draft of a "New Constitution of Japan" delivered to them a month later, Shidehara allowed them to assume that it was entirely American in origin.(17) He did not tell his cabinet the truth because his ministers were not pacifist idealists and because they might reject the article as excessive once they knew he had proposed it to the American general.(18) This concern on Shidehara's part had less to do with any doubt that his cabinet would agree on the necessity of the nation's clear demonstration of its sincere contrition than with the character of his own cabinet and the political competition taking shape then. His cabinet was a congeries of ambitious men, both liberal and conservative, some even reactionary, who had just begun to form contending political groupings and were anxious to outdo one another in the first postwar general election scheduled to be held in a few months' time. His foreign minister, Shigeru Yoshida, was his chief rival in this impending struggle that would produce a new topography of party politics. Shidehara had made the proposal without consultation with, let alone securing a consensus of, his cabinet – an unusual behavior on the part of a Japanese leader. Of course, it as a very unusual time. Still, Shidehara knew he as prime minister would be in trouble if his cabinet colleagues found out the truth. At the very least, his rivals would exploit the matter in the emerging leadership struggle and electoral competition. By remaining silent about the truth of the no-war clause's origin, he insured the smooth adoption of the crucial clause for the new Constitution. (In the end, the first postwar general election and leadership struggle resulted in the demise of the aging Shidehara and the rise of Yoshida to the premiership. Shidehara was the leader of a group called Progressives and Yoshida was head of another that entered the election as the Liberal Party.)

Shidehara's concern (which was widely shared by many Japanese) for the need of the nation to demonstrate its "sincerity" of contrition was thus incorporated into the new Constitution. However, the fact that "sincerity" had to do with repentance of past sins and was not an unconditional commitment to idealistic or dogmatic pacifism was quite evident in the deliberation of the draft Constitution in the newly elected Diet and the final wording formulated for the Constitution. The draft Constitution, approved by the Shidehara cabinet in the spring of 1946, was submitted to the new Diet after the April election by the new cabinet now headed by Yoshida. Perhaps the most important individual in the Diet deliberation of the Constitution was the chairman of the Diet's special committee on the Constitution, Hitoshi Ashida (who would later become prime minister himself). It was Ashida who was instrumental in the refinement of the wording of the Constitution, with the consensus, of course, of his colleagues. As early as October of that year, he authored an Interpretation of the New Constitution (Shin Kempo Kaishaku), in which he wrote: "Article 9's renunciation of war and the threat or use of force applies only to means of settling international disputes. Resort to force would constitute war of aggression. The article, therefore, does not renounce war and the use of force as means of self-defense. Also, war as a means of sanction against aggression falls outside the proscription of the said article."(19) The qualifying phrase, "In order to accomplish the aim of the preceding paragraph," at the beginning of Paragraph 2 of the article was added by Ashida's committee in order to allow for the maintenance of a military capability for purposes of self-defense.(20) Indeed, the article's first paragraph refers only to "means of settling international disputes" and does not mention "self-defense" or "in case of an attack or aggression from outside." During the Diet committee deliberation of the draft Constitution, a phrase "even for preserving its own security" was proposed by one of its members to be added to the article at issue, but it was dropped, for obvious reasons. The reader, if familiar with the Japanese Constitution, will recall that its Article 66, Paragraph 2 reads: "The Prime Minister and other Ministers of state must be civilians. . . ." This prescription makes sense only if we allow that the qualifying paragraph of Article 9 enables the nation to have self-defense forces and that there would, therefore, be military officers. It was reported that MacArthur's General Headquarters had directed the Diet committee to add this paragraph to Article 66 in order to insure civilian supremacy over the military.(21)

Apart from the alleged Japanese devotion to pacifism, there still persists the notion that the "pacifism" embodied in the Constitution itself, by the apparent nobility of its rhetorical quality, has inhibited Japan in realistically viewing the international environment. This notion seems to have been particularly current among those who believe Japan has not done enough for its own defense. One Japanese defense analyst observed that Article 9 "has been an obstacle to convincing the Japanese public that denouncement of war does not preclude a capacity for self-defense."(22) An American scholar noted that the effect of the pacifism of the article was "the moral cast of the debate over Japanese security in the ensuing years (an orientation accepted by all parties)," thus suggesting that it prevented Japan from doing what it should for its own defense.(23) These observations, however, are somewhat misleading. Most Japanee — officials, politicians, and citizens alike — even in the early postwar years, were realistic enough to recognize the necessity of an ability to defend their nation against attack and aggression. Nor were the Japanese people in general ignorant of the series of violent troubles that began to emerge in various parts of the world almost as soon as the war had ended, including the war in nearby Korea. Whether the Constitution permitted a self-defense capability (the point of public debate early in the 1950s) or (since then) to what extent it permitted the nation's self-defense forces to arm themselves, therefore, was really a nonissue. The real issue was the nation's fear of playing in the international arena a role that was commensurate with its increasing ability and changing circumstances until it became palpably dangerous to avoid playing it.

This was a reluctance born of a strangely reinforcing combination of that historical psychology of passive optimism and the more recent sense of national self-uncertainty that after 1945 had cumulated into a powerful collective politophobic impulse. This impulse was powerfully abetted by the amae attitude that the nation had developed toward the United States, an attitude that was based on the belief that the United States as patron and protector was indeed dependable and could be counted on to defend Japan from harm. The real issue with respect to Article 9, therefore, was psychological, not constitutional. It is precisely this that crucially affected the character, content, and pattern of security concern and defense debate that was discussed in Chapter 5. Had it not been for this amae attitude of the Japanese toward the United States or, to look at the other side of the same coin, the extraordinary patronage and protectiveness of the United States, the politophobic impulse of the postwar Japanese would most likely have been significantly tempered, at least with respect to national defense and security.

The politophobia in postwar Japan was significantly abetted and reinforced by three contributive features that could be viewed as particularly pronounced in Japanese society. One was the ethno-centric notion that the Japanese are a very unique, or more positively, uniquely blessed people (or what Riesman called the Japanese "exceptionalism").(24) All nationalistic or tribal groups of people in the world feel special or unique, somehow different from others. In the case of the Japanese, however, this feeling is extraordinarily strong, reflecting, perhaps, their history of insulation from the world and their "natural" development. Nobody can be like them or truly understand them. Japanese, for example, assume their cultural exclusivity, while Americans believe in the universality of their culture. Thus, the Japanese think that foreigners can never master their language nor really like such distinctly Japanese dishes as <u>sushi</u> and <u>sashimi</u> and are astonished when they do, while the Americans asume that everybody should speak English and love hamburgers and are disappointed when they do not. If fierce ultranationalism had made Japan unique among nations before 1945, it was "pacifism" of the Constitution that rendered it <u>sui generis</u> after the war. Before the war it had been their imperial tradition and martial spirit that in their eyes made the Japanese first among all nations; after the war, it was their "renunciation" of war and violence. This "uniqueness" was the source of national identity; and especially in a period of time when there was little else the Japanese could be proud about themselves or their country, it was perhaps natural that they should come to cling tenaciously to the "pacifist" spirit of the postwar Constitution as the only positive thing that set their nation favorably apart from the others. Pacifism, then, was not a matter of profound philosophic or ideological conviction any more than the prewar ultranationalism or devotion to the Imperial sovereignty had been; it only was a hastily appropriated new badge of national uniqueness, something that quenched the "exceptionalist" thirst of the nation at the depths of self-denigration and uncertainty.

A second phenomenon that abetted the postwar Japanese politophobia was the consensual mode of decision making and the style of political leadership that it dictated. Consensualism, like Calhoun's concurrent majority, is not very conducive to making hard decisions, since for obvious reasons, it generates a powerful pressure to avoid a problem of issue that sharply divides the group concerned as long as possible or until it becomes palpably dangerous to do so. The issue of national defense and security, given the general politophobia during much of the postwar period, was indeed of the very kind that was emotional (inasmuch as it involved the tenaciously held new national uniqueness), hence divisive, a fact that was vividly demonstrated in 1960 at the time of the ratification of the revised Japanese-U.S. mutual security pact.(25) Even though the Conservatives controlled a majority of the Diet seats, no significant external and defense policy change was perceived as feasible without a "national consensus" and especially without some degree of opposition acquiescence, and the 1960 incident only reinforced this feeling.

The role of leadership in Japan's consensual democracy is quite different from that in a majoritarian democracy such as in the United States. In the United States, a "leader" is respected, according to one analyst, "for open activism rather than for sublety."(26) He is expected to transcend division within the decisional arena and to steer supporters and recalcitrants alike in the direction he deems desirable and to produce a decision with explicit thrust. In short, he is to lead. Stepping on toes to this end is frequently admired, sometimes even by those whose toes are stepped on, for the ultimate test of his leadership is decisiveness. Thus, decisional coups de theatre are praised. In Japan, however, a leader, even the prime minister, is, or cannot but be, to borrow the words of a prominent historian, "a cooperative team player rather than a soloist."(27) The consensual culture constrains him from undertaking any independent action, for his is the role of a judicious consensus builder at best, rather than a forceful advocate. To the extent that he wishes to change the prevailing norms, preferences, or goals, he must act as an unobtrusive tactician rather than a grand strategist, seking subtle advances, not innovative moves. More often than not, therefore, the Japanese leader follows, rather than leads.

A third factor that exacerbated the tendency to skirt the issue of defense and security in Japan was the ruling Liberal Democratic Party's internal factionalism.(28) Its dynamics and logic caused a powerful compulsion to avoid disputes within the party itself as well as with the parliamentary opposition. While LDP factionalism as such had little to do with policy or political issues, any dispute or controversy would be promptly and maximally exploited by competing factions, thus affecting the party's incumbent leadership and the existing factional alignment. The 1960 security treaty dispute, among others, was a case in point. In the late spring and early summer of that year, the Diet was deliberating for ratification of the revised security treaty with the United States, which the incumbent premier, Nobusuke Kishi, had negotiated with Washington with full support of his party. Opposition Socialists, in an attempt to gain some political mileage, exploited the "pacifist" exceptionalism of the nation's Constitution and the general politophobic public orientation and boycotted the ratification debate, causing the session to drag on. Mindful that it was "undemocratic" for the LDP to prevail upon the opposition by the force of its numerical majority in the Diet, Kishi endeavored to negotiate the Socialists' return to the session, to no avail. Finally exasperated (especially since President Eisenhower was scheduled to pay a state visit soon to mark the commencement of a new chapter in Japanese-U.S. relations), the prime minister moved on his own to have the treaty ratified without the Socialists who refused to attend. Socialists cried foul ("tryanny of the majority") and inspired massive demonstrations against the treaty in Tokyo streets. Kishi's factional rivals quickly exploited this public controversy as a handy weapon to force his resignation as party president and premier, arguing that he must take the responsibility for causing the demonstrations and subsequent disorder. This experience reinforced the politophobic tendency shared by government and people alike that high-profile politics and explicit and visible political leadership should be eschewed, especially over such an emotion-inspiring issue as defense and security. Japan's head of government, therefore, "is not likely to be a man of action, even if he is temperamentally so inclined," and most LDP premiers "understandably have been prudent public figures, careful that their ties with party rivals not be unduly strained by too high a personal profile."(29)

It was thus that Japan's evasion of the issue of national defense and security, indeed realpolitik itself, was the function of politophobia that was powerfully induced by historical passive optimism and self-uncertainty, and variously abetted or reinforced by the trust in the United States as patron and protector of the nation, by the "exceptionalist" penchant of the nation, the consensual mode of decision making and leadership style, and intraparty factionalism. Much of security debate in postwar Japan, then, was something of a ritual, a domestic game in which the contestants competed to prove who was more dedicated to the nation's well-being, one through its rhetorical dedication to the idealistic pacifism and the other by its focus on material growth and prosperity. What passed for security debate was a subterfuge to avoid real security debate, because, for all their apparent disagreement and contention, both the ruling and opposition parties had an underlying agreement that they would refrain from seriously politicizing the security issue as long as possible. Government and people alike, with their politophobic inclination, felt that it was not necessary, occasional expressions of U.S. unhappiness notwithstanding, to tackle the issue so long as the United States could be safely counted on to defend their nation, and that, if it was necessary to do so, then it was necessary not to do so. It was natural, then, that Japan should have begun to show an increasingly serious concern about its defense and security once the United States, on which it had almost unquestioningly relied for the maintenance of its security, had begun to be perceived as losing its power and reliability that had once been taken for granted.

JAPAN'S EXTERNAL POLICY AS A REFLECTION OF POLITOPHOBIA

For nearly a generation after the war, Japan's politophobic posture in its external relations caused little trouble so long as it could count on the United States to protect it from potential external political and military danger. In those days, therefore, the policy of separation of economics from politics was a workable proposition since other nations, including the United States, permitted Japan to pursue such a politophobic policy. During much of this same period, the pattern of international interdependence also favored industrial states in their dealings with resource-producing Third World nations, and Japan's attempt to catch up with advanced industrial nations of the West was viewed with either admiration or tolerance by those superior to it in economic development and capability. Nature, those days, seemed quite benign to Japan.

With the accelerated decline of bipolar stability, the increase in signs of the concomitant erosion of U.S. politicomilitary influence, and the visible rise in conflicting and contentious political preferences and ideological orientations in the once-U.S.- or Western-dominated world, Japan's politophobic external posture was bound sooner or later to begin to experience growing discomfort. The sudden U.S. rapprochement with China in 1972, for example, precipitated as it at least in significant part was by Washington's desire to shore up its declining politicomilitary influence in Asia vis-à-vis the Soviet Union, forced Japan to abandon its policy of separation of economics from politics regarding Peking at the risk of antagonizing the Soviet Union and at the expense of its traditional relations with Taiwan. Even a greater discomfiture would befall Japan a year later at the time of the Yom Kippur War when the Arabs imposed their first successful threat of embargo on their oil export to industrial states that did not support the U.S. Security Council resolution demanding that Israel return all the territory it had occupied since the 1967 war and/or directly contributed to Israel's war efforts in 1973. Called the "oil shock" by the Japanese, the mere threat of the embargo was for Tokyo the first blatant case of veritable political blackmail it had been subjected to since the U.S. embargo of oil and scrap-iron exports to Japan in 1940-41. Quite unlike in the early 1940s, however, Japan had no recourse but to cave in to the Arab demand and shift its traditional follow-the-U.S.-lead Middle East nonpolicy and thus to act against a small distant state that had never committed an unfriendly act against it. It was immediately thereafter that Tokyo dispatched to the Middle East the highest official to travel to that part of the world to date, the deputy premier, for consultation and discussion with Arab leaders. Upon his return, he urged that Japan discard its traditional policy of avoiding international political problems and start playing a role commensurate with its ability. Several months later, the prime minister embarked on a highly heralded round of visits to Southeast Asian states in a posture of "positive" diplomacy, but his trip was quickly marred by anti-Japanese demonstrations in Indonesia and Thailand (these demonstrations were aimed at least as much against the corrupt regimes of Jakarta and Bangkok as against Japan's economic dominance in those countries).

Japan's response to these and other experiences, however, was an intensification of the very politophobic orientation of its traditional policy based, in the words of a concerned Japanese scholar, "solely on economic expediency and not political principles." This intensified version of traditional policy came to be called "omnidirectional diplomacy" (zenhoi gaiko) or "multidirectional peace diplomacy" (zenhoi heiwa gaiko). (An earlier version of it had been called "multidirectional diplomacy," takaku gaiko.) The major objective of this diplomacy, of course, was to diversify and secure the nation's sources of energy and industrial raw materials, as well as markets for its products. Omnidirectional diplomacy was diplomacy only in a partial and ancillary sense, for it had little political content but was underlain with a mixture of an almost unconscious wishful thinking that the ultimate course of events would somehow be benign, on the one hand, and, on the other, an uncertainty as to how any positive shift in the nation's external behavior might be received by the world at large. Thus, Japan would cultivate and expand economic relations with any nation in any region whose natural resources it requires and/or to whom it could export its products, equipment, capital, and technology. This, in itself, was nothing unusual, for even ideological adversaries trade with one another. What made Japan's diplomacy unique was its conscious eschewal of using economic power for any political purpose, denying the exercise of an ability that inhered in such power for ends that were politically principled or ideologically constant. This observation becomes apparent when we realize that, while Japan's economic relations with certain resource-producing nations and regions rose enormously in the 1970s, there was this palpable lack of any concomitant political impact or influence on the course of political events in and surrounding these nations and regions.

One of the clearer indications of the greatly intensified preoccupation on the part of Japan with having to insure constant supplies of energy and industrial raw materials in the 1970s was a sudden rise in the frequency of official visits by foremost Japanese leaders to those areas of the world that produced the bulk of those resources, but that were politically unstable and unpredictable, – in particular, the Persian Gulf region and Southeast Asia, as well as Latin America. Not only foreign ministers, but also prime ministers and ministers of finance, international trade and industry, and economic planning became unprecedentedly peripatetic abroad, promoting "international understanding," "good will," "harmony," and "mutual cooperation." In between those ministerial visits were dispatches of "special envoys" and "delegations" for discussion and consultation with leaders of those resource-producing nations. Of course, leaders of those nations were invited to Japan far more often than ever before. Reflecting this new trend of the Japanese government, the press vastly increased its coverage of those nations.

Another noticeable indication of Japan's vastly deepened concern with oil and industrial raw material supplies was the recent pattern of capital investment and distribution of direct government loans and credits abroad. The Persian Gulf states had not figured much before the "oil shock," receiving less than 7 percent of the total Japanese government loan and credit. The few years following the shock, however, witnessed the amount of official loan and credit to these states (in particular, Saudi Arabia, Iran, and Kuwait, at the very time when their oil revenues had already begun to rise by leaps and bounds) jumping to an annual average of 20 percent of the total such external loan and credit by the Tokyo government.(30) At the same time, Japanese private capital investment in these states also rose rapidly and, by 1977, well over 6 percent (nearly $1.4 billion) of total overseas Japanese capital was found in Saudi Arabia, Iran, and Kuwait, where ther had been little Japanese capital before 1973.(31) That oil was Japan's principal concern among natural resources from overseas was apparent also in Southeast Asia. Before the recent Islamic revolution led by Khomeini, Japan imported nearly as much oil from Indonesia as from Iran (for example, in 1978, $3.5 billion versus $4.2 billion), and, through 1977, total Japanese capital investment in Indonesia reached over $4 billion and accounted for over 14 percent of Japan's entire overseas private capital investment. Indonesia ranked second only to the United States in the magnitude of Japanese capital (21 percent of the total overseas Japanese capital in the United States.) (32) That Southeast Asia as a region is the closest major source of industrial raw materials for Japan was belied by the fact that fully one-third of total foreign capital annually received by the five members of the Association of Southeast Asian Nations was Japanese toward the end of the 1970s.(33) (The United States provided 23 percent of the total.) Through 1977, over 25 percent of Japan's total cumulative overseas investment was found in the region. Between 1951 and 1973, Japan's total investment in ASEAN states had amounted to only $1.4 billion, but, within a four-year period between 1974 and 1978, it quadrupled to $5.6 million.(34)

This extraordinary expansion of its economic presence in these nations and regions notwithstanding, there was no ascertainable indication that Japan exerted on any of them the kind of political influence that one would normally expect to inhere in such an expansion of economic presence and influence. The reason, of course, was simple: Japan remained averse, or at least extremely hesitant, to becoming involved in political affairs of regions concerned and, therefore, to utilize the political leverage germane to its economic presence and influence. The so-called Fukuda Doctrine promulgated by Prime Minister Takeo Fukuda in Manila during his state visits to the ASEAN nations and Burma in the summer of 1977 might serve as an illustration of this continuing Japanese problem. Couched though it characteristically was in the vocabulary of "cooperation," "equal partnership," "friendship," and "heart-to-heart understanding," the doctrine was designed to link the development of Southeast Asian nations (and Indochina) to Japan's economic security and growth by promising an expanded economic assistance and technical cooperation, that is, by rendering the region's modernization dependent on Japan's economic power. However, it still eschewed involvement in political and security affairs of the region, despite the fact that the modernization and development of the region and, by implication of the doctrine, the future supply of the region's resources to Japan were indisputably predicated upon the political stability and military security of the region. When the issue of Vietnamese "boat people" forcibly thrust itself upon the region, for example, Japan recoiled from it, unwilling to help minimize the potentially dangerous impact of refugees on internal ethnic problems in ASEAN states by offering sanctuary or financial and logistical assistance to refugees. It was only under persistent and mounting international pressures that Japan ultimately offered a financial contribution toward the construction of refugee facilities in Southeast Asia as well as "resettlement" (but not "permanent residence") to a token number of refugees.

Japan's reluctance regarding political involvement with ASEAN states had its obverse side in the form of its unwillingness to use its recently expanded economic influence in Vietnam for positive political objectives. Japan had correctly concluded that economic assistance to and trade with Vietnam would contribute toward stabilization of the region, particularly since Vietnam, with its growing influence in Indochina, would be a crucial factor for the future course of Southeast Asia. When the crisis of Vietnamese refugees exploded, however, Japan made only very timid attempts at dissuading Hanoi from its virtually extortionist program of expelling largely ethnic Chinese citizens "unsuitable for socialism." Later, both before and after the Vietnamese invasion and subsequent occupation of Cambodia, Japan again warily refrained from any attempt explicitly to use its even more expanded economic influence in Vietnam for political suasion. In mid-December 1978, when it held negotiations with Hanoi for an expanded aid program (including loans, grants in aid, and food relief), Tokyo was already aware of Vietnamese intentions regarding Cambodia, but it avoided using the negotiations as a means of exerting suasion on the Vietnamese to desist from aggression and violence, and the joint Japanese-Vietnamese communique issued at the conclusion of the negotiations contained no reference to the stability of Indochina and Southwest Asia. As one analyst noted at the time, this was viewed with considerable disappointment by the ASEAN states that had been greatly concerned with the intra-Indochinese conflict.(35) Once the Vietnamese aggression took place, Japan joined the virtually universal protest against it, but did not go beyond the level of rhetorical expression of unhappiness. After Australia, New Zealand,

and other Western states suspended their economic assistance programs in Vietnam, Japan spoke mildly of suspending its aid to Hanoi as well, but the Vietnamese, correctly, ignored the feeble threat. Some Japanese officials later told the author that, by not suspending the aid, as did other industrial states, Japan had kept the line of communication open. True enough, but for what was not apparent. (Later, as the violence in Cambodia escalated and threatened the security of Thailand, Tokyo did suspend its aid to Hanoi.) In a way, however, that was true to form: Tokyo merely followed a dominant international trend because it feared any tension with ASEAN. Whether and to what extent it would have made any difference in Vietnamese conduct either in the refugee crisis or in the Hanoi-Phnom Penh relationship had Japan made positive attempts at translating its economic presence into political influence could never be answered. That, however, is not the point here. The point is that Japan never did make any clear (clear to Hanoi as well as to others) and sustained efforts to do so.

In its relations with ASEAN and Vietnam, as in those with the Soviet Union and China, Japan's national politophobia prevented it from translating its economic power into means of political and diplomatic suasion. Put differently, there was a conspicuous absence or eschewal of linkage between economics and politics in Japan's external relations. Its policy of "separating economics from politics" (seikei bunri) was the diametric opposite of linkage policy, and thus in more ways than one gave enormous advantage to nations it dealt with, and, conversely, placed Japan at a distinct disadvantage in dealing with nations with explicit political objectives. In a very critical way, it may be argued that Japan deliberately renounced the equality of its bargaining status with those nations, because its only motive was unadulteratedly pure and simple, that is, economic, and because, as a consequence, it would use its economic capability for no other purpose than economic gain. Economic gain divorced from political leverage would be fragile, for it could be terminated or disrupted by the party providing it when that party saw political advantage in so doing. Whatever leverage Japan might have with the policy of nonlinkage would be only economic without political substance in it. In short, Japan would become a victim, an easy albeit unwilling pawn of the nation or party from which it sought such economic gain. This could be seen most clearly in its relations with the Soviet Union.

There was always an element of complementarity in economic relations between Japan and the Soviet Union over the development and exploitation of Siberia: the Soviet Union required capital and technology for its development that Japan could provide and Japan wanted energy and industrial raw materials to be extracted from the region.(36) Strictly on economic bases, there was mutually advantageous quid pro quo. The Soviet approach, of course, was not strictly economic, while the Japanese was. The Soviet Union, therefore, could turn the negotiations off and on according to political expediency, constantly changing conditions for them in order to derive maximum political advantage while Japan felt constrained against introducing political considerations (for example, the issue of the disputed northern islands, the Soviet military buildup on those islands, the Soviet hostility to the Sino-Japanese Treaty of Peace and Friendship, the expansion of the Soviet Pacific Fleet and the threat it posed to Japan's lifeline). One analyst noted that the faltering prospects of Russo-Japanese economic cooperation in the development of Siberia were in part due to Japan's unhappiness with the Soviet use of "linkage," and he observed that "Moscow has been inconsistent, separating or linking economic questions with other issues according to the needs of the moment. When it serves the purposes of Moscow, all fields are linked. . . . On the other hand, the Soviets do not hesitate to insist that Japan refrain from linkage."(37) Japan's unhappiness was entirely self-inflicted, however, for its negotiating posture (of separating economics from politics) was akin to that of a chess player who unilaterally drops his queen from the board before the match even begins. Japan had expected that, so long as it was committed to separating economics from politics in its negotiations, the Soviet Union would reciprocate. In this sense, it reflected the attitude of those Japanese referred to in Chapter 5 who felt that no nation would harm Japan because their nation lived under a pacifist Constitution. In the meantime, the Soviet Union continued to expand its military presence around Japan and East Asia, virtually fortified some of those disputed northern islands, further curtailed Japanese fishing on its territorial waters, and raised the level of threat to the security of Japan's lifeline stretching to the Middle East, and Japan failed to achieve anticipated progress in its "economic" negotiations with the Soviet Union.

Japan's relations with China were also fundamentally incongruous in that again there was this imbalance of orientation between the two, with Japan interested in China, at least in operational terms, only in terms of economic considerations, while China's primary concern was political, in which economics was the means. The slow progress in Sino-Japanese relations for several years after 1972 was at least in part due to Moscow's policy of linkage between Siberian development negotiations and Soviet political considerations with respect to China (the Sino-Japanese normalization had been greeted with marked chill in Moscow's attitude toward Japan). The necessity of a Sino-Japanese Treaty of Peace and Friendship had been voiced by a joint statement by the two governments at the time of the restoration of their diplomatic relations, but it was only in the summer of 1978 that the treaty was concluded. Japan's ultimate decision to go ahead with the treaty was in large measure motivated by its realization that, not only was it uncertain as to when and if satisfactory negotiations with the Soviet Union for its part in the Siberian development would be reached, but Peking, with its planned four-modernizations program, seemed ready to offer Japan more of what it badly needed in terms of resources, an expanded market for its products, and investment opportunities without the nettlesome impediments the Soviets had always presented. This realization was reinforced powerfully by Japan's domestic economic recession caused by OPEC petropolitics and gave irresistible impetus to the conclusion of the treaty as an expedient means for immediate alleviation of its internal economic distress, even if it temporarily annoyed the Soviet Union because of the "antihegemony clause" Peking insisted on including in the treaty. Thus far, Sino-Japanese relations were relatively free of tension because China refrained from introducing serious political issues in its relations with Japan. There are issues of great political magnitude, however, that are bound to emerge between the two nations sooner or later, among which are the status of the Senkaku Islands, the matter of the continental shelf, the issues concerning Taiwan and Indochina, and the Sino-Soviet conflict. Potentially, Japan could find Peking as nettlesome as Moscow.

Politophobia expressing itself in the exclusively economic orientation of Japanese external policy would create, because of it, a range of political problems for the nation, if it persisted. In the first place, it would run into some serious problems of communication and negotiation. The language of nations such as China, the Soviet Union, and even the United States is political, hence long range in its underlying orientation. Japan's language throughout much of the postwar period was a language of economic calculus, a language suited to short-run and immediate expediency. Any serious dissonance arising out of the fundamental incongruence of these two types of language would favor the party or parties that use the political language. Beyond that, there is a more critical consideration. Its politophobia rendered Japan ideologically color-blind and politically tone-deaf. Perhaps it did work during the period of time when Japan could hide behind the indisputably powerful and benign United States and close its eyes to realpolitik. That period disappeared quite some time past. Japan's politophobia would now expose it increasingly to the very political pressures, conflicts, and manipulations that it so judiciously tried to avoid and, at the very same time, find it without any countervailing measures. International relations are inescapably and inherently political in character. No politically inspired action (ultimately, every action is politically inspired) could be countered or countervailed by a reaction that lacks political content and potency. An economic means or action acquires political significance only if based on political calculus. Politophobic diplomacy would in the end reduce Japan to a perpetual political fence-sitter and equivocator in the international arena that is unavoidably conflictual, choosing sides when it would, not because it has a clear and voluntary political preference or is ideologically discriminating, but only because it has become absolutely impossible not to do so or only because the side it so chooses appears to promise the best immediate economic relief or gain. Such diplomacy would run the risk of alienating Japan's more reliable friends and neighbors under pressure of temptations or intimidations from others. This risk would further compound its fragility as an economic giant, for its politophobia would make it increasingly difficult for its neighbors to deal with it on the basis of trust, for they would fear that it might betray them and their interests by inaction, equivocation, or submission to temporary and immediate economic expediency.

A former vice minister of foreign affairs recently observed that Japan had no national strategy, but only business strategy.(38) A scholar told the author that Japan was "an economic power without consciousness as a nation." Both were serious indictments. It is hoped that these are indictments whose time has passed. It can be so hoped if the shift in the character and direction of security concern discussed in Chapter 5 is real. Still, we must recognize that Japan is in transition and past habits are not all gone. While those Japanese officials the author talked with all spoke of the emerging shift from the passive to the positive, or the necessity of such a shift, in the nation's foreign and defense policy and the need to translate the nation's economic power into positive political instruments, the decades-old passivity frequently crept up in their utterances. Queried about what might happen to Japan or how Japan should cope with a certain sticky problem or problems likely to arise in some contingencies, an official would sometimes conclude his reply by such observations as "things will work out somehow," "there is not much we could do except to let events take their course," or "we shall somehow be able to weather it."(39) These observations would not in themselves be unusual, but against the background of Japanese external conduct during most of the postwar period and coming from officials in whose hands the nation's policy in the immediate future rests, they sounded peculiarly troubling.

Japan, as a nation, perforce requires "strategy" or "consciousness" that cannot but be political in character. Only such strategy or consciousness would be the proper source of its conduct in a world whose internal relations are invariably political. Transition from politophobic "business strategy" to politically relevant "national strategy," then, seems to be the most crucial task Japan would have to complete with utmost dispatch.

If such a transition is indeed in the making, there clearly are a range of policy options Japan should explore and pursue in order to render its diplomacy more constructive, its defense and security more effective, and thus to enhance the prospects of orderly development, peace, and stability in East Asia. It is to some of these policy options that we will turn in Chapter 7.

NOTES

(1) Nyozekan Hasegawa, The Japanese Character: A Cultural Profile, trans. John Bester (Tokyo and Palo Alto, Calif.: Kodansha International, 1966), p. 10.

(2) Hajime Nakamura, in Ways of Thinking of Eastern Peoples: India, China, Tibet, and Japan, ed. Philip Wiener, (Honolulu: East-West Center Press, 1964), p. 18.

(3) There are many everyday Japanese expressions that reflect this trust in nature, for example, "let a matter run its own course" or "let nature take its course" (nariyuki ni makaseru), "things will work out somehow" (nantoka naru).

(4) See, for example, William W. Lockwood, "Japan's Response to the West: The Contrast with China," World Politics 9 (July 1956): 38-41.

(5) Among those explanations of Meiji Japan's success, see, for example, Robert E. Ward, "Political Modernization and Political Culture in Japan," World Politics 15 (July 1963); Taketsugu Tsurutani, "Political Leadership: Tentative Thoughts from Early Meiji Japan," Journal of Political and Military Sociology 1 (Fall 1973); and James W. White, "State Building and Modernization: The Meiji Restoration" in Crisis, Choice, and Change: Historical Studies of Political Development, ed. Gabriel A. Almond, Scott C. Flanagan, and Robert J. Mundt (Boston: Little, Brown, 1973).

(6) For this outlook of Japanese politicians, see Hajime Shinohara, Nihon no Seiji Fudo (Political Climate in Japan) (Tokyo: Iwanami, 1971), pp. 34-37.

(7) Ibid., pp. 37-38.

(8) See, for example, Tamotsu Sengoku and Atsuko Toyama, Hikaku Nihonjin Ron (Comparative Study of the Japanese) (Tokyo: Shogakukan, 1973), pp. 23-24, and Sekai no Seinen tono Hikaku kara mita Nihon no Seinen (Japanese Youths Viewed in Comparison to the World's Youth) (Tokyo: Okurasho Insatsukyoku, 1979), pp. 94-100.

(9) Japan Times Weekly, December 29, 1979, pp. 3 and 8.

(10) See an English translation of the Charter Oath in Ryusaku Tsunoda et al., eds., Sources of Japanese Tradition (New York: Columbia University Press, 1960), p. 644.

(11) Kiichi Miyazawa as quoted in Soichiro Tawara, "Soren wa kowai desuka?" (Are You Afraid of the Soviet Union?), Bungei Shunju, March 1980, p. 108.

(12) Kunio Muraoka, Japanese Security and the United States (London: International Institute for Strategic Studies, 1973) p. 2.

(13) Haruhiro Fukui, "Twenty Years of Revisionism," in The Constitution of Japan: Its First Twenty Years, 1947-1967, ed. Dan F. Henderson (Seattle: University of Washington Press, 1968), p. 54.

(14) Yoshio Kodama as quoted in William Manchester, American Caesar: Douglas MacArthur 1880-1964 (Boston: Little, Brown, 1978), p. 473.

(15) For an account of the making of the "Peace" Consitution, see Kenzo Takayanagi, "Some Reminiscences of Japan's Commission on the Constitution," in The Constitution of Japan.

(16) See MacArthur's letter quoted in ibid., pp. 87-88.

(17) For this draft, see Nihon Gendaishi Shiryo: Nichibei Ampo Joyaku Taiseishi, Kokkai Giron to Kankei Shiryo (Materials for Contemporary Japanese History: History of Japanese-American Security System, Diet Debate and Related Materials), Vol. 1, 1945-1947 Nen: Haisen to Shin Kempo no Seitei (1945-1947: The Defeat in War and the Establishment of the New Constitution), ed. Koichiro Yoshiwara and Ayazo Kubo under the general editorship of Saburo Ienaga and Hiroshi Suekawa (Tokyo: Sanseido, 1970), pp. 742-51.

(18) Takayanagi, p. 87.

(19) Quoted in Nihon Gendaishi Shiryo, Vol. 1, p. 180.

(20) Kaoru Murakami, "The Postwar Defense Debate in Review," Japan Echo 5 (Winter 1978): 18.

(21) Yasuhiro Nakasone, "Toward Comprehensive Security: Self-Defense and Article 9 of the Constitution," in ibid., p. 36.

(22) Makoto Momoi, "Basic Trends in Japanese Security Policies," in The Foreign Policy of Modern Japan, ed. Robert A. Scalapino (Berkeley: University of California Press, 1977),p. 342.

(23) Donald Hellmann, "Japanese Security and Postwar Japanese Foreign Policy," in ibid., p. 325.

(24) David Riesman, "Japanese Intellectuals – and Americans," The American Scholar 34 (Winter 1964-65): 63.

(25) See, for an excellent account of this incident, George R. Packard, Protest in Tokyo: The Security Treaty Crisis of 1960 (Princeton, N.J.: Princeton University Press, 1967).

(26) Lewis Austin, Saints and Samurai: The Political Culture of the American and Japanese Elites (New Haven, Conn: Yale University Press, 1975), p. 128.

(27) Edwin O. Reischauer, "Their Special Strengths," Foreign Policy 14 (Spring 1974): 146.

(28) For LDP factionalism, see Tsuneo Watanabe, Habatsu: Hoshuto no Kaibo (Factionalism: A Dissection of the Conservative Party) (Tokyo: Kobundo, 1958); Taketsugu Tsurutani, Political Change in Japan: Response to Postindustrial Challenge (New York: McKay, 1977), Chapter 4; and Haruhiro Fukui, "Japan: Factionalism in a Dominant Party System" in Faction Politics: Political Parties and Factionalism in Comparative Perspective, ed. Frank Belloni and Dennis Beller (Santa Barbara, Calif.: ABC-CLIO, 1978).

(29) Philip H. Trezise and Yukio Suzuki, "Politics, Government, and Economic Growth in Japan," in Asia's New Giant: How the Japanese Economy Works, ed. Hugh Patrick and Henry Rosovsky (Washington, D.C.: The Brookings Institution, 1976), pp. 763-64.

(30) Showa 54 Nen Ban Waga Gaiko no Kinkyo (1979 Diplomacy White Paper) (Tokyo: Okurasho Insatsukyoku, 1979), pp. 209-15.

(31) Asahi Nenkan 1979 Bekkan (1979 Asahi Yearbook Supplement) (Tokyo: Asahi Shimbunsha, 1979), p. 341.

(32) Ibid., and Nihon Kokusei Zue: 1979 Nen Ban (Picture of the State of Japan 1979) (Tokyo: Kokuseisha, 1979), pp. 149 and 160.

(33) Nihon to ASEAN (Japan and ASEAN) (Tokyo: Gaimusho Joho Bunka Kyoku, 1979), p. 21.

(34) Ibid.

(35) Chin Kin Wah, "The Great Powers and Southeast Asia: A Year of Diplomatic Effervescence," in Southeast Asian Affairs 1979 (Singapore: Institute of Southeast Asian Studies, 1979), p. 53.

(36) For Tokyo-Moscow negotiations over Siberian development, see David Hitchcock, "Joint Development of Siberia: Decision-making in Japanese-Soviet Relations," Asian Survey 11 (March 1971), and Gerald Curtis, "The Tyumen Oil Development Project and Japanese Foreign Policy Decision-making," in The Foreign Policy of Modern Japan, among others.

(37) Hiroshi Kimura, "Japan-Soviet Relations: Framework, Developments, Prospects," Asian Survey 20 (July 1980): 723.

(38) Shinsaku Hogen in Tawara, p. 110.

(39) Ma nantoka naru desho, Nariyuki ni makaseru hoka arimasen na, and Nantoka yatte ikeru desho, respectively.

7
Japanese Policy and East Asian Security in the 1980s

The decline of U.S. power notwithstanding, it remains axiomatic that neither Japan's defense nor East Asian security can be conceived without considering the vital functions of the United States. This is the fundamental thesis underlying this chapter. Japan has no reliable defense partner among its Asian neighbors, nor will it find one in the near future. The United States is the only nation concerned that is commonly trusted and counted on by virtually all of the region's nations. They trust it far more than they trust one another; they count on its ability and effort far more than they do one another's. Beneath the surface of their differing ideological and political orientations, including the "nonalignment" external postures of many of them, these nations earnestly look to the United States as the only guarantor of peace and stability in their region. Its past blunder in Indochina notwithstanding, none of them seems really to suspect or fear an imperialistic ambition on the part of the United States. That East Asian nations look to the United States for regional peace and security is quite understandable on at least two counts. One is their inability to manage their own regional affairs through mutual intraregional cooperation, and the other is their abiding mistrust of, or at least deep apprehension about, the Soviet Union and China. Willing or not, therefore, the United States is called upon to play the most crucial role in the region.

Because of its declined politicomilitary capability and domestic economic, social, and political constraints, however, the United States could no longer be seriously expected to do by itself all that would have to be done in order to promote, let alone guarantee, stability and security in East Asia. The era of <u>Pax Americana</u>, if there ever was one, is no more, nor will it be in the future. While it would still have to play a major, indeed decisive, role for the security of the region, the United States, in order to play its role to the best of its ability, should require assistance that is at once sustained and reliable. There is only one East Asian nation that could provide such assistance, the nation endowed with basic political stability and continuity, sufficient economic capability, and high levels of managerial and technological sophistication. That nation is Japan. It has no external political or territorial ambition; its level of political institutionalization and internal sociocultural development is such that its behavioral continuity, consistency, and predictability would be high; and it possesses vast financial, human organizational, and technological resources that could be utilized in concert with those of the United States for the benefit of the region's development and security. These vital attributes make Japan the only logical and sensible choice as the principal partner of the United States in the region. No other East Asian nation meets these prerequisites for stable and reliable partnership with the United States. Having said this, however, it has to be considered whether and to what extent the general proposition about Japan's partnership with the United States in the maintenance of regional security is acceptable to its neighbors, to the United States, and to Japan itself before some of the specifics of the partnership are discussed.

JAPAN'S REGIONAL SECURITY RESPONSIBILITY

There is a sense in which it can be said that a nation's, especially a "major" nation's, responsibility for the security of the region in which it is located is defined not by that nation's own preferences or inclinations but rather by the objective circumstances of the region. In the case of Japan this is quite clear in the immediately preceding paragraph. There is a growing recognition of this fact among East Asian states, in the United States, as well as in Japan, and this recognition generates various expectations regarding the role Japan should play and the responsibility it should shoulder.

Expectations for a Japanese Role and Responsibility

Japan's regional neighbors, especially the ASEAN states, seem to want Japan to play a significant role for the maintenance of regional security. Even as recently as 1976, there was little serious expectation of this nature, and any serious mention of such a role for Japan would have made them uncomfortable. Southeast Asians still remember Japan's conduct during World War II, but few today believe that Japan entertains an imperialistic ambition or that it may again become a dangerous military power. If anything, such fear has been replaced by ambivalence, and this ambivalence is increasingly in favor of a notion that Japan should play a significant security role in the region. Generational changes account for this in part, as well as the region's circumstances that have undergone considerable change during the last decade. Interestingly enough, however, the feelings here have also been prompted or strengthened by a growing Asian suspicion that Japan's continued pretension to moralistic pacifism and aloofness from political security issues of the region were motivated by expedient calculus of crass economic self-interest. As was discussed in Chapter 6, the Fukuda Doctrine was a good example of Japan's rhetorical fidelity to friendship, equal partnership, cooperation, and heart-to-heart understanding failing to be followed by the kind of action warranted by such protestations.(1) Put another way, Japan began to be perceived by its neighbors as a purely self-centered, resource-grabbing economic animal disguised as an above-politics, peace-loving nation but un-willing to contribute to the task of establishing stability and security in the region because it would only complicate its economic pursuit. There emerged, therefore, an increasingly pronounced feeling that "Japan should become aware that is not only an economic power, but exactly because it is an economic power, it does have a political influence and political responsibility."(2) In a sense, the traditional fear that Japan might again act dangerously in the region came to be replaced by an unhappiness, augmented by the recognition of the decline of U.S. power, that it was avoiding doing what it could and therefore should be doing for the region.

It should be noted, however, that the general contour of the role that those Asians increasingly expect Japan to play in the region's political and security affairs is quite circumscribed. In an important sense, they do not yet trust it in the way that they do the United States. For one thing, none of the Asian states (with the possible exception of China, which for its own reasons wants a militarily powerful Japan and even seems to wish a military alliance with Japan) wants Japan to acquire nuclear weapons, even though most of them want a militarily much stronger Japan.(3) Their expectation is that a militarily stronger Japan play its security role on the basis of two principal conditions: that it be played within the framework of its security relations with the United States, and that the concomi-tant military buildup be undertaken in regular consultation with its friends in the region.(4) Their desire, then, seems to be for Japan to assume its security role under restraint of its senior security partner and under close scrutiny of its neighbors. Within these limitations, even such an anti-Japanese stalwart as Carlos P. Romulo of the Philippines, the author was informed in Manila, had come to expect Japan to play an increasingly important security role in the region.

U.S. expectations for Japan playing an explicit security role in East Asia were not entirely free from ambivalence, though they have in recent years become less and less ambivalent. Well into the mid-1970s, the United States seemed to be pulled by two contra-dictory views of Japan in regard to its role in East Asian security. On the one hand, there was a veiw that Japan should assume some kind of security responsibility in the region that was consistent with its enormously expanded economic power and, on the other, there persisted an apprehension that it might become a potentially dangerous military power once it started expanding its security role.(5) It may well be that the ups and downs in the U.S. pressure on Japan to expand its defense efforts were reflective of this basic ambivalence in the U.S. attitude toward Japan's military potentials, as well as Washington's uncertainty about the feeling of its East Asian friends regarding a militarily strengthened Japan. (As recently as 1979, one American diplomat in Tokyo told the author of what he viewed as persistent fears among East Asians of a militarily expanded Japan.) By and large, however, the U.S. attitude toward Japan's potential military capability and security role in East Asia notably shifted as new kinds of conflict and new levels of tension emerged within the region as well as without in recent years,(6) a shift no doubt reinforced by a growing recognition that the United States was less and less capable of insuring East Asian security, especially the safety of the region's sealanes, in case of certain anticipatable contingencies. While not expecting Japan to substitute for its own military presence in the region, the United States clearly came to expect that an expansion of Japan's security efforts could enable its own military capability to focus on danger spots in the region as well as such adjacent areas as Southwest Asia and the Persian Gulf region.(7) In short, in Washington's eyes, it became apparent that the United States could no longer perform its crucial security function in East Asia without effective Japanese assistance and cooperation. The growth in and the new persistence of U.S. pressure on Japan to expand its defense efforts was a natural consequence of this recognition of the limitations of the United States in the face of growing international instability.

In principle, at least, the Japanese government recognizes the nation's role and responsibility as a preeminent East Asian state. In 1979 the foreign minister explicitly stated: "Japan's diplomacy henceforth must acquire depth by adding to the traditional diplomacy revolving around economic relations the political role the nation must play in the international community."(8) An internal Foreign Office memo stressed that the Japanese-U.S. security pact had come to constitute "a basic framework for international politics in Asia" and to serve "the cause of peace and stability in Asia."(9) It clearly seems at this writing that an official consensus is emerging that the nation should, on the basis of a "global perspective,"(10) adopt a "positive diplomatic direction as a member of the Western bloc" in support of the United States.(11) This would seem quite significant, for the Japanese government came not only to be concerned with the relative decline of U.S. power in the region but also to recognize that the security of the region, hence of Japan, could no longer be discussed solely in terms of events taking place within the region itself, and that, therefore, Japan should provide the United States with such support as would enable it to shift its energy to danger spots outside of the region of East Asia as occasions warrant. Thus far, however, Japan's new concern and recognition are only in principle and there remains a gap betwen its recognition of its responsibility in principle and its performance in fact.

There are a number of reasons for this gap, including the difficulty of rapidly increasing defense expenditures at a time of declining economic growth rates. Perhaps the most serious cause for the gap has to do with the uncertainty as to the kind of role Japan should play. Expectations of Japan's role on the part of the United States and its East Asian neighbors, in the eyes of the Japanese, have not gone, as one Foreign Ministry official complained, beyond the abstract and the general. One foreign policy commentator wrote: "We are waking up to the fact that we will have to play a larger role, but are not sure what this should be, or even what the U.S. thinks we should be."(12) To the extent that Japan's role would have to be supplementary and supportive to that of the United States and compatible with the needs of the region of East Asia, the specific aspects of its role would have to be spelled out through close consultation and discussion with the United States and its regional neighbors in order to maximize its effectiveness and wisdom. This remains to be done. It is to this end that the remainder of this chapter is intended to make some suggestions.

Japanese-U.S. Security Partnership: Maximizing the Effects of Cooperation

In view of persistent, albeit significantly weakened, domestic constraints, the potential militaristic or ultranationalistic residual tendencies of certain forces within, and the legitimate apprehension of its neighbors, Japan should seek to expand its own defense capability and to establish its security role in East Asia only within the context of the existing security arrangements with the United States. Moreover, for it to seek, as some Japanese have long urged, what is called an autonomous defense capability is impossible. There is no longer such a thing as autonomous national defense except perhaps for the United States and the Soviet Union.(13)   Any attempt at independent national defense, with all that it would imply in terms of the range and level of rearmament, would inescapably lead to a radical reordering of political, social, cultural, and economic systems and priorities in the country and seriously undermine, perhaps destroy, the democratic institutions and practices so painstakingly nurtured over the past 35 years. Externally, it would also surely be counterproductive more than militarily in a number of ways, with little or no gain to the nation's security or international standing.   The only reasonable general direction Japan could pursue, then, would be toward some kind of cooperative effort, or joint enterprise, with the United States in a manner that would commit the United States more confidently and comfortably to its defense and to maintenance of security in the region, and that would also maximize the effectiveness of its own defense capability and U.S. capability in the region both collectively and individually with the greatest economy and effectiveness.

The existing security arrangements between Japan and the United States are more than two decades old and, as was noted in Chapter 5, there are some indications that they have in recent years entered a new period of strengthened cooperation and mutual assistance. The Japanese government now publicly admits the inadequacy of its defense efforts of the past, treats the matter of improving the capability of the Japan Self-Defense Forces no longer as a constitutional or legal issue but as a fiscal one, and is attempting to find ways of increasing its defense spending. It has also increased its contribution to the costs of maintaining the U.S. Forces in Japan significantly beyond what the terms of the security pact prescribe. It is also in the process of undertaking an accelerated program of qualitative upgrading of the JSDF. In an effort to increase the effectiveness of their security parnership for the defense of Japan, the two nations adopted "The Guidelines for Japan-United States Defense Cooperation." Despite this evolving phenomenon of the security arrangements and the efforts that are going into their improvement, there is one question that should be asked: Are the United States and Japan individually or jointly undertaking the most effective, efficient, and economic measures for bolstering Japan's defense and for the improved maintenance of East Asian regional security? More specifically for Japan, would Japan's expansion of its defense spending, however significant (which it has not been thus far), really improve its ability for self-defense and for assistance in the maintenance of regional security? Does the presence of the USFJ help? How would the current functional division of labor between the JSDF and USFJ in defense of Japan be operational and effective in emergency? Finally, what about the safety of Western Pacific sealanes?

To state our conclusion first, we believe that some fundamental rethinking about and modifications in the security arrangements seem warranted in order for the arrangements to be really effective both for the defense of Japan and for the maintenance of security in East Asia. These are joint tasks for the two security partners and they no doubt will find them variously cumbersome.

Defense of Japan

Under the current Japanese defense policy and "The Guidelines" Japan is to cope, by itself, with limited, small-scale aggression. "When it is difficult to repel aggression alone due to the scale, type, and other factors of aggression," "The Guidelines" state, "Japan will repel it with the cooperation of the United States." Given the strong probability, as alluded to in Chapter 5, that the capability of the JSDF, especially of the Air Self-Defense Force and the Maritime Self-Defense Force, is considerably less than meets the statistical eye, the level of U.S. responsibility for Japan's defense may well be much higher than the official division of labor might suggest. In short, Japan may well be far more dependent on the United States for its own defense than is assumed.

Under these circumstances, the common proposition that Japan should undertake a significant and sustained expansion of its defense spending to increase its self-defense capability seems entirely reasonable. Let us suppose that Japan would raise its defense spending from the current 0.9 percent of its GNP by 50 percent (to some 1.4 percent), which some people in Japan do in fact favor and the United States would be pleased to see. While in itself a highly unlikely event at least in the immediate future, this would bring the defense outlay from some $11 billion to more than $16 billion per year immediately, and the figure would continue to rise in subsequent years as long as the GNP continued to grow. For reasons of constitutional limitations, domestic ideological constraints, and external political considerations, Japan would not acquire a strategic offensive capability, although there are small numbers of people in Japan who desire such a capability including nuclear weapons, as was seen in Chapter 5, and Japan is technically capable of becoming a nuclear power on short notice. This means that much of the large increment in its defense outlay would be devoted to the improvement of its tactical defense capability. At this level, some of the measures Japan should undertake to improve its self-defense capability seem obvious, for they were implied in the discussion of JSDF capability in Chapter 5. Speaking generally, they all pertain to adding to the JSDF as they exist today the kind of muscle that they should have and are obviously thought by many to have but do not. This includes, among others, an expanded ammunition inventory both for training and combat, especially of antiaircraft missiles and antisubmarine projectiles; more rigorous combat training; the hardening of radar sites and naval surface ships against enemy air attack; a vast improvement and perhaps an expansion of electronic surveillance and detection systems; the elimination of unnecessarily cumbersome administrative procedures regarding GSDF and ASDF training and maneuvers; and legislation insuring prompt response to emergency, but also carefully safeguarding the principle and practice of civilian supremacy over the military. These are among the kinds of measures that would render the JSDF only as effective as they are supposed to be at this particular point; they suggest only basic minimum improvement.

Beyond these minimal measures, the vast increase in defense spending would enable the JSDF to upgrade and expand their vital arsenal. In particular, Japan could rapidly endeavor to develop specific types of weapons more closely attuned to its unique defense requirements and its particular physical characteristics. They might include a range of small but potent weapons such as precision-guided missiles capable of being launched from land vehicles (for example, trucks and jeeps), eventually even from the shoulders of ground troops, against enemy planes and ships; mobile radar systems;

torpedoes and antisubmarine warfare mines with accurate homing devices; and the like. The defense of Japan's congested tight little industrial habitat, especially since it is without the strategic option of its own, would require its military capability to be extraordinarily versatile and mobile. This, indeed, is the crucial dimension of its security need that should command the most concentrated attention of its military experts, for the only way in which Japan by itelf could hope to discourage an attack or aggression would be to raise the anticipated costs of such a venture against it. Given the magnitude of the hypothetical expansion in defense spending, Japan could perhaps achieve a capability to cope with a "limited, small-scale aggression."

It would be possible, then, that the JSDF would in fact "cope with" a small-scale limited aggression, that is, repel it in the end. Given the "glass tower" physical and structural predicament of Japan, however, one should wonder about the extent to which this congested nation could sustain damages inflicted by a determined enemy before it is finally repelled. How quickly could Japan's civilian and military authorities accurately ascertain "the scale, type, and other factors of aggression" that would make it difficult for the JSDF to repel it alone in such an emergency? Would not the enemy, if it wanted to attack in real earnest, see to it that its scale of aggression exceeded the JSDF capability to repel it? Such "scale, type, and other factors of aggression," moreover, would not be solely in terms of JSDF capability to repel it in the end (in days? weeks? months?) but also relative to the capacity of the nation's entire life-support infrastructure to absorb disruption and chaos caused by the enemy attack in the meantime. Defensibility of Japan might have more to do with its domestic life-support infrastructure than with its military capability. Within this context of considerations, could the United States really help defend Japan?

Given the inevitable logistical difficulty, U.S. assistance in a serious emergency would have to be provided by the USFJ. With its fewer than 200 aircraft, however, it might well be that the USFJ could play only a supplementary role for the JSDF, even if it responded to the event with dispatch, especially since Japan's geographic structure would make defense against lateral enemy penetration extremely difficult. Its 43,000 ground troops would remain largely superfluous since the enemy would rely on air and perhaps naval tactical-missile attack. (The primary threat to Japan would be aerial and naval. While many Japanese fear an aggression by way of enemy troops landing on their territory, especially Hokkaido, and much of the JSDF defense effort focuses on that northern island, such an eventuality would seem extremely remote, though it should not be ruled out as a possibility at some stages of aggression. Any land invasion of Japan would be detected well before the fact, for it would require deployment of a large number of naval transport and landing craft. Invasion by airborne troops would involve extreme hazards because of Japan's topography. Moreover, land invasion of Japan as such would seem superfluous at best for its destruction and subduing. Troop landing would be essential later mainly for political and administrative purposes.) The Seventh Fleet today is spread very thin, not only because of its size reduction during the last decade but also because it now has to patrol the Indian Ocean and the Persian Gulf waters and cannot be expected to provide much assistance to Japan unless some of its major ships, especially aircraft carriers, happened to be in close proximity to the country, which would not be likely. Chances are, therefore, that the enemy would attempt to inflict a crippling blow on Japan before the United States could bring the full weight of its conventional air and naval power to rescue Japan. It would seem, therefore, that the only effective role the United States could play as Japan's security partner is as a strategic nuclear power, first to discourage any attack on Japan and, if that failed, to repel and punish the enemy promptly.

The security treaty notwithstanding, it is devoutly to be wished but not seriously to be expected that the United States would in all circumstances and unfailingly invoke its strategic capability in defense of Japan. The United States would in all likelihood be powerfully constrained by a range of military, political, diplomatic, logistical, and strategic considerations that would inevitably arise out of its multiple global security commitments and interests, of which its security relationship with Japan is but one, albeit an important one. These constraints would be all the more potent since the relative expansion of the Soviet power, on one hand, and the growing policy independence of key nations among its Western allies, on the other, would powerfully inhibit the United States in acting solely within the context of its security pact with Japan. The United States might well find itself having to choose between Japan and Western Europe (or, for that matter, the oil-rich Middle East).

A fundamental proposition here is that the only defense of Japan consists, not even in a quick and efficient military operation against the enemy attack, but in preventing it altogether. The existing security arrangements, made during the period when the United States enjoyed an overwhelming politicomilitary superiority in the world, would no longer be adequate to insure that Japan will not be attacked. They would, therefore, seem to warrant certain structural changes, for it could be persuasively argued that, whatever might be done, Japan would remain indefensible in strictly military terms. The invocation of the ultimate strategic potential of the United States in defense of Japan, as we have just noted, could not be reasonably expected except when it is part of a total Western military confrontation with the Soviet Union. Short of such a global or semiglobal conflagration, defense of Japan against a determined, well-planned, and well-executed attack, given the physical and structural features of the country, would be of utmost difficulty, to say the least, and would likely be impossible in the final analysis so long as the enemy is prepared to sustain the cost of its attack. If Japan could not be defended militarily in such an event, how could it be defended?

National defense is as much a political problem as it is a military task. A given quantity of military defense capability might be significantly augmented qualitatively in its effectiveness by political innovation. The political device we now suggest would involve a certain restructuring in the existing security arrangements between Japan and the United States. Our fundamental proposition still is that the United States is the key to Japan's defense and security, but the U.S. role we have in mind is quite different from what it has been, and would go far beyond "coordination" or "interoperability" currently envisaged between the JSDF and the USFJ, which is indeed the central operational concern of "The Guidelines." Our recommendation is that some kind and degree of Japanese-U.S. (that is, JSDF-USFJ) force integration for the tactical defense of the country be considered, particularly at the level of first-line combat operation in air and naval defense. To many, perhaps most, of the Japanese and Americans, this recommendation might sound outlandish; but we live in an extraordinarily dangerous age and the problem of Japan's defense, as was argued above, would be an extraordinarily difficult one. An extraordinary problem sometimes calls for an extraordinary solution. In any event, what kind and degree of air and naval force integration would be most desirable should be determined by relevant experts. All costs of such integration – in terms of additional aircraft and naval combatants where needed, as well as personnel expenditure, equipment, supply, and facilities involved – should be included in Japan's annual contribution to the costs of maintaining the USFJ or in the JSDF budget.

Each of the nation's front-line interceptor squadrons, for example, could be made up of ASDF and USFJ pilots flying ASDF planes or could be composed of a mix of ASDF and USFJ elements. Each surface-combatant or even submarine unit could likewise consist of either MSDF ships manned by both Japanese and American personnel or MSDF and U.S. Navy ships. The Japanese-U.S. force integration at the level of first-line air and naval defense should be accompanied by a system of joint command, with each relevant unit, group, or squadron commanded by a JSDF officer assisted by an American deputy and a staff consisting of a mix of Japanese and American officers. (Linguistic difficulties would be encountered, but they would be neither so insurmountable nor so inhibitive of the objective of the arrangement as we shall soon see.) This idea of joint command might also be applied in some form at the highest military level for the defense of the nation, with the relevant Japanese officer always playing the senior role in his relationship to his American counterpart.

The purpose of force integration loosely suggested here is not the improvement of the nation's military capability for defense, though such improvement to a degree might indeed automatically ensue. It is first and foremost political. A Japanese-U.S. force integration at the level of first-line tactical defense would create a security context in which the United States would be automatically involved in the defense of Japan from the first minute of any and every enemy attack. In the most fundamental security terms, and to the extent that the United States is committed to the defense of Japan, advantages of such force integration should be quite obvious. For Japan's potential adversary, the U.S. commitment to its defense, which in recent years has become suspect, would be definitive and fail-safe.   The enemy could no longer count on hesitation, delay, or welshing in the U.S. military response, including strategic and even nuclear, to its attack on Japan. In short, the Japanese-U.S. force integration for first-line defense of Japan would raise the level of deterrence against even the most "limited" attack on Japan far higher than the current pattern of U.S.-Japanese security arrangements could ever hope to achieve. The enemy would from the first moment of its attack on Japan be automatically engaged in a military confrontation with the United States. Such force integration for first-line defense of Japan would, therefore, constitute the most effective and direct tripwire strung along its defense perimeters. If such be the case, not only would Japan be more secure, but also the United States would reduce the risk of having to shed the blood of its USFJ in Japan's defense.

The suggested force integration would also be economical for both Japan and the United States. It would, in the first place, be less expensive than any kind of attempt to increase the JSDF and/or JSFJ capability militarily under the existing security arrangements. Under this force integration, given the character of its purpose, the focus would not be on any force expansion as such, though some degree of expansion might be required, but rather on a rearrangement of existing JSDF and USFJ personnel and resources for the purpose of a new pattern of deployment. In fact, the total force level of the USFJ could be significantly reduced (that is, a reduction of its 44,000 ground combat troops), insofar as the defense of Japan is concerned, generating a significant reduction of the current annual cost of USFJ maintenance of some $2 billion. What would be required by way of additional expenditure would be for the JSDF to acquire or, in the immediate interim, lease from the United States a certain number of tactical aircraft and naval combatants to be manned in part or in toto by American combat personnel integrated in the whole defense system, plus all equipment, facilities, and personnel costs associated with such integration. All costs so incurred, however, would most likely equal a rather minor proportion of the generally anticipated increases in Japan's defense outlay in the coming years.

Defense outlay increases that are bound to come because of the shift in security concern discussed in Chapter 5 would be rather enormous even if they seem modest as percentage points because of the magnitude of Japan's GNP. One of the modest alternative projections frequently bandied about in government circles for the military spending increases under the existing pattern of U.S.-Japanese security cooperation would have the nation increase its defense spending to 1.0 percent of GNP within five years, presumably at a steady rate and assuming that the GNP would in the meantime grow by some 6 percent per year. If this were to come about, which might well be the case, in the first year (say 1982), the defense spending would rise by nearly $2 billion and by the fifth year, the total increase over the 1981 fiscal year budget would be in the neighborhood of $30 billion. Compared to the preceding five-year period, the 1982-86 defense outlay would just about double.(14) These would be enormously large additional sums, particularly when we remember that, in 1979, the total amount of armament procurement was only $1.7 billion and that during the five-year period before 1979, the total cumulative expenditure on such procurement had amounted to only about $6.6 billion.(15) Just how much additional armament Japan would be able to acquire with these additional funds may be readily visualized on the basis of some of the weapons price tags. In 1978, to cite just a few examples from available sources, an ultramodern Spruance-class destroyer could be ordered for production at a cost ranging between $134 million and $366 million, a latest-model frigate from $147 million to $160 million, an F-15 from $17.4 million to $27.5 million, an F-16 from $7.6 million to $12.3 million (all these price differentials owing to numbers of units ordered and equipment), ASDF-compatible air-to-air missiles from $41,000 to $148,000 apiece, and a Nike-Hercules ground-to-air missile around $3 million.(16) Prices of these items may have gone up considerably in the meantime, but the potential magnitude of the increases in Japan's defense spending would render them easily manageable for the JSDF, even if they needed a large additional number of those weapons, which they would not.

The kind of Japanese-U.S. force integration, for reasons we have noted, would not require the JSDF to acquire a large amount of additional weapons. While some additions to the ASDF and the MSDF would most likely be called for, they could be relatively modest. An air-defense force integration could be promoted to a considerable extent by better utilization of the aircraft and other equipment the ASDF already has and is scheduled to acquire by policy decisions thus far, through more fuel and ammunition supply and better maintenance. Some of the nearly 200 USFJ aircraft could be shifted to the integrated air defense also. The first-line naval-force integration would seem to call for some addition to the MSDF, especially since the U.S. Seventh Fleet is understrength and spread thin. How many of what type of combatant would have to be

added would depend on the kind and degree of naval-force integration desired, but, here, too, the amount of additional funds required
might be relatively minor, especially in comparison to what would
otherwise be needed for raising the MSDF capability for effective
military defense of the nation in the absence of force integration.
(Even if, say, a combination of combatants equivalent to ten
Spruance-class destroyers were to be acquired through domestic
and/or overseas procurement over a five-year period, somewhere in
the neighborhood of $3 billion might suffice.)

Defense of Western Pacific Sealanes

Thus far, the discussion may have sounded as though we are
concerned only about how Japan could insure its security by
involving the United States in its defense against aggression and
how, by so doing, it could minimize its defense spending, with
whatever savings for the United States coming as something quite
incidental. If these were our sole concerns, the United States might
well reject our suggestion for force integration out of hand. The
security relationship between Japan and the United States could be
effectively maintained only on the basis of equity and reciprocity,
qualities that have in the past been largely lacking. The security
treaty of 1960 on which the current security arrangements are based
has itself reflected noticeable onesidedness in the two nations'
bilateral military relations. It obligates the United States to assist
Japan in defending itself but does not require reciprocal obligation
on the part of Japan, except to help defend U.S. interests on its
territory. Made at the time when Japan's per-capita GNP was one-
sixth that of the United States, it has perpetuated a situation in
which Japan, now the second largest economic power, continues to
depend for its own safety upon the United States, whose per capita
economic ability is no greater than its own and whose political and
military power has continued to decline. This affects Japan's
integrity as a full-fledged sovereign state, especially as an economic
superpower and as a nation professedly committed to the promotion
of world peace, and it causes a legitimate unhappiness on the part of
the United States, especially when Japan has been building up such
large balance-of-payments surpluses in its bilateral trade with it.
For the sake of national integrity, political consideration, the simple
principle of fairness and reciprocity, and, ultimately, enlightened
self-interest, it would seem to behoove Japan to take the initiative
in modifying its security relations with the United States in the
direction of promoting genuine mutual trust and assistance.

Apart from the consideration of fairness and reciprocity, our
suggestion regarding the defense of the Western Pacific rests on
several important considerations. One is that the U.S. naval
capability in the region – traditionally the most visible component
of its strategic security commitment in the region – has declined

rapidly over the recent decade both in absolute terms and relative to the contingent environment. At the same time, in view of its multiple security concern and commitment in other parts of the world and its increasingly intractable domestic economic, social, and political constraints, the United States would continue to be hard-pressed in its effort to restore its naval capability in the region to the level that would be sufficient for confident maintenance of sealane safety, let alone recapture its former superiority over the Soviet naval power there. Another relevant consideration pertains to the weakness of developing nations in the region. China and Taiwan possess naval capabilities approximating Japan's MSDF but they are the kind of nation with which, for obvious reasons, the United States would be well advised to avoid direct military cooperation.(17) Other nations in the region simply do not possess any naval capability to speak of except for haphazard coastal defense against smugglers,(18) and none has sufficient wherewithal to build the kind of naval capability capable of effectively partaking of the maintenance of Western Pacific security in the very near future. More importantly, endemic political instability and unpre-dictability combined with the economic underdevelopment of these developing East Asian nations render any effective military cooperation between them and the United States in the defense of the region's waters highly problematic, in any event. In addition, relations among these nations, as was discussed in Chapter 4, are at best ambiguous, frequently disharmonious, at times even hostile. Singapore's Lee Kwan Yew proposed a few years ago the formation of a joint ASEAN fleet to patrol and defend sealanes of Southeast Asia, but his proposal fell on deaf ears precisely because of the character of the mutual relations just mentioned.(19) Third, Japan is the principal beneficiary and user of Western Pacific sealanes. It benefits from their safety far more than all its neighbors combined for the simple reason that the preponderant bulk of traffic through them is to and from Japan. Japan, therefore, should make the level of contribution to their security commensurate with the advantage it derives from its use of them. Fourth, and related to their critical importance to it, Japan's sheer economic capability would seem to impose on it a responsibility for their safety that is consistent with it, particularly since other nations of the region are not as fortunate as it in the level of well-being. The ASEAN states, whose per capita income is a small fraction of Japan's, spend up to 6 percent of their meager GNPs on defense outlays while Japan spends less than 1 percent of its. Japan could not convince any of its neighbors or the United States that it is doing its best.

Our suggestion here, then, is that Japan devote a major propor-tion of whatever increases in defense spending it is currently contemplating for the improvement of its military capability under the existing security arrangements with the United States toward bolstering the security of the Western Pacific in cooperation with and in support of the United States. For reasons of imperative necessity not to aggravate the world strategic military balance and not to cause unnecessary fear and alarm on the part of its neighbors, Japan should not acquire strategic weapons and should instead confine its role to one that is supplementary to that of the United States in the Western Pacific, a role designed to provide critical assistance to the United States in the region and to enable its senior security partner effectively and flexibly to respond to strategic contingencies in the region as well as such adjacent regions as Southwest Asia and the Persian Gulf area. The existing security arrangements are at best ambiguous as to the role Japan could or should play in the maintenance of Western Pacific security.

By the end of the 1970s, the U.S. Seventh Fleet covering up to 50 million square miles of waters had been reduced to some 50 ships from over 200 at the height of the Vietnam War. The number of its ships was increased to some 58 with the emergence of crises in Southwest Asia and the Persian Gulf area, but some 20 of them, including two of the three aircraft carriers, are now permanently deployed in the Indian Ocean, leaving the Western Pacific sealanes dangerously underprotected against potential disruption. This situation is likely to continue as long as the Soviet threat in the Persian Gulf area and Southwest Asia persists. Indeed, it might further worsen should there arise some domestic upheaval in the Middle East. Under the circumstances, Japan should increase the capability of its MSDF and also of the ASDF to the point where it would be able to provide the Seventh Fleet with significant assistance in the defense of the Western Pacific sealanes. As of 1980, the MSDF maintained some 90 surface craft and 14 submarines, and the MSDF and the ASDF a combined total of some 650 aircraft. By how much these naval and air capabilities should be expanded to achieve the threshold of real effectiveness in terms of filling the security gap in the defense of Western Pacific sealanes would have to be discussed and determined by the two nations and in consultation with their friends in the region. It is here – in the participation in the maintenance of Western Pacific security – that a considerable expenditure on the part of Japan would be required, in fact far more considerable than the likely expenditure on Japanese-U.S. force integration in the defense of Japan itself. MSDF and ASDF personnel strength also would have to be expanded accordingly. Japan, however, could make a significant and visible difference in the joint Japanese-U.S. capability for the defense of the Western Pacific. The likely effect on that capability of the participation of, say, ten major MSDF surface combatants, a few submarines, and several squadrons of reconnaissance, ASW, and other tactical aircraft operating out of bases, for example, in Okinawa, Iwo Jima, as well as Japan proper (some of these bases would have to be constructed, restored, and/or expanded) in close coordination with U.S. naval units in the region would be considerable. An MSDF expansion required to this end would require some years if the needed ships were to be built, but in the interim, a certain number of them could be leased from among the modern combat craft the United States maintains in mothballs.(20) Additional aircraft could be more readily obtained. In any event, it seems that all this, even combined with the costs of the Japanese-U.S. force integration for tactical defense of Japan proper discussed earlier, would be manageable within the conservative projection of defense budget increase to a full 1 percent of the GNP mentioned above. A 50 percent increase in the current capability for the defense of Western Pacific security, as an example, would not be wide of the mark within that budgetary limit. It should be remembered, however, that we are not talking about the budget as such, but rather about security requirements.

The matter of the level of Japan's defense spending has consistently been the primary subject of security debate in Japan and of disagreement and tension between it and the United States. From the foregoing discussions in this chapter, it should by now be clear that we view the matter as an ancillary issue. The fundamental issue in Japanese-U.S. security relations is, and has always been, the specific security needs Japan, as a sovereign state and as the security partner of the United States as well as the preeminent economic power in East Asia, should meet. Whether 1 percent of its GNP is adequate or not is in itself irrelevant in the final analysis. Japan must do what it should: its level of spending ought to be determined by its security needs and responsibilities, and not the other way around. What Japan should do had better be done with greatest economy as well as efficiency. Indeed, one of the underlying purposes of this chapter is to shift the basic thrust of security debate in Japan and discussion between Japan and the United States toward the really fundamental issue.

The two general policy suggestions proposed above – Japanese-U.S. force integration for first-line tactical defense of Japan, and Japan's security participation in the defense of the Western Pacific in support of and in cooperation with the United States – would, we suspect, encounter opposition from many quarters in both nations, despite the virtues that seem to inhere in them. The first suggestion – force integration – would not be palatable to many Japanese as well as many Americans, even their governments, for different reasons. The United States would view the suggestion with understandable skepticism because it would at first glance deprive it of its national flexibility in the kind of emergency for which it is designed. In other words, the suggestion might be viewed as radically reducing the U.S. military as well as diplomatic options in the event, especially vis-à-vis the security of Western Europe from the Soviet threat. (Put differently, the NATO allies of the United States would not wish to see the United States as tied down to the defense of Japan as it is to theirs.) We submit, however, that options for the United States that it might be feared would be reduced have to do ultimately with choosing between Japan and Western Europe, that is, precisely the kind of option the Soviet Union would want the United States to retain. To the extent that the United States is really committed to the defense of Japan, then, the policy suggestion for force integration would only add the kind of political substance that it could be argued it has thus far lacked.

On the part of Japan, or many, perhaps even most, Japanese at present, the suggestion might be objected to on the ground that USFJ personnel would constitute a mercenary force with the potential to compromise the nation's "strictly defensive" stance (for example, a trigger-happy conspiracy to provoke a military confrontation) as well as the danger of logistical and command complexity accidentally provoking unnecessary combat situations. These possibilities could not be brushed away, of course, but they could be minimized or even entirely eliminated by careful selection and training of forces to be integrated into the first-line tactical defense of the country. (Incidentally, it might be argued that the putative existence of this kind of "potential" or "danger" would add to the caution on the part of any potential adversary to desist from such intimidatory "testing" acts as blatant violation of the nation's air space with its military aircraft and the jamming of Japan's radar facilities, thus further reducing the likelihood of military conflict involving Japan.)

Clearly, the suggested force integration in defense of Japan would by no means be easy and, once instituted, without difficulties and problems. Those problems and difficulties, however, would be in large measure internal rather than external, and the benefits that it would bring to the task of JSDF-USFJ cooperation for the defense of Japan would seem to outweigh them. Also, those difficulties and problems would most likely decline as the JSDF and USFJ elements so integrated learn more effectively and cooperatively to work together. In one sense, it could be said that unless Japan and the United States are prepared to encounter and manage those difficulties and problems, their cooperation in the defense of Japan would never be effective.

As for our suggestion for Japan's participation in the defense of the Western Pacific sealanes, one could, at least initially, expect a more positive reaction from the United States than from Japan, for reasons that no longer need be reiterated here. There are emerging signs, however, that Japan would not be entirely opposed to the suggestion, or some approximation thereof. For example, the Tokyo government in 1980 began for the first time publicly to talk about Japan's "right of self-defense on the high seas, "and the director-general of the Defense Agency even went so far as to state that he favored "extending the scope of Japan's defense to the Persian Gulf."(21) Only a few years earlier, the government would have been constrained from considering the matter openly for fear of an opposition charge of violating the "peace Constitution." Shortly thereafter, the prime minister himself stated in the Diet that it was constitutionally permissible for Japan militarily to defend its sealanes.(22) Equally significantly, these official statements did not provoke any serious controversy in the Diet or in the nation at large. In view of the fact that Japan could not now, as the prime minister pointed out, nor in our view could in the near future without massive strategic naval buildup (which, for reasons we discussed earlier, would not be wise), protect Japanese shipping in the Persian Gulf and the Indian Ocean, the only feasible alternative would seem to be the kind of security cooperation for the defense of the Western Pacific we have suggested, for it would enable the United States to provide better protection of sealanes in the Indian Ocean and the Persian Gulf. Indeed, the notion that Japan's positive participation in the defense of the Western Pacific would enable the United States more effectively to provide security in the Indian Ocean and the Persian Gulf is consistent though not identical with a policy recommendation recently made by a joint U.S.-Japanese policy study group consisting of security experts. The group's recommendation in this regard was that the major NATO nations cooperate with the United States in creating a military deterrent force in the Indian Ocean and Persian Gulf area (a multilateral naval force) and that other NATO states and Japan "should apply their own civil assets, including airlift and sealift, to support this allied presence" in the area.(23) Apart from the use of its "civil assets" in case of security contingencies in Southwest Asia and the Middle East to assist the United States in, for example, positioning its Rapid Deployment Force, Japan could, in the interest of preventing such contingencies, help the United States deploy as much of its naval capability currently required for the maintenance of sealane security in the Western Pacific in the Indian Ocean/Persian Gulf region precisely by adopting the kind of policy that our suggestion points to. Prevention of military conflict in Southwest Asia and the Persian Gulf region is the more immediate and less costly task than helping resolve such conflict once it has broken out.

As the study group referred to above concluded, the maintenance of Middle East/Indian Ocean security is no longer either within the sole responsibility of the United States or within its own capability and therefore is the responsibility of major industrial nations that depend on the petroleum supply from the region, namely, the United States, NATO, and Japan. The question for Japan, then, is how best to participate in that joint task. Our conclusion is that, in view of the range of problems and factors we have considered thus far in this volume, the most effective option for Japan to take would be to help the most appropriate nation for the task, namely, the United States, which happens to be its security partner in its own defense and in the defense of the Western Pacific, play its role as effectively as possible in the Middle-East/Indian Ocean area by playing its role in the defense of the Western Pacific that is commensurate with its capability, and that, in so doing, Japan would be making the greatest contribution to the prevention of open conflict in that volatile part of the world that is so vital to its economic survival. For Japan to do less than that would be to contribute to the ultimate outbreak of conflict in that region as well as to pose an indirect threat to the security of the Western Pacific.

The two general policy suggestions we have made in this chapter – a Japanese-U.S. force integration for the first-line tactical defense of Japan, and Japan's security participation in the defense of the Western Pacific in support of and in cooperation with the United States – would also contain a number of extramilitary as well as security advantages for Japan, the United States, and their friends in East Asia. For Japan, domestically, the ascertainably increased doubt about the U.S.'s will and resolve to come to its aid in case of an enemy attack would be vastly reduced, perhaps even eliminated, since force integration as suggested would in effect constitute as efficacious an insurance policy for its life and safety as could be devised under the circumstances of existing international conditions. Secondly, both force integration and Japan's participation in the defense of the Western Pacific would erode the attractiveness or relevance of the traditional and persistent militarist argument for a large independent military capability (including strategic forces) for "autonomous defense" of the nation and for the maintenance of the nation's lifeline stretching southward through the Strait of Malacca. Among the rightists and nationalists, there has always been a conviction that the existing security arrangements with the United States, because of their relative one-sidedness, treat Japan as a dependent and thus are harmful to the Japanese national integrity and pride and that Japan, therefore, should seek to defend itself in order to achieve a genuine equality in the international arena. As was noted in Chapter 5, the latent pressure within big business and industry for military expansion recently became increasingly manifest and, under stress and strain of economic problems, it would add a powerful impetus to those nationalist and rightist feelings. Our suggestions would repress or deflect some of the dangerous tendencies among these groups. By so doing, they would also help reduce the genuine leftist fears of the danger of a militarist revival in and the acquisition of strategic weapons by their nation. Moreover, while strategic defense of the nation would still militarily rest with the United States, the force integration for its tactical defense would reduce the likelihood that the United States would have to invoke its strategic capability to defend it, hence involve it in a potential superpower confrontation, by raising the political level of deterrence against an enemy attack. Japan, in short, would be much safer both from the external danger to its security and from the internal threat against its democracy.

In terms of Japanese-U.S. relations, our two suggestions would help assuage the legitimate unhappiness of the United States significantly. In security terms, the unhappiness arose out of U.S. anxiety that the JSDF, even with the ultimate backing of the USFJ, could not adequately defend Japan against even a limited, small-scale aggression, and thus in the end would force a strategic response by the United States. This fundamental unhappiness has for a number of years been expressed in criticisms of the level of Japan's military spending and thus distorted the character of the basic issue of its security requirements as such on the part of both Japan and the United States. Our suggestions, in an important sense, are an attempt, as we alluded to earlier in the present chapter, to shift the thrust of the basic issue away from fiscal disagreement, which is really ancillary. Even in fiscal terms, our suggestions would call for a significant increase in Japan's contribution to its own defense through an outlay for the cost of force integration, and the expansion of the ASDF and MSDF for the purpose of effective supportive and supplementary participation in the maintenance of Western Pacific security, which until now has been the sole responsibility of the United States. If all this could be done, as we believe it could be, within a proportion of Japan's GNP that is considerably smaller than that of the United States or any other nation's, that should not be a cause of their resentment. Effectiveness of defense and security consists not in how big a budget is expended but in efficiently and economically meeting its fundamental requirements. (In the interest of international fiscal equity, we will later in this chapter propose that Japan raise its developmental assistance and other contributions to international efforts to the level that, combined with its defense spending, would, as a proportion of GNP, approximate that of defense and developmental aid expenditures of other advanced industrial states.) Both force integration and Japan's participation in the heretofore sole U.S. task of defending the Western Pacific would help raise the level of deterrence against potential troublemakers and thus correspondingly reduce the undesirable and ultimately appalling necessity of the United States to invoke its strategic nuclear capability. As we have repeatedly observed, Japan's active participation in the defense of the Western Pacific would also afford the United States greater flexibility and mobility in responding to contingencies in the region as well as outside, and thus increase the effectiveness of the U.S. role in the strategic defense of East Asia and elsewhere.

As for Japan's East Asian neighbors, our suggestions might indeed be attractive, perhaps even to Vietnam. The principal security concern shared by most of them in recent years, especially ASEAN states, has been the pronouncedly lowered level of U.S. military presence after the Vietnam War, and this concern in the meantime has gradually given rise, as was discussed earlier in this chapter, to an expectation, albeit still characterized by ambivalence, for Japan to play a significant security role in the region. This expectation at least in part was precipitated by its neighbors' growing unhappiness about its preoccupation with economic pursuits both at home and abroad, and by ascertainable reluctance to assume diplomatic and security responsibility commensurate with its growing economic power. Many of its neighbors have come to grumble that Japan has international political responsibility precisely because it is a major economic power. To this extent, their desire that Japan play a significant security role in the Western Pacific area is becoming increasingly explicit, if not official. Their remaining ambivalence toward Japan, however, would seem to dictate, as we mentioned earlier, that it play such a security role within the framework of its security pact with the United States. It is indeed significant that there seems to have emerged a spontaneous convergence of views in this regard: The United States, Japan, as well as their East Asian friends all now regard the security pact as the basis for a stable international order in East Asia. Thus, the suggestion of Japan's supportive and supplementary participation in the defense of the Western Pacific should be entirely consistent with the East Asian expectation. Japan would not act independently and outside the framework of its security partnership with the United States. It would only be bolstering the defense of the region's sealanes and affording the United States a greater effectiveness in the performance of its strategic security role in the maintenance of stability of the region at large. Japan's role would be only functionally complementary to the primary U.S. military responsibility and thus effectively remain under U.S. restraint. Thus, our suggestion would help assuage the security concern of East Asian nations and materially improve the prospects of stability and security of the region. The Japanese-U.S. force integration for tactical defense of Japan, given its particular purpose and thrust, would also help further reduce whatever apprehension East Asian states might still entertain about the prospects of Japan becoming a major military power. In one sense, our suggestions would produce a political insurance against the rise of a militarist and expansionist Japan.

It should be obvious that all particulars and specifics germane to each of the two general suggestions would have to be thoroughly discussed and negotiated by the parties concerned. All in all, however, especially when all likely or probable alternatives in terms of policy direction, domestic consequences and ramifications, external repercussions, and fiscal and political impact are considered, the general lines of action that the two suggestions point to would seem to be far more effective in safeguarding Japan's external security and internal political health, more beneficial to the promotion of safety of the Western Pacific waters and stability of East Asia, more consolidative to Japanese-U.S. security relations, and far less costly for both nations. They would provide Japan with the best possible and most cost-effective insurance for its security without its having to become a major military power; they would therefore reduce the likelihood of the United States having to invoke its conventional or nuclear capability in Japan's behalf; they would enable the United States to perform its strategic security role in East Asia more effectively and flexibly; and, perhaps most important for Japanese-U.S. relations, they would promote equity and reciprocity, which are the vital ingredients of mutual trust and cooperation.

SECURITY THREATS AND JAPAN'S DIPLOMATIC ROLE

Military arrangements are but part of the total security provision for a nation or a region. They are made so that they may not have to be tested in battle. In an attempt to resolve disagreements, manage problems, resolve issues, and thus obviate open conflicts, what nations hope to use instead is diplomacy. In the use of this primary instrument of managing international relations, Japan ought to take a positive posture in a number of areas. It has in the past been content to rely on the "natural trend" of events and, in its relationship with the United States, to follow its lead more or less passively. This passivity, caused in large measure by its politophobic orientation as discussed in Chapter 6, deprived Japan of the use of an ability and influence that inhere in its status as an economic superpower. To the extent that the Japanese-U.S. security partnership is the key to the stability and orderly development of East Asia, Japan should determine to utilize the ability and influence at its disposal for the promotion of security in the region, and this particularly since the U.S. political and diplomatic influence has suffered a relative decline.

Japan's primary focus in diplomacy throughout the postwar period has been economic; its increasing economic power has seldom been employed as an effective means of diplomacy in the political context or for an explicitly political objective either regionally or globally. Under the changed and still changing international circumstances in and around East Asia, however, Japan, if it is to remain stable and secure, and, equally important, if it genuinely seeks "an honored place in the international community,"(24) must endeavor to do its best in order to influence the course of events in the region and to help determine the character of its outcome in the direction it apparently deems necessary and desirable. For this, Japan must translate its economic power into political influence. Officials and observers alike recognize this necessity, but there still persists anxiety about how to do it. Japan is yet to make a lasting psychological and diplomatic breakthrough in its attempt at this important power conversion.

Given its "commitment capacity"(25) both as a preeminent economic power in the region and as a "potential" military power,

Japan is clearly and inevitably in a position to play an influential role as a mediator in a number of seemingly refractory issues that have plagued the region, and, in so doing, help reduce the level of tension, instability, and uncertainty that pervade it. Several security issues readily suggest themselves as presenting opportunities and challenges for such a role to be played by Japan.

THE KOREAN PENINSULA

The conflict between North and South Korea is the oldest surviving security issue in East Asia. Virtually all parties concerned (the two Koreas, Japan, the United States, China, and the Soviet Union) desire some kind of resolution or at least peaceful management of the issue that has eluded it for a generation. The primary question has for some time now been that of how. Spasmodic attempts by the two Koreas themselves at bilateral negotiations have been precisely that – spasmodic – owing to abiding mutual distrust, although at times their concern with the need for some kind of mutual accommodation has been genuine. North Korea has also indicated from time to time in recent years its desire to open a dialogue with the United States regarding the issue, but the so-called Kissinger formula,(26) which prohibits Washington from bilateral contacts with Pyongyang (prohibition demanded by Seoul, of course), has thus far additionally reduced options available for the resolution of the issue. Japanese officials on their part have maintained that the cultivation of an appropriate "international atmosphere" around the issue ought to be the first order of business, and, to some extent, Japan's attempts to expand the range of relations with North Korea in all but the formal diplomatic area while maintaining the existing close formal as well as economic ties with South have been consistent with this objective. Characteristically, however, Japan, in these dealings with North as well as South Korea, has been wary of political discussions of the issue. It is about time it took a bolder step than it has thus far ventured to undertake, especially since the "international atmosphere" surrounding the issue has already significantly changed. The normalization of relations between Washington and Peking, China's apparent eagerness for U.S. and Japanese economic, technological, and trade assistance for its ambitious modernization program, its clearly indicated desire to avoid any recurrence of violence on the peninsula, the equally strong Soviet disinclination to support Pyongyang in another military venture,(27) and Pyongyang's ambiguous but nonetheless more restrained posture vis-à-vis Seoul in recent years, among other developments, indeed seem cumulatively to have created an atmosphere in which Japan could take discreet but critical initiative to push the issue in the direction of stabilizing the North-South relationship. In an important sense, Japan is the only one among the six nations directly concerned that not only could but should make the first critical response to this challenge. The United States is militarily aligned with South Korea, with its senior general on the peninsula in overall command of all forces there, including those of the Republic of Korea (ROK). China, however eagerly her current leaders may wish to see the Korean issue resolved, could not openly withdraw its support for Pyongyang's official goal of peninsular unification; nor can the Soviet Union. Japan, in short, is the only nation with the level of political maneuverability required for taking initiative for immediate and concrete steps toward a stable and peaceful management, if not the ultimate resolution, of the issue. Its hands are clean, so to speak, while every other concerned state's hands are still soiled from their violent involvement in the war on the peninsula three decades ago, and its subsequent military and political alignment with one or the other of the principal antagonists.

Japan should employ the economic influence it has come to possess in China, South Korea, and, to a certain extent, even North Korea to this end. Put simply, Japan should make it clear to China, South Korea, and North Korea (and also seek U.S. support in this effort) that its economic and technological assistance to their modernization program as well as trade expansion would be an integral part of the whole process of regional development, stabilization, and security. North Korea requires peninsular stability so that it may concentrate on its internal economic development, which apparently has lagged far behind its southern adversary's. It will soon face also the internal problem of succession, and political stability of its regime adequately to manage the problem would be predicated upon sufficient economic and social stability. South Korea, in turn, badly needs stability of relations with North so that it may be able to devote its energy to internal political stabilization and institutionalization. China, too, would be hard-pressed if some serious destabilizing contingency were to arise on the peninsula, for, in such an event, it could politically ill-afford to permit the Soviet Union to be Pyongyang's sole ally and supporter, and, at the very same time, Peking's involvement on the peninsula, however reluctant it may be, would have serious repercussions on its domestic modernization and on its relations with the United States. The Soviet predicament in the event would be similar to China's. For reasons discussed a bit earlier, none of these nations would be able to pursue a wholly new path of North-South reconciliation on its own initiative. They are, in one sense or another, however, all in search of pretext for departing from their respective past policies that have become so rigid as to constitute a serious constraint in seeking the peaceful management and resolution they now desire.

Even an agreement on peaceful management of the issue could not be arrived at overnight, of course. Discreet and informal negotiations could, however, be immediately initiated by Japan, first with Peking and Washington to secure their covert backing or at least acquiescence. All aspects of these negotiations with the parties concerned should be undertaken sub rosa until such time as would be politically safe for the parties to admit the goings-on. Initial Soviet backing or acquiescence would be desirable but not imperative because it would be necessary to impress on Moscow over the next several years that its role in East Asian affairs is or should be lesser than that of other nations concerned. Upon obtaining tacit support from China and the United States, Japan should commence equally discreet and informal separate negotiations with Pyonyang and Seoul, judiciously calibrating its economic commitment capacity as a major means of political suasion. Those negotiations would prove difficult and even protracted, for the mutual enmity between the two Koreas that has become deeply embedded in their attitude toward each other would pose serious psychological and political obstacles to any expeditious agreement between the principals. It might not be too far-fetched, however, to speculate that a peace conference could be convened in Tokyo participated in by the two principal antagonists, China and the United States, with Japan acting as sponsor, even as chairman. The Soviet Union, for its own sometimes unfathomable reasons, might well attempt to undermine the process of this scenario, but once a sufficient consensus were achieved among the four major combatants of the Korean War, it, too, in the end might well find it advantageous or necessary, again for its own reasons, to become part of an international arrangement guaranteeing peace and stability on the peninsula, particularly since it would quite obviously include the withdrawal of U.S. forces from the peninsula. What that arrangement would in fact be, of course, cannot be foretold, but several options or aspects of what would finally transpire might be suggested.

Given the sharp difference between the two Koreas in socio-economic structure, developmental pattern, and political and ideological orientation and given their generation-old mutual animosity compounded by fratricidal bloodshed and violence, it would be unreasonable to expect that they could agree on any kind of meaningful "national unification." The best that could be hoped for would be peaceful coexistence. To this practicable end, some kind of "German solution" would seem appropriate, with the international community recognizing both Koreas as sovereign states, preceded by the conclusion of a formal peace treaty between the principals. The UN forces in South Korea would be withdrawn. Given the potentials in each Korea for internal political instability and the danger of its spilling over their common border, however, it may well be advisable, as one Japanese expert recommended, that the current demilitarized zone (DMZ) be maintained by a UN peace-keeping force, and, at the same time, certain mutually acceptable reductions of armed forces should be undertaken by both Koreas, with all nations recognizing their regimes' pledging never to supply arms or troops to either.(28) One alternative to the last point would be a three-power (China, the United States, and the Soviet Union) or four-power (including Japan) guarantee of security and territorial integrity of each Korea, similar to the one applying to Austria since 1954. Underlying all these and other likely aspects of an international arrangement for peace and stability of Korea would be the crucial role Japan's economic power could play. Japan should use its power here as a political incentive for Pyongyang and Seoul to move toward mutual accommodation and peaceful coexistence. The kind of development suggested here – quite obviously highly inaccurate in certain specifics that would actually transpire and equally highly general in the direction and contour of what Japan in fact could do – would be extremely significant for Japanese diplomacy. Japan would, for the first time in history, be acting as a peace-maker, not as a trouble-maker as before 1945 or as a diplomatic eunuch since. It would also demonstrate its "sincere" commitment to the pursuit of peace not only to the two Koreas for whose postwar mutual conflict it had been responsible in more senses than one, but also to the rest of East Asia as well as to the world at large. Such concrete demonstration of its sincerity for peace would further reduce whatever residual fear and misgivings its neighbors may still retain toward it. Japan would become more trustworthy to them. It would also relieve the United States of the costly enterprise of maintaining its military forces in Korea. The threat to Japan's security from the peninsula would be diminished. The fear that North Korea and even the Soviet Union have been alleged to entertain of a potential ROK-U.S.-Japanese military alliance, which some circles suggested is in the offing, would also be dissipated.(29) All this would constitute a giant step toward stability and security in Northeast Asia in particular and East Asia in general.

Indochina

Apart from the Sino-Soviet quarrel that has affected it and has in turn been affected by it, the problem of Indochina involves several conflicts: Sino-Vietnamese, U.S.-Vietnamese, ASEAN-Vietnamese, and, to a lesser extent, ASEAN-Chinese. The resolution of the issue would require more or less simultaneous resolutions of these conflicts, for these different conflicts seem mutually reinforcing in terms of deterioration and complementary in terms of peaceful disposition.

The degree of visceral animosity between China and Vietnam that developed especially since mid-1977 would seem far less than that between North and South Korea that hardened over a whole generation. The extent of Sino-Vietnamese combat, destruction, and casualty during their border war in the spring of 1979 was only a fraction of what the Korean War had involved early in the 1950s.

The number of ethnic Chinese fleeing from Vietnam into China, while considerable in absolute numbers, was infinitesimal relative to the total population in China, in contrast to the impact of refugees that fled from North Korea to South before the truce in 1953.(30) The issue between Peking and Hanoi, moreover, does not seem to be the kind that would spontaneously inflame and perpetuate an abiding national passion as that between the two Koreas. It would rather appear to be of the type in which mutual animosity was provoked at least in part by differential perceptions of the policy and commitment of a third party or parties and was compounded by economic considerations. As such, it might more readily lend itself than, say, the Korean issue.

The U.S.-Vietnamese impasse, the resolution of which might prove to be the essential prerequisite for that of the Sino-Vietnamese conflict, would seem much less intractable than the Hanoi-Peking quarrel. True, the United States did not achieve "peace with honor" when it withdrew from Vietnam. True, Hanoi conquered Saigon by its arms immediately upon the U.S. withdrawal in violation of the Paris peace accords. Later, Hanoi's brutal expulsion of ethnic Chinese and other "undesirable" elements from Vietnam created the massive refugee problem forcing the United States to take in nearly 200,000 of them as permanent residents, in spite of racial, ethnic, and socioeconomic problems it already faced internally. The expulsion was followed by the Vietnamese membership in COMECON, the Hanoi-Moscow Treaty of Friendship and cooperation, and the launching of the Vietnamese invasion of Cambodia. Everything Vietnam did after the U.S. withdrawal was unacceptable to Washington. Accordingly, the United States steadfastly refused to establish diplomatic relations with Vietnam and to provide economic assistance mentioned in the Paris accords on which Hanoi had counted quite eagerly. Not everything Vietnam did,however,seemedunavoidable.Someactions,clearly,wereinevitable: for example, Hanoi's unification of Vietnam by militarily overthrowing the Saigon regime, given its decades-long commitment to it; and the military conflict with Pol Pot's Cambodia in view of the latter's utter intransigence regarding its territorial disagreement with Vietnam and forcible expulsion of Vietnamese from the disputed territory as well as from Cambodia proper (the Pol Pot regime insisted that no negotiations could be held until all Vietnamese left Cambodia and rejected Hanoi's call for a ceasefire and withdrawal of their respective forces from the border area).(31) Others, for example, Hanoi's membership in COMECON and treaty with Moscow, and the deterioration of Sino-Vietnamese relations toward their war, may well have been avoidable. The refusal of the United States to recognize Hanoi formally may have been a crucial factor abetting these developments. One senior American diplomat in Tokyo quite frankly dismissed the present author's suggestion that having a diplomatic mission in Hanoi would have given Washington some influence over Vietnamese behavior, but there is reason to believe that Hanoi's conduct (hence China's and the Soviet Union's) might have been significantly moderated if the United States had recognized Hanoi or at least had indicated its willingness to discuss the formal recognition, and at the very least entered into some kind of negotiations over economic assistance. Reasons for Washington's refusal to do so were understandable; indeed, they were not very astute politically and in terms in East Asian regional security. Hanoi had sought, even desperately, rapprochement with Washington since 1975 and tried to achieve it in a number of ways,(32) in vain. (Vietnam, in 1978, even dropped its persistent demand for "reparation" funds — originally cited as $5 billion — from the United States, clearly indicating its desire for rapprochement with the United States.) As was briefly discussed in Chapter 4, Hanoi's initial problem that led to its membership in COMECON and the treaty with Moscow, even its expulsion of ethnic Chinese, was economic, much of it its own making to be sure. Assistance that Peking had been providing Hanoi was relatively modest because of Peking's own domestic requirements. If its withdrawal indeed precipitated the rise of Soviet influence over Vietnam, then Hanoi's membership in COMECON and closer tie with Moscow might well have been prevented had the United States been forthcoming. Actual events that subsequently took place, however, only made the Hanoi-Washington rapprochement more difficult.

The tension between ASEAN and Vietnam had been dormant before the explosion of the refugee problem because of the former's anticommunism and apprehension about the latter's oft-proclaimed goal of establishing a greater federation of Indochina, and became greatly exacerbated by the refugee problem and the Vietnamese invasion of Cambodia, and, more recently, by the immediate security threat posed against Thailand as a consequence of the manner of Vietnamese pursuit of Pol Pot guerrilla forces near the Thai-Cambodian border. ASEAN is unanimous in its stand regarding defense and security of Thailand and has taken an unusually militant stand in this regard, as was reported in Chapter 4. With respect to Vietnam's virtual domination of Indochina, however, there is considerable discord among ASEAN states, again as discussed in Chapter 4. It is significant, however, that the latest (that is, as of this writing) meeting of ASEAN foreign ministers, while deploring Vietnam for threatening Thailand in the strongest language, nevertheless referred to the Cambodia issue as calling for "political solution" by ASEAN and Vietnam and that ASEAN would continue its dialogue with Vietnam.(33) Only a year earlier, ASEAN was demanding complete withdrawal of Vietnam from Cambodia.

These circumstances would seem to suggest that the resolution of the three conflicts revolving around Indochina would require several considerations that the parties concerned ought to contemplate. They include, among others: the acceptability of some kind of Indochinese federation as a more viable and stabilizing peninsular political arrangement than the traditional trifurcated division whose instability in and among its parts rendered it vulnerable to competitive external interference; an explicit pledge by Vietnam (and, if necessary, Cambodia and Laos) never to threaten the security and territorial integrity of Thailand; a similar pledge by China and Vietnam to each other; U.S. recognition of Vietnam; joint or coordinated economic, technologic and food assistance to Vietnam by Japan and the United States; and commitment by Vietnam (and Cambodia) to prevent further outflow of refugees into neighboring states and to guarantee safe return and resettlement of those already in Thailand (as well as those willing to return from elsewhere) in their home district. These would no doubt be very difficult conditions, but not insurmountable ones, unless the prevailing condition in and over Indochina were allowed to deteriorate. The continuation of the current condition would sooner or later lead to a point where it would become impossible for Vietnam to extricate itself from the Soviet grip and where the whole of Indochina might in fact become Moscow's advance base in Southeast Asia. When this point is reached, it would be irrational or otherwise impossible for other parties concerned even to acquiesce in any kind of Indochinese federation. To obviate this dangerous point is a critical task, and to this end, Japan should and could play an important mediative role.

Vietnam's desire for Japanese capital, technology, and even rice had been strong well before Japan established formal relations with Hanoi.(34) After 1975, Japan followed its recognition of Hanoi with modest but relatively significant economic and food assistance, and considerably expanded trade with it until 1980 when the international clamor over the Vietnamese military threat to Thai security forced it to suspend the aid programs to Vietnam. In the meantime, Tokyo did little to translate its economic assistance to Hanoi into an instrument of political suasion, as was noted in Chapter 6. Again, its commitment capacity should be invoked in order to link it to the resolution of the three external conflicts in which Vietnam has been engaged. To this end, Japan would have strong support from ASEAN which was earlier disappointed by its failure to exert any significant diplomatic influence on Hanoi before and after the Vietnamese invasion of Cambodia. ASEAN itself has rather limited abilities to steer Vietnamese conduct since it does not possess much by way of what Hanoi needs. Instead of supporting ASEAN efforts to influence Hanoi, therefore, Japan should take a strong diplomatic initiative that ASEAN could support. Such an initiative, of course, should be endorsed by Washington as well. Once there is a critical agreement among Japan, ASEAN, and the United States, China which maintains the most hard-lining attitude toward Vietnam among the parties concerned, would most likely be persuaded to go along.(35) In this process, Tokyo would have to use its commitment capability as a means of suasion over the Chinese whose domestic stability would clearly hinge on the success of the ongoing modernization program. Vis-à-vis Washington, which might prove to be less readily forthcoming as one may assume, Tokyo could even link the issue of Hanoi-Washington rapprochement to Japan's increased share of the security costs for East Asia (that is, its participation in the maintenance of Western Pacific security). Japan could even offer to underwrite such assistance programs to Vietnam as Hanoi had hoped in earlier years from the United States for the time being, affording the United States a "decent interval" between the time of rapprochement and the time when it would feel less domestic political constraint in providing assistance to Hanoi.

These are but a few of many alternative techniques that Japan could employ in active promotion of stability in and over Indochina, and each of them would encounter a range of difficulties. How those difficulties could be overcome would depend on the skill and discretion with which Tokyo pursues the goal. It would seem clear, however, that it could not successfully pursue the goal unless it is willing to translate its economic ability and commitment capacity into political suasion. Moscow no doubt would resist such efforts on the part of Japan through a variety of direct and indirect means, but if Hanoi were persuaded of the long-range attractiveness of what the resolution of those three major external conflicts would entail in terms of economic, technical, and other assistance from Japan and eventually from the United States and resumption of aid from other Western nations, it might well decide to reverse the direction it has taken since 1977 regarding the Soviet Union and COMECON. In an important sense, a meaningful option should be made available to Hanoi. Considering the logistical difficulties involved, the Soviet Union would be unlikely to undertake the kind of politicomilitary venture against Vietnam that it launched against Afghanistan in December 1979, Czechoslovakia in August 1968, or it would most likely launch against Poland if the current (Spring 1981) tension between the Warsaw regime and the Solidarity movement were not resolved to its liking. When it comes to competitive developmental assistance to Vietnam, Moscow would be readily outperformed by Tokyo and Washington.

The ambiguous relationship between ASEAN and China is at least in part the function of tension and instability in and over Indochina and some of its consequences and impact upon the still volatile "Chinese problem" in some of the ASEAN states. To this extent, the ambiguity of ASEAN-China relations (that is, ASEAN fear of China) would be greatly reduced if the three major conflicts discussed above were resolved.

Clearly, what has been suggested thus far regarding the positive mediative role Japan should play in steering the problems in and over Korea and Indochina in the direction of peaceful resolution is ambitious both because it would require extraordinary diplomatic skill and perseverance and because Japan, habituated to evasion of international political responsibility, would have difficulty in finding secure diplomatic footing and courage to take up such a formidable responsibility. We shall have something more to say about this in the final chapter. Suffice it at this moment to suggest that Japan really has no meaningful alternatives to assuming the responsibility because of the unique position it occupies in East Asia and the power that inheres in it. Passivity on the part of a major nation is an impediment to its long-range interest as well as to the stability of the region in which it is located. Again, a nation's, especially a major nation's, international role and responsibility are defined not by that nations own preference or inclination but by the character of its international environment.

Japan's omnidirectional diplomacy has in fact been merely an omnidirectional trade policy divorced from any identifiable long-term political considerations. If it is to mean anything at all beyond a general external trade program disguised as diplomacy, then the problems of Korea and Indochina provide unique opportunities as well as formidable challenges for Japan to test its political mettle and the sincerity of its protestations of friendship, cooperation, heart-to-heart understanding, and promotion of peace, progress, and security in East Asia. In fact, Japan does seem to enjoy some advantages, besides its economic power, that other nations in the region do not. In an important sense, the fact that Japan has in the whole postwar period abstained from external political involvement could be turned into an advantage. Past liability should not be permitted to hamper future actions of a nation; it should be turned into an asset. Japan's postwar political hands are clean and its mutually contentious neighbors who have been frustrated by the seeming intractability of their disharmony and conflict and have become wary of one another's overtures for management and resolution of their disagreements might well listen to it with the kind of open-mindedness that they could not have toward one another, precisely because Japan has said little so far and done even less. Backed by its indubitable economic ability, this liability turned into asset might confer upon Japan the kind of power and suasion it never suspected it possessed. It should endeavor to maximize this power by judiciously calibrating the levels, the kinds, and the contexts of economic inducements. Only be resolutely pursuing the task discussed above in this manner could it demonstrate to the world that it has at last come of age, a genuine major power.

JAPAN AND UN PEACE-KEEPING ACTIVITIES

Related to the necessity of an active Japanese diplomacy in the promotion of stability in East Asia is Japan's role in UN peace-keeping activities. Here, too, there is a critical need for a positive shift in Japan's approach to them, if it is to act as a major nation genuinely concerned about peace and stability in East Asia as well as elsewhere in the world, and if its credibility as such a nation is to be seriously taken. In the past, Japan never went beyond the mere act of paying amounts of financial contribution assessed by the United Nations for various peace-keeping missions and refused any further involvement in those missions. Its enormous economic ability made it quite easy, at least in the eyes of other nations, for Japan to make monetary contributions to these missions. After all, amounts assessed against Japan in those efforts were quite insignificant given the magnitude of its GNP or government revenue. Even here, however, Japan's record is not all good. For example, during a two-year period between the fall of 1973 and the fall of 1975, Japan was requested by the United Nations to contribute $11.4 million to the costs of UN Emergency Forces (UNEF) and UN Disengagement Observer Forces (UNDOF). (For the same period, the U.S.'s share was $46.2 million, the USSR's $24.0 million and West Germany's $11.3 million, to cite but a few examples.) Of the amount requested, Japan paid only $8.6 million, leaving the largest unpaid amount ($2.9 million) among relevant UN members except for China which refused to pay any part of the amount assessed against it.(36) When the United Nations dispatched a peace-keeping force to Cyprus late in 1974, Japan was among a number of nations making "voluntary" financial contributions toward the force's costs, but its contribution consisted of a piddling $300,000, which was only three-quarters of small Sweden's contribution, one-third of West Germany's, and a fraction of that of the United States (which contributed $9.6 million) and Britain's (more than $3.3 million) and only slightly larger than Holland's.(37) (How piddling a sum $300,000 in fact was might become even more distinct when we consider that, during the Liberal Democratic Party's 1972 convention held to elect its president/premier-designate, anywhere between $40,000 and $80,000 per head was reported to have been circulated among some 480 delegates. The party never denied or challenged the report.)

Japan's refusal to participate in UN peace-keeping missions was officially based on "constitutional" as well as "legal" restrictions. Its government argued that the postwar Constitution prohibited participation of any UN activity involving the use of arms and that, even when the activity did not involve the use of arms, the existing law governing the JSDF did not permit any of their elements to participate since it assigned no such duty to them. Additionally (or, at times, alternatively), the government stated that even though Article 51 of the UN Charter recognized the right of nations to collective security, the Japanese Constitution did not recognize such a right for Japan.

These arguments, however, have always seemed highly contrived, hence questionable, even though no other member of the United nations has ever publicly raised the issue against Japan. In the first place, the San Francisco Peace Treaty, which restored Japan as a sovereign state and a member of the international community, stipulated (in Article III, Paragraph 5), and a later exchange of official memoranda between the Japanese prime minister and the U.S. secretary of state (the heads of their respective national delegations to the signing of the treaty) affirmed, Japan's assumption of the UN Charter obligations, including those stipulated in Article 51. In the revised security pact with the United States (1960), Japan did reaffirm its "inherent right of individual or collective self-defense as affirmed in the Charter of the United Nations." Second, the Preamble of the postwar Constitution, which in part states "we have determined to preserve our security and existence, trusting in the justice and faith of the peace-loving peoples of the world," could not possibly mean that, while Japan should rely on other nations to help it defend itself against attack and violence, it has no reciprocal obligations or that it should always remain a special ward of the international community. (In this connection, it is important to recall that Principle 5 of the Basic Policies for National Defense quoted at the outset of Chapter 5 states the need to build up Japan's defense capability "pending more effective functioning of the United Nations in the future in deterring and repelling such aggression.") Third, if the Japanese government seriously desired to participate in UN peace-keeping activities but felt that the existing law governing the JSDF did not clearly permit such participation (a contention that in itself is dubious), then presumably it could modify the law at issue accordingly.

The arguments of the Japanese government regarding its refusal to participate in UN peace-keeping activities sounded contrived, hence questionable, precisely because they were, arising as they did out of the collective national politophobia discussed in Chapter 6 from which the nation's avoidance of realpolitik was induced. They were, therefore, neither constitutional nor legal but psychological. In any event, Japan's obvious preference to "buy" its way out of more serious kinds of contribution to UN peace-keeping efforts (perhaps one of the few vital practical functions of the world organization) has given the world an impression similar to that of the draft-age son of a wealthy South Vietnamese citizen in the 1960s or a rich merchant in Nationalist China in the 1930s and 1940s who bought his way out of the compulsory military service for the nation at war.(38) As one Defense Agency official commented to the author, Japan is rich, so it is no great sacrifice for it to give money to UN peace-keeping missions. What the Japanese as a nation should do, he went on to suggest, was to demonstrate to the world their genuine commitment to world peace and security by their readiness to shed their own blood for the defense of threatened nations. Indeed, in the eyes of the world at large and especially those nations that expect Japan to play a positive international role commensurate with its power, Japan would continue to look selfish and devious if it continued to insist on monetary expenditure as a substitute for a more serious kind of contribution to UN efforts. Japan's protestations of commitment to peace, freedom, and stability of the world would remain suspect, even blatantly hypocritical.

Fortunately, there is some evidence that suggests that Japan may be beginning to shift its attitude toward UN peace-keeping activities in the direction that the preceding paragraph implied. In the fall of 1980, the issue of whether Japan could participate in those activities, which had remained dormant for some years, was resurrected by members of parliamentary opposition, in part precipitated by a call for its consideration made in a recent policy paper prepared by the Foreign Ministry's Security Policy Planning Committee.(39) That the new key policy group within the Foreign Ministry urged such consideration was in itself significant, but more interesting was the cabinet response to the opposition query. While still claiming to adhere to the traditional official position that the Constitution did not permit JSDF participation in any UN activity involving combat, the cabinet's written "answer" stated that JSDF participation in a mission not involving combat or use of arms in discharging its objective was not necessarily forbidden, and that the government would give positive considerations to providing noncombat personnel and material to peace-keeping missions, and to dispatching civilian officials to the proposed UN observer group to Namibia to monitor its independence and free elections.(40) The extent to which the cabinet response to the issue in fact departed from past practice is difficult to ascertain, but there was clearly a kind of positive wording, as well as deliberate ambiguity, that had in the past been lacking. In a society imbued with the consensual mode of decision making and the leadership style that it dictates, it is to be expected that the government would move with utmost deliberateness and caution in bringing about any significant policy change or shift. Given the fact that even some of the more "pacifist"-oriented critics began to urge using JSDF personnel for combating international terrorist activities, medical duties, and handling refugees in various parts of the world,(41) it may well be that the Japanese government has taken a first step toward cultivating a new consensus about more positive and serious ways in which the nation could participate in vital UN peace-keeping activities.

The current intention of the Japanese government apart, it is clear that Japan should seriously consider the participation in those UN activities, in addition to complying with whatever financial requests the United Nations might make of it toward their maintenance. To this end, the current law governing the JSDF should be so modified as explicitly to permit such participation. (Since Japan refused to comply with the UN secretary general's request in 1958 for cooperation with the dispatch of an observation group, the United Nations has not made a similar request to the Japanese government. It might help push Japan in the right direction if the United Nations were to make a formal request for Japanese participation in one such of the current or future peace-keeping missions, by sending small JSDF contingents even as medical or logistical corps.) Japan's past noninvolvement would seem to render it suitable for participation in a number of peace-keeping missions in such less Cold War-sensitive areas as Cyprus, the Golan Heights, or even in the Sinai Peninsula, or, if it comes to pass, on the Thai-Cambodian border, the demilitarized zone in Korea, or even on the Sino-Vietnamese border. Japan's participation in this regard would be viewed by the world as another positive sign of Japan's seriousness as a major power worthy of its status.

JAPAN'S ROLE IN DEVELOPMENT AND MODERNIZATION: EAST ASIA AND BEYOND

Japan is in a unique position to undertake diplomatic initiative for the management and resolution of existing conflicts in East Asia. Even if successful, however, such management and resolution can be rendered durable only if nations concerned feel secure about their respective national viability and resilience. This is particularly the case in East Asia since many of the existing conflicts are rooted in problems of socioeconomic modernization and political development. The extent to which a developed nation such as Japan could help any developing nation overcome those problems is obviously circumscribed, for how and at what pace such modernization and development takes place or can be engineered depends primarily upon the character and quality of indigenous political leadership that alone can utilize and manipulate existing conditions, institutions, and resources for the purpose of progress.(42) The only way in which an advanced state could help a developing nation, then, would be to make available to it certain conditions or resources that would help reduce the obstacles it faces or increase its ability to overcome them. One such condition, of course, is a stable external environment, to the creation of which Japan, as we have suggested, could and therefore should make significant contribution. Another is economic and technological resources, and this, too, Japan can and therefore should offer in a manner that would be most contributive to the developing nation's progress and stability.

Japan's recent record of developmental assistance to Third World nations is by no means outstanding. From 1975 to 1979, Japan was one of only two major advanced industrial nations to offer less than 0.3 percent of their respective GNPs as official developmental aid (ODA) (the other was the United States), while such relatively small industrial states as Sweden, Norway, and Holland contributed over 0.9 percent of their GNPs as ODA.(43) Moreover, for the year 1978, for example, of the $1.53 billion Japan allocated for ODA, only $162 million was in the form of outright grants.(44) The Development Assistance Committee of the Organization for Economic Cooperation and Development (OECD) recommended in 1978 that its member nations raise ODA to 0.7 percent of their respective GNPs by 1985.(45) Domestic economic and political constraints would obviously make it difficult for Japan (or, for that matter, any nation today) to meet this target, but some approximation of the recommended figure should be pursued. Despite the apparently earnest contention of many Japanese officials interviewed by the author that their nation is doing the best it could to help developing nations, the contention would seem no more convincing than another traditional official Japanese protestation that the nation was doing the best it could for national defense.

Of the relatively modest ODA contribution it has been making in recent years, Japan has directed a major proportion (approximately 40 percent) to Southeast Asia. This is quite appropriate inasmuch as Southeast Asia is potentially or latently the most volatile part of East Asia and its development and stability are the key to the future of East Asia. Because of political and ideological problems involved, Japan has contributed relatively small amounts to Northeast Asia (less than 4 percent of its ODA and confined to South Korea and Taiwan) until now. China and North Korea would remain questionable areas for which Japan would undertake official developmental assistance for reasons that were discussed in Chapter 4, but these same reasons would also seem to warrant that Japan consider ODA for these communist states not only as a means of helping them modernize and thus achieve political stability but also as an instrument of political influence with the view to preventing them from destabilizing conduct. This of course, is much easier said than done, but as a general proposition, it is consistent with and integrative of the kind of direction in which we argued that Japan's positive diplomatic role vis-à-vis security threats in the region should be projected. Japan should carefully consider ways in which it could be most effectively implemented.

Beyond East Asia, Japan's ODA, as did its private investment, focused on oil-rich nations in the Persian Gulf and Middle East areas (nearly one-quarter of the total), but relatively little in Africa and Latin America. To a considerable extent, both in East Asia and elsewhere, Japan's ODA program reflected its economic preoccupation in its external policy. ODA, however, is an economic means of diplomacy, that is, of promoting international stability and, in order to achieve its goal, its implementation should be based ultimately on political consideration. Part of Japan's ODA policy, then, should be based, not on response or reaction to the occurrence of events (for example, threat of Arab petropolitics, manifest political instability in a nation on which Japan already depends for the supply of some key resources, or the current attractiveness or necessity of a key commodity in a region or a nation) but rather on a long-range anticipation of occurrence of alternative events relating to the issue of international stability and instability. In East Asia itself, this is the kind of consideration that might lead to an expanded ODA program, however phrased or channelled, for, say, Vietnam, no matter how unpalatable to Japan its current policy and orientation may be.   ODA is, first and foremost, a political investment (and, like any investment, it is accompanied by risk of failure).   In regions beyond East Asia, long-term considerations would surely warrant that Japan pay more attention to various selective parts of Africa and Latin America that are variously volatile and unpredictable as to future behavior.

Given its past record with respect to ODA, one way of demonstrating its genuine commitment to the promotion of international stability and orderly development of Third World nations would be for Japan to increase its ODA to the level that, when combined with its defense spending, would reasonably approximate that of spendings by its OECD peers on defense and ODA combined.   Japan's ODA in recent years was approximately 0.26 percent of its GNP. It would be politically impossible for the government immediately to expand Japan's ODA several folds, but even if Japan only doubled it to 0.52 percent (which incidentally would equal Britain's ODA relative to its GNP),(46) the total of its ODA allocation would reach approximately $5.5 billion.   Not only would it enable Japan to reach its helping hand out to areas of the world where it has been rather neglectful as a foremost economic power, but, in an important sense, it would also increase its "political" capability enormously.   What Japan could do with it, of course, would depend entirely on its will, sense of purpose, and skill. To the extent that the Japanese government, as well as the Japanese people in general, view economic cooperation as "the only positive means available to Japan in international relations,"(47) it is all the more imperative that it increase its ODA drastically in order to perform the role and responsibility that are not only consistent with but also are warranted by its power and status for the promotion of world stability and peace.   International fiscal equity, especially among the advanced industrial democracies, would seem to require that Japan's total international peace efforts as a proportion of its GNP (that is, for military security as well as ODA for the promotion of development and stability in Third World nations) be comparable to those of its advanced industrial and democratic peers.   Otherwise it would be difficult for Japan to escape its peers' view that it is doing less than it should and could be.

An integral part of Japan's entire ODA program should be the cultivation of "human resources" in target nations.   This   is important, especially for Japan, which, because of its "exceptionalist" outlook and the exclusivist character of its society, has historically neglected the vital value of fostering close human relations with other nations and cultivating skills and knowledge among people from countries with which it deals. The United States and European states have been notably attentive in this regard and, as a consequence, find influential politicians, officials, technicians, and other professionals in Third World nations who have been trained in their institutions of higher learning and who have close human ties with their own politicians, officials, technicians, and other professionals. The extent to which these educational and human experiences and ties positively affect relations between Third World nations and these advanced industrial states, of course, is impossible to ascertain. It nonetheless seems axiomatic that genuine "cooperation" and "heart-to-heart understanding" between Japan and those developing nations it wants to help would be impossible without first cultivating their human resources in and thus developing human ties with them. In this connection, a projected plan by the Japanese government to establish by 1984 an ASEAN North-South Center in Okinawa, with a branch center in each of the the five ASEAN states, to foster "human resources for nation building" is a step in the right direction, at least in principle.(48) The purpose of the plan, according to the government, is to respond to the need of ASEAN states for human resources needed for modernization and development through training in such fields as medical science and agriculture and to enhance human intercourse and ties between Japan and these developing nations. This concept, however, should be expanded to include people from other parts of the Third World, and at a vastly expanded scale. This sort of effort on the part of Japan is long overdue, for, in more senses than one, Japan has been part of the problem that was discussed in Chapter 4 about the low level of development of multiple channels of communication and interaction among East Asian nations and the lack of adequate tradition of purposeful mutual interactions.

NOTES

(1) The Doctrine in part declared: "the government and people of Japan will never be skeptical bystanders in regard to ASEAN's efforts to achieve increasing resilience and greater regional solidarity but will always be with you as good partners, walking hand in hand with ASEAN." From a translation by the Ministry of Foreign Affairs, n.d.

(2) Jusuf Wanandi, Security Dimensions of the Asia-Pacific Region in the 1980s (Jakarta: Center for Strategic and International Studies, 1979), p. 97.

(3) See, for example, observations by Japanese ambassadors to ASEAN states in Asahi Shimbun, November 30, 1980, p. 4, and a report on Southeast Asian perceptions of Japan in Asahi Shimbun, August 14, 1980, p. 3.

(4) See, for example, Jusuf Wanandi, "Dimensions of Southeast Asian Security," Indonesian Quarterly 2 (January 1980): 50; his Security Dimensions of the Asia-Pacific Region in the 1980s, pp. 98-99; and the New York Times, January 11, 1981, p. E5.

(5) See, for example, a discussion of this ambivalence in Yonosuke Nagai, "Some Observations on the Perception Gap," in Discord in the Pacific: Challenge to the Japanese-American Alliance, ed. Henry Rosovsky (Washington, D.C.: Columbia Books, 1972), pp. 208-09, and Joint Working Group of the Atlantic Council of the United States and the Research Institute for Peace and Security, Tokyo, The Common Security Interests of Japan, the United States, and NATO (Washington, D.C.: and Tokyo: Atlantic Council of the United States, December 1980), p. 20.

(6) See, for example, a report of opinion surveys in Yomiuri Shimbun, September 15, 1980, as reprinted in Shimbun Geppo 407 (October 1980): 74.

(7) See United States-Japan Security Relationship - The Key to East Asian Security and Stability (Washington, D.C.: U.S. Government Printing Office, 1979), p. 2; Nihon Keizai Shimbun, March 17 as reprinted in Shimbun Geppo 401 (April 1980): 32; Mainichi Shimbun, March 28 and 29 as reprinted, ibid.

(8) In the preface of Waga Gaiko no Kinkyo: Showa 54 Nen Ban (1979 Diplomacy White Paper) (Tokyo: Okurasho Insatsukyoku, 1979).

(9) New Considerations on Security Treaty: Meaning of the Security Treaty Today (an internal Foreign Ministry memo for limited official use, April 1979), pp. 2-3. Emphasis added.

(10) See the summary of "Security Policy in the 1980s," prepared by the Foreign Ministry's Security Policy Planning Committee as reported in Nihon Keizai Shimbun, July 28, 1980 and reprinted in Shimbun Geppo 405 (August 1980): 69-70.

(11) See, for example, Asahi Shimbun, September 17, 1980, p. 2, and September 12, 1980, p. 2. Emphasis added.

(12) Hideaki Kase, "Northeast Asian Security: A View from Japan," Comparative Strategy 1 (1978): 101.

(13) Shujiro Kotani, Kokubo no Ronri (Logic of National Defense) (Tokyo: Hara Shobo, 1970), esp. pp. 86-88.

(14) Adapted from tables in Shoji Takase, "Takamaru Boei Rongi no Naiatsu to Gaiatsu" (Internal and External Pressures on the Rising Defense Debate), Asahi Janaru, April 11, 1980, p. 112.

(15) Showa 54 Nen Ban Boei Hakusho (1979 Defense White Paper) (Tokyo: Okurasho Insatsukyoku, 1979), p. 238.

(16) See Tom Gervasi, Arsenal of Democracy: American Weapons Available for Export (New York: Grove Press, 1978), pp. 42-230.

(17) In 1978, China had 11 destroyers and 85 submarines, plus escort, patrol, and other minor craft, and Taiwan had 21 destroyers, 10 frigates, 5 submarines, plus other minor surface craft. See Barry Blechman and Robert Berman, eds., Guide to Far Eastern Navies (Annapolis: Naval Institute Press, 1978), pp. 94-95 and 234.

(18) None of the ASEAN states has anything more devastating than a few frigates and patrol craft. See Asia Research Bulletin, November 10, 1980, pp. 744-46.

(19) For Lee's proposal, see Takuya Kubo, "Kaijo Boei to Kaijo Kotsu no Kakuho" (Maritime Defense and Security of Maritime Traffic), Kokusai Mondai 217 (April 1978): 46.

(20) For the types and numbers of moth-balled naval craft in the United States, see Francis P. Hoeber, David B. Kassing, and William Schneider, Arms, Men, and Military Budgets: Issues for Fiscal Year 1979 (New York: Crane, Russak, 1978), p. 67. They include at least 30 modern destroyers.

(21) See, for example, Japan Times Weekly, October 25, 1980, p. 1.

(22) Japan Times Weekly, November 15, 1980, p. 1.

(23) Joint Working Group of the Atlantic Council, p. 35.

(24) In the Preamble of the postwar Constitution.

(25) This phrase is borrowed from Coral Bell, "Security Preoccupations and Power Balances After Vietnam," in Conflict and Stability in Southeast Asia, ed. Mark W. Zacher and R. Stephen Milne (Garden City, NY: Doubleday, 1974), p. 478.

(26) For the Kissinger formula as well as Pyongyang's recent overtures to the United States, see Gareth Porter, "Time to Talk with North Korea, "Foreign Policy 34 (Spring 1979): 52-73.

(27) As an indication of this disinclination, the Soviet military aid to North Korea dropped by nearly 90 percent between 1973 and 1976. Ibid., p. 59.

(28) For a comprehensive set of recommendations for establishing peace and stability on the Korean peninsula, see Hisashi Maeda, "A Peace Area of Korean Peninsula," Korea Review 22 (April 1979): 23-33.

(29) See, for example, Yasuhiro Maeda, "Nikkan Gunji Jidai no Sutato" (The Beginning of a Japan-Korea Military Era), Sekai, October 1979, pp. 177-80, and his "Nikkan Gunju Kyotei no Genjo" (The Present Condition of Japan-Korea Military Cooperation), Sekai, December 1980, pp. 107-13.

(30) By an official Chinese estimate, about 250,000 by mid-1979 and an additional 10,000 per month thereafter in that year. See Sekai, September 1979, p. 155. South Korea claimed "millions of North Korean refugees" even before the Chinese intervention in October 1950. A Handbook of Korea, 3d ed. (Seoul: Korea Overseas Information Service, Ministry of Culture and Information, 1979), pp. 160-61.

(31) For these events preceding Vietnam's invasion of Cambodia, see, for example, J. L. S. Girling, "Politics in Southeast Asia: A Year of Conflict," in Southeast Asian Affairs 1979 (Singapore: Institute of Southeast Asian Studies, 1979), pp. 5-10.

(32) See Asia Research Bulletin, September 30, 1978, pp. 489-503.

(33) Asahi Shimbun, June 25, 1980, evening edition, p. 1.

(34) See Alvin Coox, "Japan and Southeast Asian Configuration," in Southeast Asia under the New Balance of Power, ed. Sudershan Chawla, Melvin Gurtov, and Alain-Gerard Marsot (New York: Praeger, 1974), p. 88.

(35) For China's posture toward Vietnam, see, for example, a report on the Japanese foreign minister's talk with his Chinese counterpart in Peking in Asahi Shimbun, December 5, 1980, p. 2.

(36) See Masatake Okumiya, Nihon Boei Ron (A View of Japanese Defense) (Tokyo: PHP, 1979), p. 207.

(37) Ibid.

(38) For some examples of convoluted and obfuscatory debate on whether the nation's participation in UN peace-keeping activities was permissible, see Atarashii Nichibei Kankei eno Tenkan (Transition to a New Japanese-American Relationship), Vol. 4 of Nihon Gendaishi Shiryo: Nichibei Anzen Hosho Taiseishi, Kokkai Rongi to Kankei Shiryo (Materials for Contemporary Japanese History: History of Japanese-American Security System, Diet Debates and Related Materials), ed. Hiroshi Suekawa and Saburo Ienaga (Tokyo: Sanseido, 1971), pp. 19-20.

(39) For this policy paper, see Nihon Keizai Shimbun, July 28, 1980, or its reprint in Shimbun Geppo 405: 69-70.

(40) See Asahi Shimbun, October 28, 1980, p. 1, or its reprint in Shimbun Geppo 408 (November 1980): 56-58.

(41) See, for example, Shimpei Fujimaki and Yonosuke Nagai, "Gendai Shakai ni okeru Guntai to Gunjiryoku" (The Military and Military Power in Contemporary Society), Kokusai Mondai 247 (October 1980): 10.

(42) For the crucial, often catalytic role of political leadership in modernization and development, see Taketsugu Tsurutani, The Politics of National Development: Political Leadership in Transitional Societies (New York: Chandler, 1973).

(43) New York Times, April 20, 1980, p. E3, and March 1, 1981, p. E5.

(44) Waga Gaiko no Kinkyo: Showa 54 Nen Ban, pp. 504-05.

(45) See Takuya Kubo, "Gemba kara no Boei Ron" (Defense Argument from the Field), Chuokoron, January 1979, p. 127.

(46) New York Times, March 1, 1981, p. E5.

(47) Sogo Anzen Hosho Kenkyu Gurupu, Sogo Anzen Hosho Senryaku (Strategy for Comprehensive Security) (Tokyo: Okurasho Insatsukyoku, 1980), p. 40.

(48) See <u>Asahi Shimbun</u>, November 20, 1980, p. 1, and December 27, 1980, p. 2.

8
Conclusion

Our plea that Japan adopt a positive, indeed "activist" posture and orientation in its defense and external policy in its own interest as well as in the interest of East Asian security is not entirely without elements of risk, which many thoughtful Japanese fear. This fear was expressed several years ago by a prominent Japanese scholar, Chie Nakane, in an interview with <u>Newsweek</u>:

> The Japanese way of thinking depends on the situation rather than principle – while with the Chinese it is the other way around. . . .we Japanese have no principles. Some people think we hide our intentions, but we have no intentions to hide. Except for few leftists or rightists, we have no dogma and don't ourselves know where we are going. This is a risky situation, for if someone is able to mobilize this population in a certain direction, we have no checking mechanism. . . .If we establish any goal we will proceed to attain it without considering any other factors. It is better for us to remain just as we are. For if we are set in motion toward any direction, we have just too much energy and no mechanism to check its direction.(1)

Nakane's observation is accurately reflective of Japan's experience before 1945 and, therefore, suggestive of potential risk that perhaps necessarily inheres in the kind of direction that our policy recommendations discussed in Chapter 7 warrant of it in the new decade.

The Japanese had had no history of collective aggressive behavior or missionary zeal prior to their modern century. Instead, as was noted in Chapter 6, they had been deeply habituated to moderation and passivity in behavior and thought. Yet, once determined that they should emulate and catch up with advanced Western states and some of their colonial dominions in order to insure their national survival and safety, and pointed in a particular direction by their leaders, whether it be the imperialistic aggrandizement in Korea or China or the more ambitious "Greater East Asia Co-Prosperity Sphere," they did indeed proceed in that direction with headlong tenacity. In so doing, they failed to consider scrupulously the ramifications of either the goal pursued or the process of attaining it. The ultimate result of this pattern of modern Japan's external behavior was the holocaust of Hiroshima and Nagasaki.

Japan's consensual mode of decision making and the leadership style it dictates, as was discussed in Chapter 6, have the inherent tendency to inhibit radical departure from the prevailing norms, preferences, and orientations, and thus to incline toward moderation, vacillation, and even inaction in the face of pressures of events. The formation of consensus for a policy that significantly departs from the prevailing norms, preferences, and orientations is extremely difficult, cumbersome, and time-consuming. Once such a consensus is formed, however, and aimed at a specific direction, that consensus feeds on itself and gathers an irresistible momentum; and precisely because it is the consensus, there is no internal mechanism to check its direction. This was what happened in Japan before the war. Neither the fundamental character of the Japanese nor the consensual mode of decision making has basically changed in the meantime. Hence Nakane's fear. What, then, about the policy suggestions in Chapter 7?

These policy suggestions are rooted in two interrelated considerations that should obviate the risk that may otherwise be seriously feared. One, of course, is that Japan, in spite of itself, is called upon to perform a certain international role and shoulder a certain responsibility warranted by its environment and by its power and status because, unless it did so, it would in effect contribute to the erosion of international peace and stability by inaction and passivity. The other consideration is that its dangerous potential to which Nakane referred (but which we believe is not so uniquely Japanese even though its tendency may be more obvious in the Japanese, owing to their recent and devastating experience) could be curbed and contained by certain structural and procedural safeguards. In other words, the kind of necessary "mechanism" that Nakane believed was absent could be provided so as to enhance Japan's positive contributive performance and minimize the danger of its acting in a destabilizing manner.

The only alternative to this consideration would be that the fear of the risk on the one hand and the requirement for Japan to pursue an activist defense and external policy on the other would place the nation in an insoluble quandary, the kind of quandary in which many Americans found their nation in the immediate post-Vietnam era and which generated a certain isolationist sentiment. The restraining "mechanism" or safeguard concerning Japan's new policy direction was discussed in Chapter 7 without so calling it, but perhaps it needs reiteration here. One important aspect of such a safeguard is the proviso that Japan undertake its security responsibility within the framework of the Japanese-U.S. security pact in which the United States remains the senior security partner. To the extent that there is a relevant consensus on the matter, Japan could or would take no unilateral action either with respect to its own national defense or with regard to the security of the Western Pacific. Second, insofar as the maintenance of Western Pacific security is concerned, there is an additional restraining element, that is, close consultation with and scrutiny by the ASEAN states as well as the United States. Japan's role in it is not primary but supplementary and supportive of the United States. Third, we are quite specific about urging that Japan not acquire strategic weapons for reasons that were discussed in Chapter 7 as well as Chapter 5. Besides, the United States and ASEAN nations with whom it would have to consult and cooperate would not countenance Japan's acquisition of such weapons in any event. Japan's diplomatic efforts within East Asia as well as without could be fruitful only if it makes them a member, in the words of its own government, of "the Western bloc" seeking stabilization of the world situation, the reduction of East-West conflict, and the North-South developmental gap. For Japan to depart from these specific contexts of international conduct would be only to invite its political, military, and even economic isolation in a world where such isolation would be immediately disastrous to it. In short, we believe that our plea for Japan to adopt a positive, activist posture and direction in its defense and external policy must be accompanied by the kind of restraining mechanism that was lacked before the war.

Before 1945 Japan made mistakes — ultimately terrifyingly devastating mistakes at that. Inaction and passivity, however, are not the signs of having learned the lesson; they are signs that the lesson has not been learned or that a wrong lesson has been learned. The lesson consists not in inaction or passivity or pusillanimity, but rather in judiciously avoiding the blindness, arrogance, and misjudgment that were the causes of those past blunders, while actively performing the role and shouldering the responsibility that are commensurate with one's power and status. This, of course, requires courage, an appropriate national will, which a nation would have difficulty finding, especially when it has been burned badly once before and when it is in that self-inflicted quandary. Japan, however, has no alternative if it, as it professes, wishes to contribute to and promote peace and stability in East Asia and, ultimately, beyond. Japan cannot contribute to it in a manner of its own choosing; it can contribute to it only in a manner that the international environment requires. The only alternative for Japan is to remain passive politically, diplomatically, and in security affairs, while expanding its economic power and wealth, and so to watch, from the sidelines, its international environment and its own safety stumble along toward possible disaster. There is no guarantee, of course, that, if Japan did what it should, security and peace in East Asia would be assured. There is certainty, however, that, if it did not, Japan would eventually find itself having been a contributor to the destruction of regional peace and security. This is the predicament of every responsible major nation in international affairs.

In addition, there is a sense in which it could be argued that Japan's continued avoidance of realpolitik would even hasten the worsening of the condition of its external environment. Apart from the prospect of some "inappropriate" nation or nations being tempted to fill the vacuum caused or perpetuated by Japan's inaction, we have in particular the potential attitude and policy direction of the United States in mind. The particular character of postwar Japanese-U.S. relations discussed in Chapter 5 instilled in the minds of the Japanese a self-complacent, hence erroneous, notion that their country, especially its security, is indispensable to the United States and that, for that reason, the United States would never abandon their country. True, Japan has maintained the closest overall relations with the United States among the East Asian nations thus far and, objectively speaking, they should and most likely would maintain them in the future. Nations act, however, not always on the basis of objective conditions and requirements of their external environment; there is always the possibility that they act on the basis of their narrowly and dangerously subjective impulses and judgments, as Japan most palpably has done in the past. There is no assurance, therefore, that the United States would always act in the common interest between itself and Japan. This prospect would be far more likely for Japanese-U.S. relations than, say, Anglo-U.S. relations.

Americans and British often refer to their ties as a "special relationship," for they share a common language, civilization, tradition, history, and heritage. Theirs is indeed a blood relationship, with all that it implies in terms of mutual perspective, valuation, and sense of common destiny. Japanese-U.S. relations, however fervently the Japanese may wish otherwise, are not of the same kind. There is no commonality or consanguinity of language, civilization, tradition, history, or heritage. They are not "natural" in the sense that Anglo-U.S. (and, perhaps to a lesser but nonetheless significant extent, Euro-U.S.) relations may be said to be natural. Postwar Japanese-U.S. relations are, in a sense, an unnatural creature of an extraordinarily unusual and, from a historical perspective, momentary combination of circumstances. Mutual harmony and trust that are essential for viable and enduring relations in times of increasing international stress and strain do not come very naturally here; they must be deliberately cultivated and judiciously maintained. One high State Department official concerned with relations with Japan told the author, "The United States and Japan do not have an option not to get along," but any statement like this is a "formulism" and does not necessarily reflect the fundamental character of future Japanese-U.S. relations.

Particularly when its own power has significantly declined relative to world security contingencies and its policy flexibility and mobility additionally curtailed by growing domestic economic and sociopolitical constraints, it is safe to assume that the United States is also declining in its capacity for equanimity toward its allies. If this is indeed the case, the kind of attitude Japan adopts toward its own defense as well as East Asian security becomes crucial in shaping the attitude of the United States toward these issues.

It is entirely probable, therefore, that the failure on the part of Japan to develop a positive, activist direction in its defense and external policy and to shoulder the kind of burden that has been discussed will push the United States toward a narrower definition of its national interests and security responsibility, especially since the equilibrium between its multiple security commitments and its ability to sustain them is no longer as secure as it once was. When this happens the United States might well find it necessary to reassess the value of its continued commitment to the defense of Japan and its lifelines. Conversely, Japan's adoption of the kind of positive direction we have suggested for its defense and external policy would help the United States move in the direction of greater confidence in its continued commitment to its defense and East Asian regional security. Quite unlike during the first three postwar decades, Japan in the 1980s could expect the United States to maintain such commitment only by helping it effectively perform its security role in East Asia and elsewhere through its active partici-pation in diplomatic, security, and developmental tasks in the region and beyond. Japanese-U.S. relations should henceforth be a genuine partnership, based on equity and reciprocity, qualities indispensable for its endurance. It is only on this basis that Japan also could expect to exert positive and constructive influence on the inter-national conduct of the United States.

Our plea for Japan to adopt a new direction might be objected to on the ground that there is not yet a sufficiently strong popular consensus in its support. Since Japan is a democratic nation, there is indeed a legitimate concern about the necessity of a popular consensus for any significant policy change. This issue, however, should also be considered from the practical perspective relevant to the nation's past conduct in the postwar period. Postwar experiences pertinent to defense and external policy making in Japan indicate that the relationship between government policy and popular ap-proval or support has been of a particular kind: popular support emerges or is strengthened only after the fact. To cite a few examples: The establishment of the JSDF, the normalization of relations with the Soviet Union, and the ratification of the revised Japanese-U.S. security pact of 1960 were all controversial before each took place. It cannot be said that there was any significant popular consensus or approval prior to the government decision, but each was followed by a rapid rise in popular approval sufficiently strong enough to insure its institutionalization and its termination as an issue. Regarding the normalization of relations with the People's Republic of China, too, there was a considerable shift in the public attitude after the event. Before normalization, the PRC used to be quite unpopular among the Japanese except for the leftists, one of the least-liked foreign countries, even though a majority of the Japanese favored trade relations with it. Only a small minority favored recognition of the Peking regime as the sole legitimate government of China at the expense of the Nationalist regime in Taiwan. After the normalization of Sino-Japanese relations, which involved Japan's severance of diplomatic ties with Taiwan, however, the Japanese public opinion of the PRC quickly improved and little public objection was raised against the normalization with Peking or the diplomatic severance with Taipei.

In part, this tendency of the Japanese public to accept an event or decision once it takes place or is made may be a reflection of their passive optimism or reliance on the course of events discussed in Chapter 6, which predispose them to make the best of the new situation and adjust to the fact. Perhaps it was with this in mind that the distinguished scholar whom we quoted several pages earlier in a different context observed that the Japanese, in their views, "change more easily with the shift of the time when compared with the peoples of other societies."(2) If these observations are correct, it is more likely than not that once the government undertakes a necessary change in policy direction regarding national defense and regional security, the people will soon accept it and the change will cease to be an issue. To the extent that national policy making is a matter of creative political leadership in the face of obstacles and resistance, the particular relationship between government and popular approval that was noted in postwar Japan is neither extraordinary nor inordinate. Indeed it is the responsibility of the government, as the guardian of national interests and the commonweal, to lead the people in the direction it deems necessary while at the same time patiently persuading them of its necessity.

In order to take a new direction and embark upon a course of positive contribution to international stability, it is necessary that the Japanese recognize that theirs is a "major" nation, one of a handful of such nations in the world, with enormous potentials for doing good. Fortunately, this recognition may be emerging already, albeit slowly and hesitantly. In an important sense, it may be argued that Japan has already entered a period of historic transition in its outlook, self-image, and search for its place in the world community toward a genuine major power. Such a nation could achieve the mastery of self and a firm grasp of the direction of its destiny. It would then be able to act with composure and assurance in the international arena, composure and assurance that Japan has never been able to acquire in its modern century. This lack of composure and assurance in the past led it to act aggressively and arrogantly, hence dangerously, before 1945, and timidly and passively since. Self-recognition as a major power is the first step for Japan toward accepting that power imposes upon itself responsibility that cannot be evaded. Power whose responsibility is evaded becomes ultimately as dangerous as power that is abused. Before the war, Japan more often than not abused the power it possessed; since then, it has evaded the responsibility that inheres in its growing power. Its enlightened self-interest warrants that Japan use its power at once resolutely and wisely in pursuit of its own safety and well-being as well as East Asia's security and orderly development in the new decade and beyond. For Japan's destiny is inextricably bound up in the future course of the entire region, a course that would remain volatile, unpredictable, and pregnant with danger, unless it uses its considerable power to help steer it through the perilous waters of chance, contingency, and accident.

NOTES

(1) Chie Nakane as quoted in Kei Wakaizumi, "Japan's Dilemma: To Act or Not to Act," Foreign Policy 16 (Fall 1974): 31.

(2) Chie Nakane, Japanese Society (Berkeley: University of California Press, 1970), p. 151.

Bibliography

Abegglen, James. The Japanese Factory. Glencoe, Ill.: The Free Press, 1958.

Akasaka, Taro. "Boei Rongi no Kuruizaki" (Unseasonable Flowering of Defense Debate). Bungei Shunju, March 1978, pp. 164-67.

Anzen Hosho Kyokai, ed. Kaiyo Nihon no Shorai: Ampo Kenkyu 17 Nen no Kiroku (The Future of Maritime Japan: Seventeen-Year Record of Security Studies). Tokyo: Hara Shobo, 1970.

Asahi Shimbunsha. Asahi Nenkan 1979 Bekkan (1979 Asahi Yearbook Supplement). Tokyo: Asahi Shimbunsha, 1979.

Auer, James E. The Postwar Rearmament of Japanese Maritime Forces 1945-71. New York: Praeger, 1973.

Austin, Lewis. Saints and Samurai: The Political Culture of the American and Japanese Elites. New Haven, Conn.: Yale University Press, 1975.

Axelbank, Albert. Black Star Over Japan. New York: Hill and Wang, 1972.

Baerwald, Hans. "The Diet and Foreign Policy." In The Foreign Policy of Modern Japan, edited by Robert A. Scalapino, pp. 37-54. Berkeley: University of California Press, 1977.

_____. Japan's Parliament: An Introduction. New York: Cambridge University Press, 1974.

Bell, Coral. "Security Preoccupations and Power Balances after Vietnam." In Conflict and Stability in Southeast Asia, edited by Mark W. Zacher and R. Stephen Milne, pp. 469-89. Garden City, N.Y.: Doubleday, 1974.

Bell, Daniel. "The Public Household – On 'Fiscal Sociology' and the Liberal Society." Public Interest 37 (1974): 29-68.

Bellak, Leopold. Overload: The New Human Condition. New York: Human Sciences Press, 1975.

Blechman, Barry, and Robert Berman, eds. Guide to Far Eastern Navies. Annapolis: Naval Institute Press, 1978.

Boei Sangyo Kyokai. Jieitai Nenkan 1977 (1977 JSDF Yearbook). Tokyo: Boei Sangyo Kyokai, 1977.

Boulding, Kenneth E. Stable Peace. Austin: University of Texas Press, 1978.

Brendle, Thomas M. "Recruitment and Training in the SDF." In The Modern Japanese Military System, edited by James H. Buck, pp. 67-96. Beverly Hills, Calif.: Sage Publications, 1975.

Brittan, Samuel. "The Economic Contradictions of Democracy." British Journal of Political Science 5 (1975): 129-59.

Buck, James H., ed. The Modern Japanese Military System. Beverly Hills, Calif.: Sage Publications, 1975.

Campbell, John C. Contemporary Japanese Budget Politics. Berkeley: University of California Press, 1977.

Chawla, Sudershan, Melvin Gurtov, and Alain-Gerard Marsot, eds. Southeast Asia under the New Balance of Power. New York: Praeger, 1974.

Cole, Robert E. Japanese Blue Collar: The Changing Tradition. Berkeley: University of California Press, 1971.

Conquest, Robert. Present Danger: Toward a Foreign Policy. Stanford, Calif.: Hoover Institution Press, 1979.

Coox, Alvin. "Japan and Southeast Asian Configuration." In Southeast Asia under the New Balance of Power, edited by Sudershan Chawla, Melvin Gurtov, and Alain-Gerard Marsot, pp. 80-93. New York: Praeger, 1974.

Craig, Albert. "Functional and Dysfunctional Aspects of Government Bureaucracy." In Modern Japanese Organization and Decision-Making, edited by Ezra Vogel, pp. 3-32. Berkeley: University of California Press, 1975.

Curtis, Gerald. "The Tyuman Oil Development Project and Japanese Foreign Policy Decision-Making." In The Foreign Policy of Modern Japan, edited by Robert A. Scalapino, pp. 147-74. Berkeley: University of California Press, 1977.

Destler, I. M., Hideo Sato, Priscilla Clapp, and Haruhiro Fukui. Managing an Alliance: The Politics of U.S.-Japanese Relations. Washington, D.C.: The Brookings Institution, 1976.

De Vos, George. Socialization for Achievement: Essays on the Cultural Psychology of the Japanese. Berkeley: University of California Press, 1973.

Doi, Takeo. Amae no Kozo (The Structure of Dependence). Tokyo: Kobundo, 1975.

Ebashi, Takashi. "Jieitai: 25 Nen no Kiseki" (JSDF: The Locus Problem of Their 25 Years). Sekai, October 1979, pp. 84-103.

Emmerson, John K. Arms, Yen and Power: The Japanese Dilemma. New York: Dunellen, 1971.

Endicott, John E. Japan's Nuclear Option: Political, Technological and Strategic Factors. New York: Praeger, 1975.

Fujimaki, Shimpei, and Nagai Yonosuke. "Gendai Shakai ni Okeru Guntai to Gunjiryoku" (The Military and Military Power in Contemporary Society). Kokusai Mondai 247 (October 1980): 2-12.

Fukui, Haruhiro. "Japan: Factionalism in a Dominant-Party System." In Faction Politics: Political Parties and Factionalism in Comparative Perspective, edited by Frank Belloni and Dennis Beller, pp. 43-72. Santa Barbara, Calif.: ABC-CLIO, 1978.

_____. "Policy-Making in the Japanese Foreign Ministry." In The Foreign Policy of Modern Japan, edited by Robert A. Scalapino, pp. 3-36. Berkeley: University of California Press, 1977.

_____. "Twenty Years of Revisionism." In The Constitution of Japan: Its First Twenty Years, 1947-1967, edited by Dan F. Henderson, pp. 41-70. Seattle: University of Washington Press, 1968.

Gervasi, Tom. Arsenal of Democracy: American Weapons Available for Export. New York: Grove Press, 1978.

Gibney, Frank. Japan: The Fragile Superpower. New York: Norton, 1975.

Girling, J. L. S. "Politics in Southeast Asia: A Year of Conflict." In Southeast Asian Affairs 1979, edited by Institute of Southeast Asian Studies, pp. 3-12. Singapore: Institute of Southeast Asian Studies, 1979.

Gurtov, Melvin. "The Soviet Presence in Southeast Asia: Growth and Implications." In Conflict and Stability in Southeast Asia, edited by Mark W. Zacher and R. Stephen Milne, pp. 275-91. Garden City, N.Y.: Doubleday, 1974.

Halliday, Jon, and Gavan McCormack. Japanese Imperialism Today. New York: Monthly Review Press, 1974.

Hasegawa, Keitaro. "Chuso ga wakai suru hi" (The Day China and the Soviet Union Will Achieve Reconciliation). Bungei Shunju, May 1979, pp. 260-91.

Hasegawa, Nyozekan. The Japanese Character: A Cultural Profile, translated by John Bester. Tokyo: Kodansha International, 1966.

Hayashi, Risuke. Ajia no naka no Nihon: Heion no naka ni hisomu Fuan (Japan in Asia: Apprehension beneath Tranquility). Tokyo: Tairyusha, 1978.

Hellman, Donald. Japan and East Asia: The New International Order. New York: Praeger, 1972.

_____. "Japan and Southeast Asia: Continuity Amidst Change." Asian Survey 19 (December 1979): 1189-98.

_____. "Japanese Security and Postwar Japanese Foreign Policy." In The Foreign Policy of Modern Japan, edited by Robert A. Scalapino, pp. 321-40. Berkeley: University of California Press, 1977.

Henderson, Dan F., ed. The Constitution of Japan: Its First Twenty Years, 1947-1967. Seattle: University of Washington Press, 1968.

Hitchcock, David. "Joint Development of Siberia: Decision-making in Japanese-Soviet Relations." Asian Survey 11 (March 1971): 279-300.

Hoeber, Francis P., David B. Kassing, and William Schneider. Arms, Men, and Military Budgets: Issues for Fiscal Year 1979. New York: Crane, Russak, 1978.

Holbrooke, Richard. "U.S. Posture in the Pacific in 1980." Current Policy 154 (March 27, 1980): 1-5.

Hoon, Khaw Guat. "Recent Development in China-ASEAN Relations." In Southeast Asian Affairs 1979, edited by Institute of Southeast Asian Studies, pp. 61-71. Singapore: Institute of Southeast Asian Studies, 1979.

Hopper, David R. "Defense Policy and the Business Community: The Keidanren Defense Production Committee." In The Modern Japanese Military System, edited by James H. Buck, pp. 113-47. Beverly Hills, Calif.: Sage Publications, 1975.

Ienaga, Saburo, and Hiroshi Suekawa, eds. Nihon Gendaishi Shiryo: Nichibei Ampo Joyaku Taiseishi, Kokkai Giron to Kankei Shiryo (Materials for Contemporary Japanese History: History of Japanese-American Security System, Diet Debates and Related Materials). 4 vols. Tokyo: Sanseido, 1970.

Institute of Southeast Asian Studies. Southeast Asian Affairs 1979. Singapore: International Institute of Southeast Asian Studies, 1979.

International Institute for Strategic Studies. Military Balance 1978-1979. London: International Institute for Strategic Studies, 1978.

_____. Military Balance 1979-1980. London: International Institute for Strategic Studies, 1979.

_____. Strategic Survey 1978. London: International Institute for Strategic Studies, 1979.

Ishiwara, Shintaro, Susumu Hani, and Hirotatsu Fujiwara. Ikani Kuni o Mamoruka (How to Defend the Nation). Tokyo: Nisshin Hodo Suppansha, 1970.

Janowitz, Morris. Social Control of the Welfare State. New York: Elsevier, 1976.

Japan, Government of. Defense of Japan, n.d.

_____. Indonesia Gaikyo (Indonesia Outline). Embassy of Japan: Jakarta, January 1980, mimeo.

_____. Japan Statistical Yearbook. Tokyo: Statistics Bureau, Prime Minister's Office, 1979.

_____. Kokumin Seikatsu Hakusho (White Paper on People's Livelihood). Tokyo: Keizai Kikakucho, 1971.

_____. Kokusai Tokei Yoran 1975 (International Statistical Abstract, 1975). Tokyo: Okurasho Insatsukyoku, 1975.

_____. Nihon no Tokei (Statistics of Japan). Tokyo: Okurasho Insatsukyoku, 1979.

_____. Nihon to ASEAN (Japan and ASEAN). Tokyo: Gaimusho Joho Bunka Kyoku, 1979.

_____. Sekai no Seinen to no Hikaku kara mita Nihon no Seinen (Japanese Youths Viewed in Comparison to the World's Youths). Tokyo: Okurasho Insatsukyoku, 1979.

_____. Showa 53 Nen Ban Boei Hakusho (1978 Defense White Paper). Tokyo: Okurasho Insatsukyoku, 1978.

_____. Showa 54 Nen Ban Boei Hakusho (1979 Defense White Paper). Tokyo: Okurasho Insatsukyoku, 1979.

_____. Showa 55 Nen Ban Boei Hakusho (1980 Defense White Paper). Tokyo: Okurasho Insatsukyoku, 1980.

_____. Showa 52 Nen Ban Kagaku Gijutsu Hakusho (1977 Science and Technology White Paper). Tokyo: Okurasho Insatsukyoku, 1978.

_____. Showa 48 Nen Ban Kosei Hakusho (1973 Health and Welfare White Paper). Tokyo: Koseisho, 1973.

_____. Showa 53 Nen Ban Yoron Chosa Nenkan (1979 Public Opinion Survey Yearbook). Tokyo: Okurasho Insatsukyoku, 1979.

_____. Waga Gaiko no Kinkyo: Showa 54 Nen Ban (1979 Diplomacy White Paper). Tokyo: Okurasho Insatsukyoku, 1979.

Joint Working Group of the Atlantic Council of the United States and the Research Institute for Peace and Security, Tokyo. The Common Security Interests of Japan, the United States and NATO. Washington and Tokyo: Atlantic Council of the United States, December 1980.

Kahn, Herman. The Emerging Japanese Superstate. Englewood Cliffs, N.J.: Prentice-Hall, 1970.

Kaihara, Osamu. Nihon Boei Taisei no Uchimaku (Inside Japan's Defense System). Tokyo: Jiji Tsushinsha, 1977.

_____ and Takuya Kubo. Genjitsu no Boei Rongi (Real Defense Debate). Tokyo: Sankei Shuppan, 1979.

Kamo, Takehiko. " 'Gunkaku no Shiso' sasaeru Keizai Nashonarizumu" (Economic Nationalism That Sustains 'The Ideology of Military Expansion'). Asahi Janaru, May 2, 1980, pp. 6-11.

Kaplan, Morton, and Kinhide Mushakoji, eds. Japan, America, and the Future World Order. New York: The Free Press, 1976.

Kase, Hideaki. "Northeast Asian Security: A View from Japan." Comparative Strategy 1 (1978): 95-101.

Kato, Yozo. Shiroku: Jieitaishi (Personal Record: A History of the Self-Defense Forces). Tokyo: Gekkan Seisaku, 1979.

Kempo Chosakai Jimukyoku. Nichibei Anzen Hosho Kankei Bunshoshu (Collected Documents Relating to the Japan-U.S. Security Arrangements). Tokyo: Kempo Chosakai Jimukyoku, 1959.

Kimura, Hiroshi. "Japan-Soviet Relations: Framework, Developments, Prospects." Asian Survey 20 (July 1980): 707-25.

Kimura, Tetsusaburo. "Indoshina Higeki no Kozo" (Structure of Indochinese Tragedy). Sekai, September 1979, pp. 14-19.

King, Anthony. "Overload: Problems of Governing in the 1970s." Political Studies 23 (1975): 284-96.

Kishida, Junnosuke. "Senshin Shakai no Sogo Anzen Hosho towa nanika" (What Is Comprehensive Security of Advanced Society). Chuokoron, January 1979, pp. 96-107.

Kodama, Susumu. "Zaikai-jin no Boei Hatsugen" (Defense Proposals by Big-Business Leaders). Asahi Januaru, April 11, 1980, pp. 15-18.

Kojima, Tomoyuki. "Chuso Wakai to Tairitsu no Kozu" (Structure of Sino-Soviet Reconciliation and Confrontation). Asahi Janaru, April 27, 1979, pp. 92-97.

Kokuseisha. Nihon Kokusei Zue (Picture of the State of Japan). Tokyo: Kokuseisha, 1979.

Kondo, Koichi. "Betonamu Shakaishugi no Satetsu" (Fiasco of Vietnamese Socialism). Chuokoron, September 1979, pp. 66-90.

Kotani, Shujiro. Kokubo no Ronri (Logic of National Defense). Tokyo: Hara Shobo, 1970.

Kubo, Takuya. "Gemba karano Boei Ron" (Defense Argument from the Field). Chuokoron, January 1979, pp. 118-27.

_____. "Kaijo Boei to Kaijo Kotsu no Kakuho" (Maritime Defense and Security of Maritime Traffic). Kokusai Mondai 217 (April 1978): 42-50.

Kurisu, Hiroomi. Watakushi no Boei Ron (A Personal View of National Defense). Tokyo: Takagi Shobo, 1978.

Kuroyanagi, Yoneiji. "ASEAN's Security Position and Its Policy Implications for Japan." In Japan-Indonesia Relations: Past, Present, Future, pp. 26-47. Jakarta: Center for Strategic and International Studies, 1979.

Kusumi, Tadao. "Japan's Defense and Peace in Asia." Pacific Community 4 (1973): 415-36.

Langdon, Frank C. Japan's Foreign Policy. Vancouver: University of British Columbia Press, 1973.

Lockwood, William W. "Japan's Response to the West: The Contrast with China." World Politics 9 (1956): 37-54.

Macrae, Norman. "Pacific Century, 1975-2075? Economist, January 4-10, 1975, pp. 15-35.

Maeda, Hisashi. "A Peace Area of Korean Peninsula." Korea Review 22 (1979): 23-35.

_____. A View of International Disarmament Problems. Research Papers Series A-35. Tokyo: Institute of International Relations, Sophia University, 1979.

Maeda, Yasuhiro. "Nikkan Gunji Jidai no Sutato" (The Beginning of a Japan-Korea Military Era). Sekai, October 1979, pp. 177-80.

_____. "Nikkan Gunji Kyotei no Genjo" (The Present Condition of Japan-Korea Military Cooperation). Sekai, December 1980, pp. 157-61.

Marsh, Robert, and Hiroshi Mannari. Modernization and Japanese Factory. Princeton, N.J.: Princeton University Press, 1976.

Mendel, Douglas H. The Japanese People and Foreign Policy: A Study of Public Opinion in Post-Treaty Japan. Berkeley: University of California Press, 1961.

Mendl, Wolf. Issues in Japan's China Policy. London: Royal Institute of International Affairs, 1978.

Miyawaki, Mineo. "Nihon no Boei Seisaku Kettei Kiko to Kettei Katei" (Structure and Process of Defense Policy Making in Japan). Kokusai Mondai 247 (October 1980): 34-62.

Miyazawa, Kiichi. "To Meet the Challenge." Asian Survey 20 (July 1980): 677-82.

Momoi, Makoto. "Basic Trends in Japanese Security Policies." In The Foreign Policy of Modern Japan, edited by Robert A. Scalapino, pp. 341-64. Berkeley: University of California Press, 1977.

Morimoto, Yoshio. "Ajia no Sinjosei to Soren Gaiko" (New Asian Situation and Soviet Diplomacy). Sekai, March 1979, pp. 106-13.

Morris, Ivan. Nationalism and the Right Wing in Japan: A Study of Postwar Trend. London: Oxford University Press, 1960.

Morrison, Charles E. and Astri Suhrke. Strategies of Survival: The Foreign Policy Dilemma of Smaller Asian States. New York: St. Martin's Press, 1979.

Murakami, Kaoru. "MiG-25 Jiken kara nani o mananda ka" (What We Have Learned from the MiG-25 Incident). In 1977 Jieitai Nenkan, pp. 31-49. Tokyo: Boei Sangyo Kyokai, 1977.

_____. Nihon Boei no Koso (A Plan for Japan's Defense). Tokyo: Simul, 1976.

_____. "The Postwar Defense Debate in Review." Japan Echo, Winter 1978, pp. 18-31.

Muraoka, Kunio. Japanese Security and the United States. London: International Institute for Strategic Studies, 1973.

Nagai, Yonosuke. "Some Observations on the Perception Gap." In Discord in the Pacific: Challenge to the Japanese-American Relations, edited by Henry Rosovsky, pp. 199-211. Washington, D.C.: Columbia Books, 1972.

Nakajima, Mineo. "Boei Senryaku to shite no Nihon Gaiko" (Japanese Diplomacy as Defense Strategy). Chuokoron, January 1979, pp. 82-94.

_____. "Taiheiyo o koeta Shinwaryoku" (Power of Friendship over the Pacific). Chuokoron, February 1979, pp. 80-86.

Nakamura, Hajime. Ways of Thinking of Eastern Peoples: India, China, Tibet, and Japan. Honolulu: East-West Center Press, 1964.

Nakane, Chie. Japanese Society. Berkeley: University of California Press, 1970.

Nakasone, Yasuhiro. "Toward Comprehensive Security: Self-Defense and Article 9 of the Constitution." Japan Echo, Winter 1978, pp. 32-39.

Nakayama, Hiromasa. "Soren Shakaishugi Bocho no Genkai" (Limits of Soviet Socialist Expansion). Asahi Janaru, April 25, 1980, pp. 10-20.

Niizawa, Yoshisuke. "Seisaku Kettei Kiko to Posuto Burejunefu" (Policy Decision Structure and the Post-Brezhnev Era). Asahi Janaru, April 25, 1980, pp. 21-26.

Ogata, Sadako. "Some Japanese Views on United States-Japan Relations in the 1980s." Asian Survey 20 (July 1980): 694-706.

Ohashi, Ryuken. Nihon no Kaikyu Kosei (Japan's Class Structure). Tokyo: Iwanami, 1972.

Oka, Yoshiteru. "Questioning the 1% of Japan's Defense Budget." Business Japan, July 1979, p. 57.

Okabe, Tatsumi. Tonan Ajia to Nihon no Shinro: "Hannichi" no Kozo to Chugoku no Yakuwari (Southeast Asia and Japan's Road: Structure of "Anti-Japanism" and the Role of China). Tokyo: Nihon Keizai Shimbunsha, 1976.

Okimoto, Daniel. "Security Policies in the United States and Japan: Institutions, Experts, and Mutual Understanding." In U.S.-Japan Relations and the Security of East Asia, edited by Franklin Weinstein, pp. 9-48. Boulder, Colo.: Westview Press, 1978.

Okita, Saburo. "China, Japan and the United States: Economic Relations and Prospects." Foreign Affairs 57 (1979): 1090-1110.

Okumiya, Masatake. Nihon Boei Ron (A View of Japanese Defense). Tokyo: PHP, 1979.

Ominato, Taro. "Boei Mondai ni kansuru Kokumin Ishiki no Doko" (Trend of Popular Perception of the Defense Issue). Kokubo 315 (May 1979): 35-58.

Ono, Toru, ed. Tonan Ajia to Kokusai Kankei (Southeast Asia and International Relations). Tokyo: Koyo Shobo, 1979.

Osanai, Hiroshi. Nihon no Kakubuso (Japan's Nuclear Armament). Tokyo: Daiamondo, 1975.

Otsuka, Hidesuke. Kore ga Uyoku da (This is the Right Wing). Tokyo: Eru Suppansha, 1970.

Packard, George R. Protest in Tokyo: The Security Treaty Crisis of 1960. Princeton, N.J.: Princeton University Press, 1967.

Patrick, Hugh, and Henry Rosovsky, eds. Asia's New Giant: How the Japanese Economy Works. Washington, D.C.: The Brookings Institution, 1976.

Pike, Douglas. "Communist vs. Communist in Southeast Asia." International Security 4 (1979): 20-38.

Porter, Gareth. "Time to talk with North Korea." Foreign Policy 34 (Spring 1979): 52-73.

Reischauer, Edwin O. The Japanese. Cambridge: Harvard University Press, 1977.

_____. "Their Special Strength." Foreign Policy 14 (Spring 1974): 142-51.

Republic of Korea, Government of. A Handbook of Korea. Seoul: Korean Overseas Information Services, Ministry of Culture and Information, 1979.

Riley, John. "The American Mood: A Foreign Policy of Self-Interest." Foreign Policy 24 (Spring 1979): 74-86.

Roherty, James M., ed. Defense Policy Formation: Towards Comparative Analysis. Durham, N.C.: Carolina Academic Press, 1980.

Rosovsky, Henry, ed. Discord in the Pacific: Challenge to the Japanese-American Alliance. Washington, D.C.: Columbia Books, 1972.

Saeki, Kiichi. "Japan's Security in a Multipolar World." In United States-Japanese Relations, edited by Priscilla Clapp and Morton Halperin, pp. 183-202. Cambridge, Mass.: Harvard University Press, 1974.

Saito, Akira. "Changing Japanese Attitude on Security Treaty." Look Japan, March 10, 1980, pp. 4-5.

Sakanaka, Tomohisa. "Military Threats and Japan's Defense Capability." Asian Survey 20 (July 1980): 763-75.

_____. "A New Phase of Japan's Defense Policy." Japan Quarterly 27 (1980): 461-70.

_____. "'Soren kyo' no Kento" (A Study of "Soviet Threat"). Kokusai Mondai 247 (October 1980): 63-76.

Salisbury, Harrison. "How a Nuclear War Can Start in East Asia." Bulletin of the Atomic Scientists 35 (April 1979): 21-22.

Sankei Shimbun Shuzaihan. Nihon no Anzen (Japan's Security). Tokyo: Sankei Shimbunsha, 1976. 2 vols.

Sato, Eiichi. "Nihon ni okeru Boeiryoku Koso" (Defense Buildup Plans in Japan). Kokusai Mondai 247 (October 1980): 13-33.

Scalapino, Robert A. "Asia at the End of the 1970s." Foreign Affairs 58 (1980): 693-737.

_____, ed. The Foreign Policy of Modern Japan. Berkeley: University of California Press, 1977.

Seki, Haruhiro. "Hendo suru Ajia to Nihon Gaiko" (Changing Asia and Japanese Diplomacy). Sekai, February 1979, pp. 27-39.

Sengoku, Tamotsu, and Atsuko Toyama. Hikaku Nihonjin Ron (Comparative Study of the Japanese). Tokyo: Shogakukan, 1973.

Shaplen, Robert. "A Reporter at Large: From MacArthur to Miki — II." The New Yorker, August 11, 1975, pp. 105-23.

Shinohara, Hajime. Nihon no Seiji Fudo (Political Climate in Japan). Tokyo: Iwanami, 1971.

Shirai, Hisaya. "Mosukuwa de miru Taikoku no pawa gemu" (Superpower Power Game Viewed from Moscow). Asahi Janaru, January 16, 1979, pp. 30-35.

Sogo Anzen Hosho Kenkyu Gurupu. Sogo Anzen Hosho Senryaku (Strategy for Comprehensive Security). Tokyo: Okurasho Insatsukyoku, 1980.

Stockholm International Peace Research Institute. World Armaments and Disarmament: SIPRI Yearbook 1978. Stockholm: Stockholm International Peace Research Institute, 1978.

Suryandinata, Leo. "Indonesia: A Year of Continuing Challenge." In Southeast Asian Affairs 1979, pp. 105-18. Singapore: Institute of Southeast Asian Studies, 1979.

Swearingen, Roger. The Soviet Union and Postwar Japan: Escalating Challenge and Response. Stanford, Calif.: Hoover Institution Press, 1978.

Takahashi, Takeo. "Oil and Japan's 'Energy-Weak' Economy." Look Japan, June 10, 1979, pp. 4-6.

Takase, Shoji. "Takamaru Boei Rongi no Naiatsu to Gaiatsu" (Internal and External Pressures on the Rising Defense Debate). Asahi Janaru, April 11, 1980, pp. 10-14.

Takayanagi, Kenzo. "Some Reminiscences of Japan's Commission on the Constitution." In The Constitution of Japan: Its First Twenty-Years, 1947-1967, edited by Dan F. Henderson, pp. 71-88. Seattle: University of Washington Press, 1968.

Tawara, Soichiro. "Soren wa kowai desuka?" (Are You Afraid of the Soviet Union?). Bungei Shunju, March 1980, pp. 92-113.

Trezise, Philip H., and Yukio Suzuki. "Politics, Government, and Economic Growth in Japan." In Asia's New Giant: How the Japanese Economy Works, edited by Hugh Patrick and Henry Rosovsky, pp. 753-811. Washington, D.C.: The Brookings Institution, 1976.

Tsou, Tang, Tetsuo Najita, and Hideo Otake. "Sino-Japanese Relations in the 1970s." In Japan, America, and the Future World Order, edited by Morton Kaplan and Kinhide Mushakoji, pp. 49-90. New York: The Free Press, 1976.

Tsukamoto, Tetsuya. "Nisso Zenrin Joyaku no Wana" (The Trap in a Russo-Japanese Treaty of Good Neighborhood). Bungei Shunju, April 1980, pp. 92-111.

Tsunoda, Jun. "Is Japan's Defense Posture Adequate?" Asian Affairs 5 (March-April 1978): 199-215.

Tsunoda, Ryusaku, et al., eds. Sources of Japanese Tradition. New York: Columbia University Press, 1960.

Tsurutani, Taketsugu. "Causes of Paralysis." Foreign Policy 14 (Spring 1974): 126-41.

_____. "80 Nen dai ni okeru Beikoku no Tainichikan to Nihon no Taio" (America's View of Japan and Japan's Response in the 1980s). Kokusai Mondai 250 (January 1981): 16-29.

_____. "Japan's Security, Defense Responsibilities, and Capabilities." Orbis 25 (Spring 1981):

_____. Political Change in Japan: Response to Postindustrial Challenge. New York: McKay, 1977.

_____. The Politics of National Development: Political Leadership in Transitional Societies. New York: Chandler, 1973.

_____. "The Security Debate." In Defense Policy Formation: Towards Comparative Analysis, edited by James Roherty, pp. 175-94. Durham, N.C.: Carolina Academic Press, 1980.

United Nations. Yearbook of National Account Statistics 1978. New York: Statistical Office of the United Nations, 1979.

United States, Government of. Department of Defense Annual Report: Fiscal Year 1980. Washington, D.C.: U.S. Government Printing Office, 1979.

_____. U.S. Foreign Policy for the 1970s. Washington, D.C.: U.S. Government Printing Office, 1971.

_____. The United States, China, and Japan. Washington, D.C.: U.S. Government Printing Office, 1979.

_____. United States-Japan Security Relationship - The Key to East Asian Security and Stability. Washington, D.C.: U.S. Government Printing Office, 1979.

_____. United States Military Posture for FY 1980. Washington, D.C.: U.S. Government Printing Office, 1979.

_____. U.S. Relations with Japan and China. Washington, D.C.: U.S. Government Printing Office, 1979.

van der Kroef, Justus M. "ASEAN: The View from Hanoi, Moscow and Peking." Contemporary Asia Review 1 (1977): 19-30.

Van Zandt, Howard. "Japanese Culture and the Business Boom." Foreign Affairs 48 (1970): 344-57.

Wah, Chin Kin. "The Great Powers and Southeast Asia: A Year of Diplomatic Effervescence." In Southeast Asian Affairs 1979, pp. 45-60. Singapore: Institute of Southeast Asian Studies, 1979.

Wakaizumi, Kei. "Japan's Dilemma: To Act or Not to Act." Foreign Policy 16 (Fall 1974): 30-47.

Wanandi, Jusuf. "Dimensions of Southeast Asian Security." Indonesian Quarterly 8 (1980): 39-52.

_____. Security Dimensions of the Asia-Pacific Region in the 1980s. Jakarta: Center for Strategic and International Studies, 1979.

_____. A View from ASEAN on the Interest and Role of the United States in Southeast Asia. Jakarta: Institute for Strategic and International Studies, n.d.

Ward, Robert E. "Political Modernization and Political Culture in Japan." World Politics 15 (1963): 569-96.

Watanabe, Tsuneo. Habatsu: Hoshuto no Kaibo (Factionalism: A Dissection of the Conservative Party). Tokyo: Kobundo, 1958.

Weinstein, Franklin, ed. U.S.-Japan Relations and the Security of East Asia. Boulder, Colo.: Westview Press, 1978.

Weinstein, Martin. Japan's Postwar Defense Policy 1947-1968. New York: Columbia University Press, 1971.

White, James W. "State Building and Modernization: The Meiji Restoration." In Crisis, Choice, and Change: Historical Studies of Political Development, edited by Gabriel Almond, Scott Flanagan, and Robert Mundt, pp. 499-559. Boston: Little, Brown, 1973.

Whiting, Allen S., and Robert F. Dernberger. China's Future: Foreign Policy and Economic Development in the Post-Mao China. New York: McGraw-Hill, 1977.

Yano, Toru. "Soren Betonamu Joyaku no Kikendo" (Dangerous Potentials of the Soviet-Vietnamese Treaty). Chuokoron, January 1979, pp. 108-17.

Yuize, Yasuhiko. "Taikoku no Shokuryo Senryaku to Nihon no Anzen Hosho" (Superpower Food Strategy and Japan's Security). Asahi Janaru, April 11, 1980, pp. 32-37.

Zacher, Mark W., and R. Stephen Milne, eds. Conflict and Stability in Southeast Asia. Garden City, N.Y.: Doubleday, 1974.

Index

203

About the Author

TAKETSUGU TSURUTANI is a Professor of Political Science at Washington State University, Pullman, Washington.

Dr. Tsurutani has published extensively in the areas of comparative politics and international relations. He is the author of The Politics of National Development: Political Leadership in Transitional Societies and Political Change in Japan: Response to Postindustrial Challenge, and his articles have appeared in the Journal of Politics, the Review of Politics, Asian Survey, Foreign Policy, The Journal of Political and Military Sociology, and Orbis, among others.

Dr. Tsurutani holds a B.A. from Lawrence College and an M.A. and Ph.D. from the University of Wisconsin, Madison.